DEMCO

INTERPRETING
ELECTIONS

INTERPRETING ELECTIONS

BY STANLEY KELLEY, JR.

PRINCETON UNIVERSITY PRESS • PRINCETON, N.J.

Copyright © 1983 by Princeton University Press

Published by Princeton University Press, 41 William Street,
Princeton, New Jersey 08540
In the United Kingdom: Princeton University Press,
Guildford, Surrey

Library of Congress Cataloging in Publication Data will be
found on the last printed page of this book

This book has been composed in CRT Times Roman

Clothbound editions of Princeton University Press books
are printed on acid-free paper, and binding materials are
chosen for strength and durability. Paperbacks, while satisfactory for
personal collections, are not usually suitable for library rebinding

Printed in the United States of America by Princeton University Press,
Princeton, New Jersey

FOR
STELLA E. KELLEY

CONTENTS

LIST OF TABLES AND FIGURES

TABLES

FIGURES

PREFACE

In "The Simple Act of Voting," published in 1974, Thad Mirer and I proposed a theory of voting and tested it with data drawn from the University of Michigan's surveys of voters in the six presidential elections from 1952 to 1968. Our objective was "to improve upon current explanations of voters' choices," and in our concluding remarks we argued that our view of voting had "immediate implications for those who interpret elections" and "consequences of importance for one's view of the American electorate." This book shows in detail what some of those implications and consequences are.

The central ideas of the book reflect three distinct sets of influences. The academic study of voting is the first and most obvious of these, and, like most other students of that subject, I owe a particularly great intellectual debt to the authors of *The American Voter*—Angus Campbell, Philip Converse, Warren Miller, and Donald Stokes. The ideas of professional campaigners—interpreters of elections in progress—have also been a strong influence. The efforts of campaigners to understand how the many particular concerns of voters translate into victory and defeat at the polls have interested me for a long time and have shaped my own conception of that process in many ways. Political philosophy, my first love in the study of politics, has been a third important influence, one that has urged me continually toward attempts to puzzle out how elections contribute to, or impair, the health and stability of democratic government. My attention in this book to electoral mandates and to the quality of electoral decisions arises out of a concern for the meaning of elections in this larger sense.

Surveys of opinion have provided most of my data on the attitudes and behavior of voters. My heaviest reliance is on eight studies of presidential elections conducted by the Center for Political Studies (and various antecedent organizations) of the Institute of Social Research of the University of Michigan;

indeed, the reader may assume that the information presented
in tables and figures comes from these studies unless I have
specifically noted otherwise. The Michigan surveys, financed
in recent years by the National Science Foundation (and in
earlier ones by the National Institute of Mental Health and
the Rockefeller Foundation) are made widely available by the
Inter-University Consortium for Political and Social Research. They have become a virtually indispensable resource
for the empirical study of elections, and this book, certainly,
could not have been written without access to them. In Chapter 9, which examines the press's interpretations of the 1980
elections, I have also taken data from surveys by the *New
York Times* and CBS News, NBC News and the Associated
Press, ABC News, ABC News and Louis Harris and Associates, the Gallup Poll, the *Los Angeles Times, Newsweek,* and
Time. For helping to make information from these surveys
available I am grateful to Jeffrey D. Alderman, David M. Alpern, Michael Kagay, Andrew Kohut, Patricia McGann,
Mark A. Shulman, Linda Simmons, and John F. Stacks.

Friends have done a great deal to make this book a better
one than my efforts alone could have produced. The manu-
script was read in whole or in part by Douglas Arnold, James
DeNardo, Harold Feiveson, Fred Greenstein, Amy Gutmann,
Jennifer Hochschild, Walter F. Murphy, Richard Shapiro,
and Dennis Thompson, all of Princeton University, and by
Michael Kagay of Louis Harris and Associates, C. Anthony
Broh and Gerald Pomper of Rutgers University, Thomas
Ferguson of the Massachusetts Institute of Technology,
Howard Husock of WGBH Television (Boston), Glenn
Shafer of Kansas University, Michael Stoto of Harvard Uni-
versity, and Edward Tufte of Yale University. Both for their
encouragement and for their detailed and pointed criticisms, I
am extremely grateful.

I am also personally indebted to many others. Asif Agha,
Robert Bennett, Daniel Feinstein, John G. Geer, Wendy
Gerber, John Hass, Ken John, Uday Mehta, Richard Sobel,
Michael Stoto, Jan Viehman, and Acquila Washington have
served as research assistants; individually and collectively,

they have shown phenomenal energy, diligence, patience, and intelligence. Carol Treanor and Douglas Danforth of the Center for Advanced Study in the Behavioral Sciences helped me with computing while I was a Fellow at the Center and even taught me something of the art of computing. Judith Rowe and J. R. Piggott have facilitated my work at the Princeton Computer Center. June Traube was mainly responsible for typing the manuscript and otherwise readying it for the publisher. Her speed, sense of humor, and good spelling—the latter finely honed by much playing of Scrabble—make it a pleasure to work with her. She was ably assisted on occasion by Joan Carroll, Chen Chien, Nils Dennis, Dorothy Dey, and Mildred Kalmus. For financial support, and for making time available for my research, I am grateful to the Center for Advanced Study in the Behavioral Sciences and to Princeton University. William Hively and Sanford Thatcher of Princeton University Press deserve great credit for their handling both of the manuscript and its author. Finally, I thank my mother, to whom this book is dedicated. For several long periods she provided me with a quiet retreat in which to write, companionship, much good food, and a degree of tolerance that I could not have asked even from my best friends.

For the interpretations of the data I have used and for the shortcomings of this book, I alone am responsible.

Stanley Kelley, Jr.
Princeton, N.J.

INTERPRETING
ELECTIONS

CHAPTER ONE

INTRODUCTION

The belief that elections carry obvious messages is widely shared in democratic nations. It is held by many protest voters, surely, and evidently by those politicians, reporters, editors, scholars, and promoters of causes and interests who, in the immediate aftermath of an election, say with great assurance what it means. The same belief has been a premise of democratic theorists, many of whom, like John Stuart Mill, have seen elections as a "periodical muster of opposing forces, to gauge the state of the national mind, and ascertain, beyond dispute, the relative strength of different parties and opinions."[1]

The wide acceptance of this view of elections is puzzling. Unquestionably, voters have reasons for voting as they do and, in that sense, send messages. One may, for example, reasonably think of a blindly partisan voter as saying, "I like any Democrat better than any Republican" (or vice versa). But why should anyone believe that the content of the millions of messages sent in a national election (or that of the tens of thousands in any large constituency) is easily grasped? Certainly, election *returns* convey very little information. In Walter Lippmann's words,

> We call an election an expression of the popular will. But is it? We go into a polling booth and mark a cross on a piece of paper for one of two, or perhaps three or four names. Have we expressed our thoughts on the public policy of the United States? Presumably we have a number of thoughts on this and that with many buts and ifs

[1] John Stuart Mill, *Considerations on Representative Government*, Gateway Edition (Chicago: Henry Regnery Company, 1962) p. 230.

and ors. Surely the cross on a piece of paper does not express them.[2]

A vote is only an avowal of support at a particular time, very often of support with reservations. The count of votes tells no one how far voters will follow the victorious candidate, or for how long, or in what direction. Of course, election returns come to us in a context—particular candidates have raised particular issues against a background of particular events—and we also have crude rules of thumb that relate this context to voting; for instance, we believe that voters care most about matters touching their personal interests, that partisans tend to vote for their party's candidates, that honesty in candidates is highly valued, and so on. Given only such contextual information and such rules, however, anyone who is reasonably clever can easily "explain" an election's outcome in several different ways, all equally convincing. Consider a critical election like that of 1860: It will be forever unknown how much the slavery issue contributed to its outcome and how much economic interests did, because we have no specific knowledge of the considerations that the voters of that time brought to their choices and no way of ascertaining them. Our legitimate confidence in interpreting the elections of small clubs and caucuses underlines the point. In that setting one can find out what voters saw at stake, how firmly they stood behind candidates, and how pleased voters were with their choices. In large constituencies this kind of information is lacking, unless it is deliberately acquired by research. In the absence of such, mass electorates imply massive ignorance about the meaning of elections.

Sampling is a practical answer to this problem of numbers, and sample surveys of the electorate are a way to acquire for large groups of voters information that is easily acquired for very small ones. Thus, the advent of the sample survey has been a development of major importance for the interpreta-

[2] Walter Lippmann, *The Phantom Public* (New York: Harcourt, Brace, 1925), pp. 56–57.

tion of elections, though much of that importance remains potential, as the many conflicting interpretations of recent elections suggest. Of course, some disagreement about an election's meaning is to be expected no matter how much knowledge exists about it—different explanations affect political interests differently—but political motives are by no means the only source of disagreement, as I shall show. To a large extent the difficulty is conceptual. Analysts have thought less carefully than they should have about how to identify the considerations that matter to voters, how voters translate these considerations into votes, and how to discover the relative contributions of particular issues and events to the way the vote divides. Answers to long lists of questions about candidates, policies, and parties do not of themselves tell us the conditions that voters *as voters* may attach to their support for candidates. Consider a poll, commissioned by the Republicans in 1964, which found that 55 percent of the respondents thought that Lyndon B. Johnson was "warm and friendly" and that only 17 percent thought the same of Barry Goldwater.[3] What did this finding mean? Do voters care whether a president is warm and friendly? Do some care and others not? For those who care (if there are such), how strongly do they care? Is warmth and friendliness the only consideration they have in mind, or are there others? If there are others, do they weigh as heavily as warmth and friendliness? Are perceptions of warmth and friendliness a concern only of voters already strongly committed to the candidates or do such perceptions matter to undecided voters as well? Without answers to these and other questions, a finding of this sort advances the understanding of an election very little. The huge amounts of survey data that exist for recent presidential elections limit the number of stories that can be believably told about them, but it remains quite possible, consistently with those data, to vary substantially the elements of such stories, and the stress given

---

[3] Thomas W. Benham, "Polling for a Presidential Candidate: Some Observations on the 1964 Campaign," *Public Opinion Quarterly* 29 (Summer 1965), pp. 185–199.

them. Minor themes of one account can become major themes of another.

How to reduce the indeterminacy of our interpretations of elections is the central problem of this book, and in it I propose some new ways to do so. These procedures derive from an explicit theory of voting, are applicable to any election for which the right kinds of data exist, and involve relatively uncomplicated techniques for identifying the concerns and opinions that figure in voting and for tracing their consequences for the electorate's collective decision. The questions that these procedures are designed to answer are not new. Like most analysts, I am interested in explaining the outcomes of elections, ascertaining the content of any mandates issued to winning candidates, gauging the decisiveness with which parties and opinions have won or lost favor, and assessing the quality of the judgments that enter into voting.

Better interpretation of elections has an important contribution to make to the writing of political history, and the desire to make such a contribution is one motive for my efforts here. To illustrate my analytical methods concretely, and as an exploration of recent political history, I examine two elections in detail—the Johnson and Nixon landslides. Contemporary analysts saw both as particularly decisive. The winners of both claimed popular mandates. Both were thought to teach a lesson in practical politics—that the electorate prefers centrists to extremists. Many also saw the electorate in 1972 as reversing its decision of 1964. Johnson's great victory seemed to reaffirm the allegiance of voters to the New Deal. Then came the expansion of the war in Southeast Asia, the heightening of racial tensions, the weakening of party ties, and increasing prominence for such issues as abortion, the use of drugs, the control of crime, and the rights of women. When the electorate reelected Richard Nixon in 1972, giving the Republicans as large a plurality as that given the Democrats eight years earlier, these observers concluded that the New Deal tide had finally ebbed.

I have reached rather different conclusions than these about the two elections. No one can deny that new issues in the late sixties and early seventies played a part in the swing away from Democratic leadership after 1964, but more remarkable is the continuity in the major concerns of the voters from 1964 to 1972 that my analysis reveals. The electorate's concern with the issues of the New Deal was an important feature of that continuity. The evidence also shows that these two landslides, outwardly so similar, were inwardly much less so. Landslides can differ greatly in their meaning, as I shall show, so much so, in fact, that one of these—the election of 1972—can aptly be called a *close* landslide.

A better understanding of what voters mean to say in voting, and of how individual judgments translate into a collective judgment, can help us also to evaluate the governmental consequences of elections. Among the institutions of democratic states it is elections that give political leaders the most direct and obvious incentive to take note of the wishes and views of ordinary people. This fact arouses uneasiness in many intellectuals and politicians otherwise strongly committed to democratic government; a well known contemporary student of politics, for instance, distrustful of popular pressures on public officials, has written with approval of a party system that can resolve "disagreements in ways which reduce to a minimum the number of commitments elective officials must make to policy positions, many of which perforce would be unattainable, unwise, or contradictory."[4] Such uneasiness has been fed by studies of public opinion which have shown that many voters are badly informed about public affairs and that those voters who shift their votes most easily from one candidate to another are particularly ill-informed. But *electoral* opinion and *public* opinion are not the same thing, if by the one we mean opinion that counts in elections and, by the other, responses to questions put to voters in surveys. An examination of the concerns that entered into voting in 1964 and 1972 suggests that electoral opinion is more fo-

[4] James Q. Wilson, *The Amateur Democrat* (Chicago: University of Chicago Press, 1962), p. 357.

cused and less casual than public opinion, that the points voters raise in choosing between candidates usually make good sense. Whatever more extensive studies may show in this regard, however, the distinction between electoral and public opinion, and careful adherence to that distinction in interpreting elections, is crucial for any realistic assessment of the way elections work.

A more accurate decoding of the messages of elections can contribute something of importance to better leadership, as well as to better political history and a better understanding of elections. Applied over time to many elections, techniques well designed for such decoding can help us to build a kind of case law of elections, a set of generalizations about what voters can be expected to do in varying circumstances. The same techniques can also be used in advance of elections, to show politicians where voters are, attitudinally, and how they feel about being there. It is true that the information produced by such methods can be misused; unhappily, those who mislead draw on much the same knowledge as those who lead. Nonetheless, democracy is not served except by accident if politicans are ignorant of, or misread, the concerns and beliefs that voters bring to their choices. While many people doubt that voters' wishes ought always to be *obeyed,* most would agree that they should be *heeded.* A leader ignorant of those wishes is apt to see his followers dwindle away, as he tries to lead them where they will not go. Failed leadership is a failed opportunity for worthwhile collective action and, if it is chronic, a danger to the survival of a democratic regime. To last, a democratic regime, like any other, must come to terms with the power that resides in the great mass of the people. By definition it must do so without repression, and for that reason it must either concur or convince, trim or lead, or else in the long run seem unworthy of support to its citizenry.

These general observations on what I seek to do and why should suffice to introduce the chapters that follow. Chapter 2 sets forth the theory of voting on which I rely and the reasons to believe that it is a good one for my purposes. Applying certain features of that theory, Chapter 3 assesses the extent to

which the elections of 1964 and 1972 can properly be called
decisive, comparing them in that regard with other presidential elections from 1952 to 1976. Chapter 4 introduces concepts useful for thinking about the relationship between the
concerns of individual voters and the outcomes of elections,
and Chapters 5 and 6 trace in detail the impact of voters' concerns on the division of the vote in 1964 and 1972. Chapter 7
considers the theory of electoral mandates as it has evolved in
the United States and examines the evidence for the mandates
claimed by Presidents Johnson and Nixon. Chapter 8 assesses
the reasoning and evidence which support the proposition
that poorly informed voters play a peculiarly decisive role in
elections. Chapter 9 evaluates common methods of interpreting elections, alternatives to my own, as they figured in the
press's interpretation of the election of 1980.

CHAPTER TWO

A THEORY OF VOTING

A good starting point for thinking about the interpretation of elections is a quite simple conception of the way people make choices, in voting and more generally. One may conceive of any choice as involving a set of *considerations* (or prima facie reasons for choosing in one way or another) and a *rule* for combining (or weighing) them. To know both the considerations and the rule is to explain the choice, if it has already been made, or to predict it, if it has not. Thus, the first two commandments for the interpreter of elections are: Look for the considerations and look for the rule. The considerations that enter into the collective decision that we call an election are just the sum of those that enter into the decisions of individual voters, and the rule that voters use to translate considerations into votes is one key to understanding the impact of particular considerations on an election's outcome.

Survey research has taken two general approaches to identifying the considerations that go into voting. One is to encourage voters to state their motives in their own words, for instance, by asking them to specify the good and bad points of the candidates and parties. The second is to pose specific questions about specific matters—the honesty of the candidates, for example, or the health of the economy—which the researcher believes will influence voting. In my analyses of the elections of 1964 and 1972 I rely almost entirely on data produced by the first approach. I shall note two reasons for that choice here, reserving additional comments until later: Because the opinions of American voters are very heterogeneous, any list of questions about particular considerations, even a long list, is almost certain to omit important ones. Moreover, virtually all the questions that such a list includes will concern matters that some voters see as relevant to voting while others do not. If the responses of the latter go unidentified and undiscounted—and it is hard to identify them—a survey's results can yield a quite misleading picture of the influences at work in an election.

Of the many conceivable decision-rules that might be used to combine considerations, I attribute to voters one on which several studies of voting have converged.[1] This rule is a simple one:

> The voter canvasses his likes and dislikes of the leading candidates and major parties involved in an election. Weighing each like and dislike equally, he votes for the candidate toward whom he has the greatest net number of favorable attitudes, if there is such a candidate. If no candidate has such an advantage, the voter votes consistently with his party affiliation, if he has one. If his attitudes do not incline him toward one candidate more than toward another, and if he does not identify with one of the major parties, the voter reaches a null decision.[2]

I shall call this decision-rule the *Voter's Decision Rule* (or, simply, the Rule) and the theory of which it is a part the rule-consideration account of voting.

Note the following features of that account: (1) By assumption, the Voter's Decision Rule holds for all voters, always, but the number and content of the considerations to which voters apply it may vary from voter to voter and from election to election. For instance, the ideological stance of candidates may seem important to a voter in one election but not in another, and in the same election may matter to some voters but not to their neighbors. (2) By assumption also, the Rule, a set of considerations, and party affiliations determine voters' choices immediately and wholly. These proximate causes of a

[1] See particularly Richard A. Brody and Benjamin I. Page, "Indifference, Alienation and Rational Decisions: The Effects of Candidate Evaluations on Turnout and the Vote," *Public Choice* 15 (Summer 1973), pp. 1–17; Stanley Kelley, Jr., and Thad W. Mirer, "The Simple Act of Voting," *American Political Science Review* 68 (June 1974), pp. 572–591; and William R. Shaffer, *Computer Simulations of Voting Behavior* (New York: Oxford University Press, 1972), pp. 65–68.

[2] Kelley and Mirer, "The Simple Act of Voting," p. 574.

vote, however, have causes also, and any effort to elucidate a voting decision fully would attempt to find them. (3) The Rule involves an important assumption that is counterintuitive, namely, that all the considerations which enter into a voting decision are weighed equally. This assumption does not imply, however, that voters may not discard possible considerations as unimportant and in that way give greater weight to some than to others. (4) Once the considerations which enter into a decision are known, the Rule produces two sorts of predictions: *Predictions from considerations,* when these yield an advantage to a candidate, and *predictions from partisanship,* when there is no such advantage. Null decisions are simply those for which this account of voting can make no prediction, though they might be interpreted either as decisions to choose at random among the candidates or decisions to abstain. (5) No "probablys" are involved in this way of predicting (or explaining) a voter's choice. If a voter's count of likes and dislikes and his party affiliation give any advantage at all to a candidate, he receives the voter's vote, regardless of the size of the advantage.[3] The application of the Rule tells one, however, how close to indifference a voter is in choosing between candidates. The difference in the net number of favorable attitudes that a voter has toward each of any pair of candidates (I shall call that difference a *net score* and show how to compute it later) may be large or small. When it is small, the voter (in this account of voting) is almost as ready to vote for one candidate as for the other. Thus, one may think of voters with low net scores as weakly committed to their choices and those who reach null decisions as uncommitted.

TESTS OF THE THEORY

To be a useful basis for interpreting elections, a theory of voting should be internally consistent, unambiguous, and accurate in its predictions, the last of these criteria being important

---

[3] Brody and Page, "Indifference, Alienation and Rational Decisions," p. 13.

not for its own sake but because it is an important test of a theory's explanatory value.[4] Parsimony and a believable account of the way voters arrive at decisions should also count in a theory's favor. The rule-consideration account of voting is obviously clear, consistent, and parsimonious. How believable is it, and how accurate are its predictions?

Some aspects of the theory are readily believable. In partisan elections candidates and parties are the objects of choice, and to canvass one's likes and dislikes of these objects is simply, in the language of economics, to compare their utilities. Both the importunities of campaigners and the need to choose by a known future date impel voters to such a canvass, even if it is only a brief one. Some voters find a choice hard, others do not, and the former often end by invoking a standing preference for a party.

That voters must apply the Rule unconsciously, if they apply it at all, does not in any way impeach its believability. There is nothing odd in the idea of unconscious choice, and even when we speak specifically of conscious choice we usually do not mean to imply that the entire process is conscious. It can be nearly so, as when we put down on paper the pros and cons of taking another job and try to assign each consideration a weight, or when a business applies cost-benefit analysis in the search for an optimum mode of operation. Such procedures, however, are almost always reserved for decisions that we see as particularly consequential. Ordinarily, how we combine considerations into choices is hazy to us; between identifying the considerations and arriving at a decision, there is an unconscious leap.

Almost certainly, the nonintuitive assumption that voters weigh all considerations equally does not always hold true,

[4] C. G. Hempel observes, ". . . it may be said that an explanation . . . is not complete unless it might as well have functioned as a prediction: If the final event can be derived from the initial conditions and universal hypotheses stated in the explanation, then it might as well have been predicted, before it actually happened, on the basis of a knowledge of the initial conditions and the general laws." C. G. Hempel, *Aspects of Scientific Explanation* (New York: The Free Press, 1965), p. 234.

but one can easily see why many voters might tend to follow such a procedure much of the time. Consider, first, the kinds of things—the honesty of candidates or their stands on issues of policy—that figure as considerations in voting. While it is extremely hard to assign a precise importance to such matters in utiles or in any other unit of measurement, the mind can construct a set of considerations that strike us as roughly comparable. A voter might equate one candidate's integrity with another's experience, for example, but would be unlikely to think, "I like Candidate A's integrity but I like Candidate B's two years in the state assembly *and* his four years in the state Senate *and* his three terms as U.S. Representative *and* his two terms as U.S. Senator." Second, consider the consequences of voting. In two-party systems candidates frequently fail to take clearly opposed stands on issues important to voters, and in any case an individual voter's vote has a trivial impact on the outcome of any election in a large constituency. Thus, both the nature of voting decisions and their small individual consequence make rational for the voter a simple decision-rule that conserves time and thought. The Rule is a formula, a mental program, for making decisions of just that sort.

Since tests of the accuracy of the Rule's predictions are reported in detail elsewhere, I shall limit myself here to a brief summary of their results.[5]

The most extensive set of tests applied the Rule to data drawn from surveys conducted by the Center for Political Studies of the University of Michigan. Before each presidential election since (and including) 1952, Michigan interviewers have asked respondents to state their likes and dislikes of the major parties and the good and bad points of major candidates, putting down as many as five responses to each question.[6] Treating these responses as the considerations that re-

[5] See Appendix I below and the works cited in footnote 1 above. See also Thomas E. Mann, *Unsafe at Any Margin: Interpreting Congressional Elections* (Washington, D.C.: American Enterprise Institute for Public Policy Research, 1978), pp. 63–71.

[6] In 1952 the questions about parties were as follows: "I'd like to ask you what you think are the good and bad points about the parties. Is

spondents brought to their choices, one can apply the Rule straightforwardly to predict each respondent's vote and, by summation, the division of the vote in the sample and the electorate. Table 2.1 shows the accuracy of such predictions for presidential elections from 1952 to 1980. These results are much better than those one obtains by basing predictions on party identification, the social and demographic characteristics of voters, or ideological affiliation, and slightly better than those one gets by basing predictions on respondents' statements of their voting intentions. Clearly, the great majority of voters act *as if* they were using the Rule, and the accuracy with which the division of the vote is predicted shows that the Rule's predictions of individual votes are nearly unbiased, with errors canceling out.

Moreover, by no means all of the errors of the Rule's predictions count against it. The timing of preelection interviews, for instance, was surely a major source of such errors. Consider these facts: (1) Among voters who say how they intend to vote, intentions and the Rule's predictions agree about 96 times out of a hundred.[7] (2) The Survey Research Center typically interviews respondents over a period of a month and a

---

there anything in particular that you (like, don't like) about the (Democratic, Republican) Party? What is that?" The questions about the candidates were, "Now I'd like to ask you about the good and bad points of the two candidates for President. Is there anything in particular about (name of candidate) that might make you want to vote (for him, against him)? What is that?" With trivial variations interviewers have asked the same questions in later studies of presidential elections, and those for the elections of 1968 and 1980 also included questions about George Wallace and John Anderson, respectively.

In the data made available to members of the Inter-University Consortium for Political and Social Research from all the University of Michigan's national election studies except that for 1972, up to five responses to each of the likes-dislikes questions have been coded; in the 1972 study, up to three only were coded. A second version of the data for 1972 exists, however, in which up to five responses were coded, and, unless I specifically note otherwise, the reader may assume that this second version is the one on which I am relying. I am grateful to Michael Kagay for making these five-response data available to me.

[7] Kelley and Mirer, "The Simple Act of Voting," p. 580.

TABLE 2.1

**Predicting the Presidential Vote with
the Voter's Decision Rule**

Election	Sample Size	% of Individual Votes Correctly Predicted*	% of Vote Predicted to Be Democratic minus Actual % Democratic in the:	
			Sample	Population
1952	1184	87.1	+ 3.3	+ 0.4
1956	1266	85.5	+ 4.6	+ 2.6
1960	1413	88.2	+ 0.4	− 0.7
1964	1113	90.3	+ 2.1	+ 8.2
1968	1027	80.9	+ 1.0	− 0.8
1972	834	83.7	+ 3.2	+ 1.2
1976	1662.5	84.1	+ 1.9	+ 1.9
1980	972	75.1	− 0.1	+ 4.3

Mean for all elections 84.4   2.1   2.7
                                    (abs. value) (abs. value)

* Automatically counted as errors are all votes for minor-party or independent candidates (except those for Wallace in 1968 and Anderson in 1980) and null predictions, as well as those votes that were incorrectly predicted. Voters who refused to say how they voted or said that they did not remember how they voted, however, have been excluded from the samples that figure in this table.

half in its preelection surveys. (3) Roughly 85 percent of the Rule's errors occur when it predicts the votes of respondents with net scores at or near zero, that is, when it predicts a null decision or identifies a voter as weakly committed.[8] Furthermore, errors occur with more (or much more) than average frequency in predicting the votes of those interviewed early,[9] those undecided at the time of their interview,[10] and those who changed their choices after being interviewed.[11] Taken

[8] Ibid., pp. 578–579.
[9] Ibid., pp. 581–583.
[10] Ibid., p. 581.
[11] Ibid.

together, these facts suggest that a great many of the Rule's errors arise because predictions do not take into account changes in the considerations that enter into the choices of voters *after* they have been interviewed.

That conclusion is consistent with other evidence as well. Consider a voter interviewed two weeks before election day whose preference for a candidate is weak. The more such a voter exposes himself to campaign arguments, the more likely he is to encounter some that will change his preference and falsify the Rule's prediction for him. Furthermore, this change of preference should be toward the side (if any) favored by the flow of argument that reaches him. This reasoning squares nicely with three findings about the Rule's errors. In predicting the votes of weakly committed voters, errors are more frequent for those who express a large number of likes and dislikes than for those who do not.[12] One would expect that result, since the former tend to be more interested in the election and thus more likely to expose themselves to arguments that introduce new considerations into their calculations. Further, the Rule shows greater than average rates of error when it predicts votes inconsistent with party affiliation and votes for the losing candidate in a landslide election.[13] In both cases the flow of argument toward such voters is likely to be biased, in the latter case toward the victor, in the former toward the candidate of the voter's party as his friends and family suggest reasons for remaining loyal to it.[14]

Errors that arise from the timing of preelection interviews do not count against the Rule's validity, and neither do those from two additional sources. Interviewing most probably

---

[12] Ibid., p. 579.

[13] Ibid.

[14] John G. Geer, in an as yet unpublished paper that draws upon data from the University of Michigan's 1952 National Election Study, shows that an indicator of the homogeneity and partisan direction of opinion among a respondent's friends and family can increase the proportion of cases correctly predicted by the Rule by as much as 6 percentage points. Geer argues that this indicator in part forecasts postinterview changes in the opinions of respondents, as they are subjected to pressures from friends and family, though his results suggest an independent role for this "discussion factor" as well.

stimulates some respondents to vote who would not do so otherwise; these voters have no counterparts in the electorate being sampled. A tendency also exists for respondents to report a larger proportion of votes for the winning candidate than the official count shows, since some, apparently, attach importance to picking winners and say they have done so either in forgetfulness of how they actually voted or because they believe such a claim is somehow more acceptable than the truth. The stimulation effect is probably not a major cause of error; when one removes from the sample those respondents most likely to have been subject to it, rates of error are reduced, but not greatly.[15] The misreporting of votes, however, may lead to a considerable exaggeration of the true rate of error. As I have just noted, the Rule in fact shows a larger rate of error in predicting votes for the losing candidate than for the victor. Moreover, among weakly committed voters there is a strong relationship between the probability of an erroneous prediction and the time of the postelection interview; the later the interview, the greater the chance of error.[16]

Unequal weighting of considerations by voters seems *not* to be a major cause of error in the Rule's predictions. Regression analysis permits one to compare the Rule's success in predicting (more properly, postdicting, when regression is used) votes with that of alternative models of voting decisions in which the weight of different sorts of considerations can vary. Such comparisons yield only trivial differences in rates of error, and it is easy to suggest why.[17] Across a large population of voters, differences in the ranking of considerations occur but cancel out. While Voter A ranks peace above inflation, Voter B assigns the two issues the reverse ordering, thus giving them equal weight on the average.

Data from the University of Michigan national elections studies of 1960 and 1964 permit a still more direct test of the impact on predictions of the assumption of equal weighting.

[15] Kelley and Mirer, pp. 583–584.
[16] Ibid., p. 585.
[17] See Appendix I.

In those years interviewers asked respondents to name the most important problems facing government and to identify the party best able to handle each problem; respondents could name as many as three problems in 1960 and as many as six in 1964. It is reasonable to treat these problems as considerations in respondents' votes and, further, to suppose that the problem a respondent named first is likely to have been the one most important to him. Parallel regressions—one in which the weights of problems are constrained to be equal, the other in which those weights are allowed to vary—show two things: First-named problems do have the greatest impact on voting, but constraining the weights of the problems does *not* reduce one's ability to postdict votes correctly.[18] This last result argues strongly for the assumption of equal weighting as a convenient approximation of the truth.

As Table 2.1 shows, the Rule's predictions of individual votes yielded an unusually large proportion of errors for the elections of 1968 and 1980. The Wallace and Anderson candidacies were a great part of the trouble: Large percentages of those predicted to vote for these candidates did not, and a considerable proportion of the votes each received came from the respondents who had been predicted to vote for someone else. If Wallace and Anderson voters are excluded from consideration, the percentage of votes correctly predicted by the Rule becomes 88.5 for 1968 and 86.5 for 1980, results comparable in their accuracy to those reported in Table 2.1 for other elections. That the Rule makes better predictions for two-candidate elections than it does for three-candidate elections is not surprising; as formulated, it makes no special allowance for voters' expectations about the candidates' chances. In an election with two candidates, voting for one's second choice because one expects one's first choice to lose makes no sense; in a three-candidate election, it may be sensible to do just that.[19]

[18] See Table A.I.7, Appendix I.
[19] Votes for minor candidates (with Anderson not counting as such) also account for an appreciable proportion of the Rule's errors (5 to 12 percent) in the elections of 1972, 1976, and 1980.

Two other possible sources of error in the Rule's predictions—unconscious considerations and conscious considerations which voters leave unstated in their interviews—seem likely to be occasional, rather than frequent, causes of error. Campaigns and the fixed dates of voting, as I have already noted, push voters toward a conscious canvassing of likes and dislikes. Moreover, interviewers give respondents many opportunities to express likes and dislikes (in a two-candidate race as many as forty). Thus, respondents are likely to remain silent only about those considerations which they find particularly hard to articulate, which they regard as mean or embarrassing, or which they have forgotten.

CRITICISMS

Critics of these tests of the Rule have acknowledged its success as a formula for predicting votes but have contended that voters' likes and dislikes fail to *explain* voters' choices in any useful sense. Some critics argue also that the latter may explain the former, that is, that voters' likes and dislikes may be rationalizations of voters' choices.

Ian Budge and Dennis Fairlie have advanced the first contention with this argument: (1) To say that A explains B is to claim that there is "a reasonable correspondence between the two" and that A is not the same as B.[20] (2) These criteria are interdependent; if "there is a one-to-one correspondence between A and B we should think they were probably the same."[21] (3) The successes of the Rule's predictions arouse the suspicion that no interesting explanation is involved: "Given that likes and dislikes, elicited directly by questions about the parties, stand so close to the vote, one doubts that the two are at all distinguishable."[22]

As it stands, this argument has obvious flaws. In principle a cause and its effect *should* have a one-to-one relationship; the perfect correspondence between the earth's rotation and the

[20] Ian Budge and Dennis Fairlie, *Voting and Party Competition* (New York: John Wiley and Sons, 1977), pp. 93–94.
[21] Ibid., p. 94.
[22] Ibid., p. 96n.

apparent movement of the sun across the sky, for example, is quite reasonably accepted as evidence that the one causes the other. Moreover, expressing likes and dislikes in a preelection interview is plainly not the same thing as pulling a lever in a voting booth, saying what lever one has pulled, or intending to pull a particular lever. If this argument is not to be dismissed out of hand, we must reformulate it. Its gist is that (1) success in predicting votes is an insufficient basis for regarding the facts used for prediction as a good explanation of voting, and (2) proximate causes do not provide interesting explanations.

The first point is correct. For example, while one can predict voters' choices with great accuracy (usually) from their stated intentions, few would think the statement, "He voted for Jones because he said he was going to vote for Jones," a good explanation of a vote. The second point, however, is simply wrong, unless Budge and Fairlie regard the "interest" of an explanation as a matter of taste. We continually look for motives or reasons to explain human actions, the usefulness of doing so is obvious, and these motives or reasons stand as close to the actions that they are intended to explain as voters' likes and dislikes of parties and candidates do to their choices at the polls. If voters' likes and dislikes reveal the *reasons* for a voter's choice, they usefully explain it, no matter how close they stand to it or how deep an explanation they are.

That voters' likes and dislikes simply *measure* the voter's intention to vote in a particular way is an objection much like the one just discussed, but it differs sufficiently to merit discussion on its own. In measurement, so this argument goes, multiple readings produce more accurate results than single readings; thus, a chemist will dip a thermometer into a solution several times, averaging the results, to find the solution's true temperature. Similarly, a voter's expressions of likes and dislikes are so many readings of his preference for one candidate or another; these readings of preference yield quite accurate forecasts of the voter's choice but no more explain it than thermometer readings explain temperature.

Two things are wrong with this argument. First, direct statements of preference for a candidate in response to a single question in fact yield more *accurate* predictions of choices than likes and dislikes do. The latter yield a *higher proportion of correct predictions* for a sample of voters only because one can make predictions for undecided respondents and those who refuse to express preferences. Second, the argument confuses prediction with measurement. While a response to the question, "How do you intend to vote," is legitimately conceived of as a measure of a voter's true intention, responses to the "likes-dislikes" questions cannot be; the latter *measure* true likes and dislikes, though they reliably *predict* voters' choices. Why do they do so? Maybe because voters' likes and dislikes are the reasons for their choices, and motives are usually good indicators of actions.

A third objection challenges any such conclusion directly by suggesting that voters' expressions of likes and dislikes may be mere rationalizations. Clearly, they could be: A voter might say that he liked a candidate's stand on an issue, for instance, when in fact he cared only about the candidate's party or religion. Moreover, if likes and dislikes were in fact mere rationalizations, they might predict voting, and might appear to explain it, nearly as well as genuine motives.

While this argument is in a sense irrefutable—true motives are nonobservable—it is less formidable than it at first appears. In everyday life our need to understand and influence others involves us continually in attempts to discover motives. We infer these either from observation or, more often, from testimony, whether volunteered or elicited by direct or indirect questioning. In our efforts to distinguish the true from the false motive in such testimony, we apply tests: Is the hypothetical motive sufficient to explain a decision or action? Is the motive appropriate and normal for the circumstances? Has a person who tells us his motives any reason to mislead us? Does he advance only respectable reasons, calculated to win our esteem or bolster his self-esteem? Would other motives better explain his actions? While these tests will not save us from all error in assigning motives, no sensible person will for that reason give up the effort to explain by motives.[23]

---

[23] Cf. Suzanne Duvall Jacobitti, "Causes, Reasons, and Voting," *Political Theory* 7 (August 1979), pp. 390–413.

By such tests voters' statements of their likes and dislikes are hard to dismiss, wholesale, as misrepresentations of their motives. The questions that elicit these likes and dislikes do not ask directly for motives or for any statement of preference that might seem to require justification; instead, interviewers encourage voters in their interviews to go through the process by which voting choices are reached in real life. The questions about likes and dislikes occur early in interviews, before any questioning about preferences for candidates or views on issues. Interviewers are strangers, and respondents are given anonymity. The likes and dislikes expressed are overwhelmingly those that one would expect to play a part in voting, and many voters express likes and dislikes that run counter to their choices, something that we usually do not do when trying to justify a decision already taken. If voters were rationalizing, one might expect attempts to hide partisan or self-interested motives, but neither partisanship nor group interests account for voting as well, either singly or together, as the full array of likes and dislikes;[24] moreover, large numbers of voters show no hesitancy in citing partisanship or self-interest as reasons for liking or disliking parties and candidates. The behavior of voters in the aggregate squares well with their likes and dislikes: Those whose net scores have high absolute values almost all vote as predicted; those whose net scores are near zero show a strong tendency to be undecided, to delay decision, to change their minds, and to abstain from voting. It seems quite improbable that respondents not warned of questions in ad-

[24] Cf. Donald E. Stokes, Angus Campbell, and Warren E. Miller, "Components of Electoral Decision," *American Political Science Review* 52 (June 1958), pp. 367–387. Stokes and his associates note that "it is quite clear that fixed party loyalties and sociological characteristics cannot account fully for the vote. In particular, neither of these factors, relatively inert through time, can account for the short-term fluctuations in the division of the vote which are of such great significance in a two-party system . . . the movement [toward the Republicans from 1948 to 1952] can be quite easily explained if we accord genuine motivational significance to attitudes toward the candidates and issues, and observe that the popular response to the Republican candidate and to the configuration of issues salient in the campaign was far more favorable to the Republicans in 1952 than in 1948" (pp. 368–369).

vance could fabricate misleading or rationalized motives so consistent in detail with the preferences and behavior that they report.

In what is to come, my prime objective is to demonstrate the usefulness of the theory just discussed for the interpretation of elections. The next chapter, in which I assess the decisiveness of the elections of 1964 and 1972, is the first step in that demonstration. In my analysis of decisiveness, and in other applications as well, the net scores to which I have already referred figure prominently. For that reason, I shall indicate here precisely how such scores are computed.

Suppose that a respondent gives two reasons for liking the Democratic candidate, three reasons for disliking the Democratic Party, four reasons for liking the Republican Party and candidate, and one reason for disliking the Republican candidate. We can classify his attitudes thus:

KIND OF RESPONSE	NUMBER OF RESPONSES
D^+ (favorable to the Democratic Party or candidate or both)	2
D^- (unfavorable to the Democratic Party or candidate or both)	3
R^+ (favorable to the Republican Party or candidate or both)	4
R^- (unfavorable to the Republican Party or candidate or both)	1

Given these figures, the net number of favorable attitudes that the respondent has toward the Democratic candidate ($D^+ - D^-$) is -1; toward the Republican candidate ($R^+ - R^-$) it is 3. The respondent's *net score*, ($D^+ - D^-$) − ($R^+ - R^-$), therefore, is -4. Had ($D^+ - D^-$) been equal in this case to ($R^+ - R^-$), that is, if the difference between them had been zero, one would take into account the respondent's party identification,

assigning him a score of +0 if he was a Democrat, of −0 if he
was a Republican, and of 0 if he was an independent.[25] In a
sample of voters, net scores typically range from −19 to +19.

Three assumptions figure in an important way in my interpretation of respondents' net scores. They are:

1. That the sign of a respondent's net score indicates the
   candidate that he preferred at the time of his preelection interview (the Democratic candidate if the sign
   was positive, the Republican candidate if it was negative, a null decision if it was zero).
2. That the fraction of the vote for the Democratic candidate (or the Republican candidate) by respondents
   with the same net score gives the probability with
   which an individual voter with that score would vote
   Democratic (or Republican) on election day.
3. That the absolute value of a respondent's net score
   measures the strength of his commitment to the candidate he preferred at the time of his preelection interview.

The first of these assumptions seems justified by the number
of cases in which the sign of respondents' net scores coincided
with their statements of how they intended to vote (in 88.7 per
cent of the cases in 1972, in 97.4 per cent of those in 1964).
The second assumption seems a reasonable interpretation of
the meaning of net scores on election day, in cases in which
that is of interest, and the third assumption is consistent with
the strong association of scores of low absolute value with late
decisions, changes of intention, indecision, and high rates of
nonvoting.

[25] The symbols +0 and −0 are, of course, simply a notational convenience. Each can be thought of as two paired symbols (+, 0) and (−, 0) in
which the sign indicates the partisan identification of the respondents
(minus for Republican, plus for Democratic) and the zero indicates the
difference between the net number of favorable attitudes the respondent
has toward each candidate of any pair of candidates.

CHAPTER THREE

THREE TESTS OF DECISIVENESS

The term *landslide* entered the language of politics in the nineteenth century. Used by geologists as a synonym for avalanche, landslip, or slide, the word came to mean any particularly one-sided election, and that is still its connotation today,[1] though in actual usage elections have attained landslide status rather easily. According to Max Frankel, "The term has been applied to cases in which a Presidential candidate lost no more than ten states or carried eighty per cent of the electoral votes or at least fifty-three per cent of the popular vote. By those standards, there have been twenty-four landslides in the previous [before 1972] forty-six Presidential contests."[2] Table 3.1 lists the presidential elections since 1828 which satisfy at least one of these criteria for votes received or a somewhat stricter criterion than Frankel's for states carried.[3] Clearly, several of these landslides buried no one very deeply, and usage has been even looser than Frankel suggests. The *New York Times,* for instance, declared the election of 1896 a "landslide for honest money," though it met none of his tests.[4]

The presidential elections of 1964 and 1972, however, were landslides by anyone's reckoning. Those who call today's counterparts of the stars of the 1930s superstars would have to call these two elections superlandslides, or "landslides of his-

---

[1] Hans Sperber and Travis Trittshuh, *American Political Terms* (Detroit: Wayne State University Press, 1962), p. 234.

[2] *New York Times,* November 8, 1972.

[3] In our early history, to lose ten states was to lose a great part of them. Unless it qualified as a landslide on one of the other grounds that Frankel suggested, no election was included in Table 3.1 if its victorious candidate lost more than 20 percent of the states (with the District of Columbia counting as such after 1960).

[4] *New York Times,* November 4, 1896.

TABLE 3.1

Presidential Elections by Unusual Majorities, 1828–1980

Election	Winning Candidate	Popular Vote	Major-Party Vote	Electoral Vote	Potential Vote	States
1828	Andrew Jackson	56.0%	56.2%	68.2%	32.3%	62.5%
1832	Andrew Jackson	54.2	59.2	76.0	30.0	70.8
1840	William H. Harrison	52.9	53.0	79.6	42.4	73.1
1852	Franklin Pierce	50.8	53.7	85.8	35.4	87.1
1864	Abraham Lincoln	55.0	55.0	90.6	40.6	88.0
1872	Ulysses S. Grant	55.6	55.9	78.1	39.6	82.9
1904	Theodore Roosevelt	56.4	60.0	70.6	36.8	71.1
1912	Woodrow Wilson	41.8	60.4	81.9	24.6	83.3
1920	Warren G. Harding	60.3	63.8	76.1	29.7	77.1
1924	Calvin Coolidge	54.1	65.2	71.9	26.5	72.9
1928	Herbert Hoover	58.2	58.8	83.6	33.1	83.3
1932	Franklin D. Roosevelt	57.4	59.2	88.9	32.7	87.5
1936	Franklin D. Roosevelt	60.8	62.5	98.5	37.1	95.8
1940	Franklin D. Roosevelt	54.7	55.0	84.6	34.2	79.2
1944	Franklin D. Roosevelt	53.4	53.8	81.4	29.9	75.0
1952	Dwight D. Eisenhower	55.1	55.4	83.3	34.9	81.3
1956	Dwight D. Eisenhower	57.4	57.8	86.1	34.8	85.4
1964	Lyndon B. Johnson	61.1	61.3	90.3	37.8	86.3
1972	Richard M. Nixon	60.7	61.8	96.7	34.7	96.1
1980	Ronald Reagan	50.8	55.3	90.9	28.0	86.3

SOURCES: The data in the first three columns of the table and the last come from *Congressional Quarterly, Presidential Elections since 1789* (Washington, D.C.: Congressional Quarterly, 1975) and *Guide to 1976 Elections* (Washington, D.C.: Congressional Quarterly, 1977); and *New York Times*, January 6, 1981. Figures for candidates' share of the potential vote are based on Walter Dean Burnham's estimates of participation in presidential elections. Professor Burnham's estimates for elections from 1828 to 1968 may be found in Bureau of Census, *Historical Statistics of the United States: Colonial Times to 1970* (Washington, D.C.: 1975); those for elections since 1968 he kindly provided me.

NOTE: This table includes all elections since 1828 in which the winning candidate received at least 53 percent of the popular vote or won 80 percent of the electoral vote or carried 80 percent of the states. A state (or the District of Columbia after 1960) has been counted for a candidate if he carried a majority of its electoral votes. Delaware did not choose its presidential electors by popular vote in 1828, and South Carolina did not do so until 1868. The eleven states of the Confederacy did not participate in the election of 1864.

toric proportions."[5] As Table 3.1 shows, only four candidates
have won as much as 60 percent of the popular vote since
1828, and Lyndon Johnson and Richard Nixon were two of
the four. Their victories were of almost equal magnitude:
Johnson won 61.1 percent of the popular vote, 61.3 percent of
the major-party vote, and 90.3 percent of the electoral vote;
the comparable figures for Nixon were 60.7 percent, 61.8 percent, and 96.7 percent. These massive margins of victory led
observers to declare that Johnson had received the " 'loud and
clear' national mandate he had said he wanted"[6] and to call
the 1972 election "one of the most decisive victories in the
history of American presidential politics."[7]

But large victory margins alone do not justify such claims.
To call an election decisive implies that it has removed uncertainty about "the relative strengths of parties and opinions"
(to use Mill's phrase) to an unusual degree; one cannot sensi-
bly apply the term *decisive* to an election that might easily
have gone the other way, that demonstrated only feeble support for the winning candidate, or that was devoid of meaning
for the outcome of future contests between parties or opinions.
In these senses of the word, landslides (even superlandslides)
need not be decisive. Counts of electoral votes and of states
carried are so loosely related to the way *voters* divide that they
often give a quite misleading impression of the support that
candidates enjoyed: Warren G. Harding's share of the popular and major-party vote in 1920 far exceeded that of Franklin
Pierce in 1852 or of Ronald Reagan in 1980, yet both Pierce
and Reagan carried a considerably larger proportion of the
states and won considerably larger shares of the electoral vote
than Harding. In a less obvious but more important way the
division of the popular and major-party vote can also be misleading. A large plurality in either is consistent with a freakish
turnout (one candidate's followers were snowed in), with a
very weak commitment of voters to the winning candidate
(most voters preferred him to his opponent but usually the

[5] A term used by an editorial writer of the *New York Times*, November
6, 1980.

[6] Tom Wicker, *New York Times*, November 4, 1964.

[7] James Reston, *New York Times*, November 8, 1972.

preference was slight), with an unpopular victor (few people liked either candidate), or with issues that were wholly transient.

For a better indication of decisiveness one needs answers to these four sets of questions: (1) How fully did each side mobilize its adherents, and on what scale would the losing side have had to mobilize its adherents to have changed the outcome of the election? (2) For how many voters was the choice between candidates a close question? To what extent did the winning candidate's victory depend on the votes of such weakly committed voters? (3) How favorable were the attitudes of individual voters toward the winning candidate? Did many see him only as the lesser of evils? (4) Were the issues that contributed most to the outcome transient or enduring? If the latter, were the positions that the parties assumed on such issues likely to become identified as partisan? I shall apply the first three of these tests to the elections of 1964 and 1972 in this chapter, the fourth in later chapters.

VULNERABILITY TO CHANGES IN TURNOUT

If on election day the preferences of eligible voters were fixed (a condition that may hold approximately), three factors would substantially determine the fortunes of presidential candidates: how many adherents each had; the turnout of the adherents of each; and the distribution of the adherents of each among the fifty states and the District of Columbia.[8] One can estimate the quantities involved in the first two factors from data that are easily obtained. The same cannot be said of the third factor, unfortunately, and that fact precludes a conclusive examination of the impact of turnout on the elections of 1964 and 1972.

Enough is known, however, to make some points that are nearly conclusive. We may begin by computing what I shall call the *loser's mobilization ratio* for the two elections. This ratio—the turnout of the losing candidate's adherents that

[8] I am assuming that there is a reasonably honest casting and counting of ballots and that other possibilities—for example, mistakes in voting— have a minimal impact on the voting tallies.

would have been required for his vote to have equaled that of the winner—may be expressed as $V^W/(V^L + N^L)$, where V^W is the number of votes received by the winning candidate, V^L is the number of votes received by the losing candidate, and N^L is the number of nonvoters who preferred the losing candidate. The official election returns give the number of votes for each of the candidates. The sum of those numbers and the Census Bureau's estimates of the population of voting age give one the number of nonvoters. One needs to rely on survey data, which notoriously exaggerate turnout, only for an estimate of the losing candidate's support among nonvoters; I use respondents' net scores in making that estimate and, in doing so, assume that in each election voters and nonvoters with equal net scores would have cast their ballots for the losing candidate at the same rate.

Table 3.2 reports the losers' mobilization ratios for the elec-

TABLE 3.2

Losers' Mobilization Ratios for Four Postwar Landslides

Election	Mobilization Ratio
1952	73.9%
1956	84.5
1964	111.9
1972	88.7

NOTES: The *loser's mobilization ratio* is the percentage of the loser's adherents (both those who voted and those who did not vote) who would have had to cast ballots for his vote to have equaled that of the winning candidate. The preferences of nonvoters that figure in calculations of the ratio have been estimated from net scores. Of course, one could also base these estimates on nonvoting respondents' preelection statements of how they intended to vote or on their postelection statements of how they would have voted, though both these alternatives yield an indication of preference for fewer cases than net scores. Following are the ratios estimated in each of these ways for the elections of 1964 and 1972:

Election	Intentions	Postelection Statement
1964	111.2%	118.9%
1972	90.8	90.4

Obviously, the three procedures give about the same result.

TABLE 3.3

**Estimated Rates of Turnout of Candidates'
Adherents in Four Postwar Landslides**

Election	Candidate	Estimated Turnout Rate
1952	Eisenhower	65.4%
	Stevenson	59.5
1956	Eisenhower	59.1
	Stevenson	61.8
1964	Johnson	58.5
	Goldwater	70.5
1972	Nixon	55.0
	McGovern	54.8

NOTE: Preferences of nonvoters have been estimated from net scores.

tions of 1964 and 1972 and for the two Eisenhower landslides as well. Of the four elections, the 1964 election was surely the most secure against greater efforts to mobilize the losing candidate's following. Even if all Goldwater's adherents had voted, Johnson's actual vote would have given him a comfortable popular majority nationwide, an ironic fact, given the belief of some Republicans that stay-at-home conservatives had been robbing the party of victory in earlier elections. The next highest mobilization ratio (88.7 percent) is that for 1972. To interpret that figure, consider how realistic it would be for a party to set an 89 percent turnout of its candidate's adherents as the goal of a nationwide get-out-the-vote effort. The rates of turnout reported in Table 3.3 are useful benchmarks for this exercise: They show that the highest *actual* turnout of any candidate's followers in the four landslides was far below 89 percent. Note also that neither Johnson's nor Nixon's adherents voted at unusually high rates. The rate for the former was at the Democratic average for the four elections; that for the latter was considerably below average for Republican candidates. This analysis shows, *ceteris paribus,* that it would have been impossible for Goldwater, and next to impossible for McGovern, to have obtained a majority of the two-party vote nationally by a more effective mobilization of his adherents.

Given the support that each had, and given our ignorance of its precise distribution among states, it is *conceivable* that Goldwater and McGovern each could have won a majority of the electoral vote solely by increasing the turnout of supporters in the right places. Conceivable but not at all likely. Johnson would have won an electoral-vote majority even if, in addition to the states he actually lost, he had lost all those that he carried by less than 62 percent of the popular vote. Nixon would have lost only narrowly (by five electoral votes) even if he had lost all the states that he carried by less than 60 percent of the vote.

The Johnson and Nixon victories were both nearly invulnerable to a countermobilization of their opponents' followings.

Electoral Vulnerability and Intensity of Preferences

The two elections present a very different picture, however, if one examines the strength of voters' commitments to the candidates, as measured by net scores.

Figure 3.1, which shows the distribution of voters over net scores in the two elections, gives a first indication of the difference. In 1964 the median voter had a net score of +3, and the mean score was +2.4. In 1972 the net score of the median voter was −2; the mean score, −1.3. If we define as "strongly committed" those respondents whose net scores have an absolute value of 10 or more, then the proportion of strongly committed voters on the winning side in 1964 was nearly double that in 1972. If one gives "weak commitment" any of three reasonable definitions, it was substantially more prevalent in 1972. That point is driven home by Table 3.4, which shows the proportion of weakly committed voters to have been greater in 1972 than in *any* of the other elections that figure in the table, except that of 1976. The election of 1960, the closest election by conventional measures in this century, was not so close in these terms as Nixon's landslide. And Table 3.5 shows

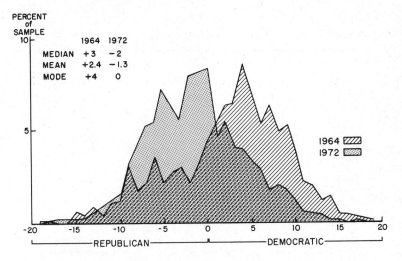

PERCENT
of
SAMPLE

	1964	1972
MEDIAN	+3	−2
MEAN	+2.4	−1.3
MODE	+4	0

1964
1972

-20   -15   -10   -5   0   5   10   15   20

REPUBLICAN ———————— DEMOCRATIC ————————

3.1   Distribution of Respondents over Net Scores

that commitment to candidates was weaker in 1972 than in 1964 as measured not just by net score but by other indices as well.

The high proportion of weakly committed voters in 1972 reflects in part the number of McGovern supporters whose preferences for him were lukewarm. If one examines only the vote for the winners in the two landslides, however, the pattern suggested by Figure 3.1 and the tables just examined remains. Table 3.6 shows that weakly committed voters contributed a considerably larger share of Nixon's vote than Johnson's, and a somewhat larger share of Nixon's vote than of Kennedy's in 1960, Nixon's in 1968, or of Eisenhower's in 1952 or 1956.[9]

Did either Johnson or Nixon need the votes of weakly

[9] In Tables 3.6 and 3.7, I have treated votes that were predicted incorrectly as weakly committed votes. Two considerations speak for this procedure: (1) In general, the probability of voting for the winner declines regularly from the high to the low end of the scale; (2) incorrect predictions are highly correlated with indecision and changes of intention. See Appendix I and Kelley and Mirer, "The Simple Act of Voting," pp. 580–585.

TABLE 3.4
Weakly Committed Voters in Presidential Elections, 1952–1976

Election	Sample Size*	% of Respondents with Net Scores between:		
		±1	±2	±3
1952	1184	14.3	22.9	32.7
1956	1270	18.1	28.7	37.6
1960	1413**	14.6	25.5	33.1
1964	1113	12.9	21.6	30.9
1968	1027	16.6	25.1	34.2
1972	830	20.8	34.2	43.9
1976	1650**	22.6	34.7	47.1

* Samples are samples of respondents who voted, excluding those who refused to say how they voted or who said that they did not remember how they had voted. The figures for 1968 take account of attitudes toward Nixon and Humphrey only.
** Weighted sample.

TABLE 3.5
Additional Indices of Strength of Commitment in the Elections of 1964 and 1972

Index of Commitment	1964	1972
Percent of respondents who:		
Expressed no preelection preference	11.3	13.7
Did not vote as intended	4.6	11.0
Did not vote	22.3	29.1
Decided late how they would vote*	12.0	12.4

* Decided how they would vote within two weeks of election day.

committed voters to win? One's answer depends on the way in which weak commitment is defined, but in brief it is this: Johnson needed few or none; Nixon needed a considerable number. Table 3.7 shows, for the two-candidate elections since 1952, the proportion of the weakly committed votes received by winning candidates that each needed for a majority.

TABLE 3.6

Percentage of Winner's Vote Received from Weakly Committed Voters in Presidential Elections, 1952–1976

Candidate	Votes Received from Sample	Weakly Committed Voters Defined as Those with Net Scores of:*		
		≤ +1 or ≥ −1	≤ +2 or ≥ −2	≤ +3 or ≥ −3
Eisenhower '52	687	21.7	28.7	36.1
Eisenhower '56	755	26.2	33.4	40.7
Kennedy	693**	18.5	29.1	35.8
Johnson	750	14.1	21.2	29.6
Nixon '68	490	18.4	24.1	31.4
Nixon '72	531	27.1	37.7	45.0
Carter '76	834**	25.7	38.3	51.2

* *Weakly committed voters* are defined differently, but symmetrically, for Democratic and Republican candidates. For the former, the weakly committed are all those with net scores *less than* a positive number; for the latter, they are all those with net scores *greater than* a negative number. The figures for 1968 take account of attitudes toward Nixon and Humphrey only.

** Weighted sample.

TABLE 3.7

**Percentage of Winner's Vote Received from Weakly
Committed Voters Required for a Majority in
Two-Candidate Presidential Elections, 1952–1976**

Candidate	*Weakly Committed Voters Defined as Those with Net Scores of:*[*]		
	$\leq +1$ or ≥ -1	$\leq +2$ or ≥ -2	$\leq +3$ or ≥ -3
Eisenhower '52	36.9	52.3	62.1
	(55)[**]	(103)	(154)
Eisenhower '56	39.9	52.8	61.2
	(79)	(133)	(307)
Kennedy[***]	100.0	100.0	100.0
	(128)	(202)	(248)
Johnson	0.0	0.0	12.6
	(106)	(159)	(222)
Nixon '72	20.1	42.5	51.3
	(144)	(200)	(239)
Carter '76[***]	90.7	93.5	95.2
	(201)	(286)	(393.5)

[*] The notation is the same as that for Table 3.6.
[**] Numbers in parentheses are the numerical base for the percentage figures. Note that respondents voting for McCarthy and Maddox do not figure in the calculations for the election of 1976.
[***] Weighted sample.

These data show that Lyndon Johnson's victory was by this measure by far the most secure of any since 1952. Richard Nixon's was very much less secure. He needed one-half of the votes that he received from the weakly committed (as defined most broadly in the table), while Johnson needed about one-eighth of their votes. By comparison with 1964 the election of 1972 was a *close landslide* and its voters—on both sides—among the least enthusiastic of recent history.

THE POLITICAL CREDIT OF SUCCESSFUL CANDIDATES

What a presidential election means for the later conduct of government depends significantly on voters' attitudes toward the victorious presidential candidate and his party. Favorable attitudes are political credit on which the victor can draw in exercising leadership; unfavorable attitudes may be obstacles to the acceptance of his policies and programs. Neither the count of votes nor net scores, however, are of much use in distinguishing successful candidates with much credit from those with little. Both votes and net scores tell us something important about voters' comparative evaluations of candidates but nothing about the evaluations that went into the comparison.

Recall, however, that a net score is the difference, for any voter, between the net number of his attitudes that are favorable to the Democratic candidate and party, $(D^+ - D^-)$, and the net number that are favorable to the Republican candidate and party, $(R^+ - R^-)$.[10] Each of these components of a net score—let us call them *credit ratings* for convenience—range in value from $+10$ to -10, that is, from extremely favorable to extremely unfavorable. We can use them to compare voters' attitudes toward successful candidates in different elections and, incidentally, toward the choices that different elections offered.

Table 3.8 makes both applications. For each of the elections between 1952 and 1976 the table's first column reports the percentage of voters who gave *both* candidates credit ratings of zero or less. These *lesser-of-evils* choices are a sign of weakness in the winning candidate's support, since voters making such choices see (at best) as many things to dislike as to like about him. More than one-fifth of all voters gave both candidates a zero-or-less rating in 1972, the highest proportion to do so in any of these elections. Read together, the two columns of Table 3.8 show an increasing disenchantment of voters with the choices offered them. In the first three elections that figure in the table, voters who rated both candidates positively outnumber those who made lesser-of-evils choices considerably; in the last four, it is the other way around.

Nonetheless, of the winning candidates in these elections, it was Lyndon Johnson who had the most political credit on

---

[10] See the discussion of net scores in Chapter 2.

TABLE 3.8

**Lesser-of-Evils and Better-of-Goods Choices in
Presidential Elections, 1952–1976**

| Election | Respondents Choosing the: | |
	Lesser of Evils	Better of Goods
1952	7.3%	12.6%
1956	9.3	15.4
1960	5.9	14.4
1964	12.3	5.5
1968	19.4	7.1
1972	21.2	7.0
1976	20.1	10.2

NOTE: A voter's choice counts as one between the *lesser of evils* when neither $(D^+ - D^-)$ nor $(R^+ - R^-)$ is greater than zero; when neither is less than +1, the choice counts as one between the *better of goods*. The figures for 1968 take account of attitudes toward Nixon and Humphrey only.

TABLE 3.9

Credit Ratings for Six Winning Candidates, 1952–1976

Candidate	% Net Positive Credit Ratings	Mean Credit Rating	Median Credit Rating	Quartile Ratings
Eisenhower '52	56.9	1.42	+1	−1, +4
Eisenhower '56	59.1	1.37	+1	−1, +4
Kennedy	53.9	.97	+1	−2, +4
Johnson	64.3	1.45	+2	−1, +4
Nixon '68	47.1	.58	0	−2, +3
Nixon '72	53.4	.53	+1	−1, +3
Carter '76	48.8	.29	0	−2, +3

NOTE: Credit ratings range from −10 to +10. Net positive ratings are those of +1 or greater.

election day. Sixty-four percent of all respondents gave him a positive credit rating (see Table 3.9); the comparable figures for the other two landslide winners, Nixon and Eisenhower (1952 and 1956), were 53 percent, 57 percent, and 59 percent, respectively.[11] The mean and median ratings for Johnson also exceeded those for Nixon and Eisenhower. In this table as in the last, Nixon in 1972 makes a poor showing. His credit rating in his landslide victory shows a greater resemblance to those of Kennedy and Carter, winners by narrow margins, than to the ratings given Johnson and Eisenhower.

Figure 3.2, which shows the distribution of respondents in 1960, 1964, and 1972 over the full range of values that credit ratings can assume, permits a detailed comparison of voters' evaluations of Johnson and Nixon, on the one hand, and of Nixon and Kennedy, on the other. That Johnson had greater strength among respondents than Nixon is obvious: The curve for Johnson is like that for Nixon, moved about two points toward the positive end of the scale. More than 20 percent of all respondents gave Johnson a rating of +5 or better, and 55 percent gave him a rating of +2 or better. The comparable figures for Nixon are 11 percent and 40 percent. Nixon's ratings in 1972 gave him no clear advantage over Kennedy in 1960. The major difference in the curves for the two men is in the degree of consensus among voters in rating them. Almost 60 percent of the sample gave Nixon a rating between −1 and +3. Kennedy was given considerably fewer ratings in that range (47 percent) and more toward both the positive and negative ends of the scale.

One would expect positive evaluations of a candidate to

[11] In interpreting this result, bear in mind that credit ratings reflect attitudes toward parties and policies as well as evaluations of the personal qualities and qualifications of candidates. General Eisenhower was the most popular, personally, of these three candidates, but his party and some of the policy positions with which he was identified hurt his candidacy, whereas party and policies helped Johnson. See Michael R. Kagay and Greg A. Caldeira, "A 'Reformed' Electorate? Well at Least a Changed Electorate, 1952–1976," tables 1.1 and 1.2, pp. 8 and 12, in William J. Crotty (ed.), *Paths to Political Reform* (Lexington, Mass.: Lexington Books, 1980).

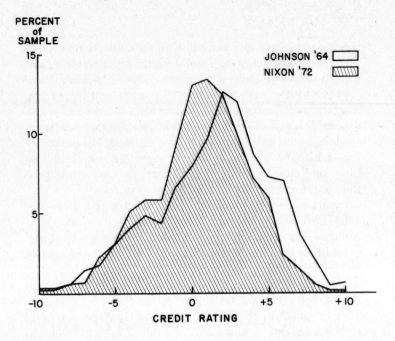

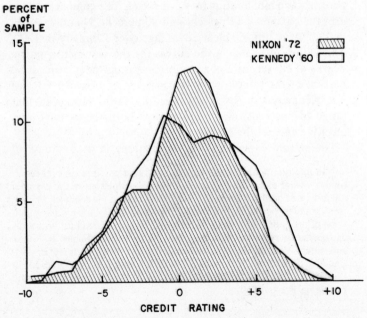

3.2   Comparison of Credit Ratings: Johnson and Nixon, Nixon and Kennedy

TABLE 3.10

Credit Ratings by Strength of Commitment to the Winning Candidate in Presidential Elections, 1952–1976

Candidate	Respondents Giving Positive Credit Ratings in:		
	Half of Sample Most Favorable to Candidate	Next Most Favorable Fourth of Sample	Least Favorable Fourth of Sample
Eisenhower '52	96.3%	32.9%	2.3%
Eisenhower '56	96.4	38.8	4.0
Kennedy	93.8	27.2	1.2
Johnson	97.7	58.1	3.8
Nixon '68	85.6	17.0	0.5
Nixon '72	89.7	32.6	1.8
Carter '76	85.8	21.6	1.9

NOTE: Net scores have been used to measure strength of commitment.

predominate among his adherents and negative evaluations to be most frequent among opposition voters, and the data confirm this expectation (see Table 3.10). There are variations on this theme, however, which indicate in still another way the relative strength of the candidacies that we have been examining. For each candidate, Table 3.10 reports the percentage of positive credit ratings in the half of the sample most favorable to his candidacy, in the next most favorable fourth of the sample, and in the least favorable fourth. In this array of data Johnson shows the strongest base of support: Ninety-eight percent of those in the half-sample most favorable to him gave him a positive credit rating. His credit also shows greater penetration beyond his base. Nixon's position in 1972, in contrast, was the weakest of any of the landslide winners and clearly superior only to that which he occupied in 1968 and to Jimmy Carter's in 1976.

Our review of the credit ratings of victorious candidates shows quite forcefully that Nixon's landslide was not only closer, attitudinally, than either Johnson's or Eisenhower's, but also more *negative*. His huge margin of victory owed less to positive evaluations of him by voters than theirs did, and more to negative evaluations of his opponent. Clearly, equal margins of victory do not necessarily indicate equal support in the electorate.

CHAPTER FOUR
ISSUES AND OUTCOMES

In assessing the extent to which the elections of 1964 and 1972 were decisive, I have ignored so far the substance of the concerns that underlay net scores and credit ratings. No full account of the decisiveness of an election can properly do so. In politics, as in everyday life, we rightly take the grounds for preferences as indicators of their durability: Some issues that affect voting are specific to particular elections and imply nothing for later ones or even for later support for the winning candidate, while other issues arise again and again, and parties and candidates become identified with the positions that they take. And, of course, knowledge of the considerations that figure in voting is of central importance for interpreting elections, quite apart from gauging their decisiveness. For most people, to ask what an election means is to ask what beliefs and attitudes made voters pull one lever and not another.

In the next two chapters I shall examine in detail the concerns of voters in the elections of 1964 and 1972 and show how those concerns comingled and interacted to produce two monumental landslides. These analyses will be easier to understand and to evaluate if they are prefaced by a discussion of some issues of method. For that reason I shall note in this chapter some features of the data I have drawn upon and introduce some concepts that are helpful in thinking about the relationship between the decisions of individual voters, on the one hand, and the decisions of the electorate as a whole, on the other.

DATA

As I have noted already, I identify the considerations that entered into voting in 1964 and 1972 with the likes and dislikes that voters expressed in answering eight free-answer questions put to them by interviewers of the University of Michigan's Survey Research Center. I have not worked directly with the statements of voters that the interviewers recorded, however, but with coders' classifications of those statements. In both years coders assigned likes and dislikes to a large number—in 1972 more than 400—of mutually exclusive categories, so the codes preserve a great deal of the concreteness of voters' responses. The categories in the code vary in specificity from "don't agree with his policies" to "like his stand on aid to parochial schools." The distribution of responses over the categories of the codes is testimony to the great heterogeneity of the American electorate, or at least to the heterogeneity with which it expresses itself: Eighty to 90 percent of the categories describe the likes and dislikes of fewer than 5 percent of the respondents.

For analytical purposes most students of voting have grouped these coded entries of likes and dislikes into a much smaller number of categories. Donald E. Stokes and his associates, for instance, treated virtually all likes and dislikes as pertaining to the personal attributes of the candidates, the relation of population groups to the major parties and their candidates, issues of domestic policy, issues of foreign policy, or the records of the major parties in the management of government.[1] Other analysts have used a different, but usually a comparably small, number of categories.[2] Probably no

---

[1] Stokes, Campbell, and Miller, "Components of Electoral Decision," and Donald E. Stokes, "Some Dynamic Elements of Contests for the Presidency," *American Political Science Review* 60 (March 1966), pp. 19–28. See also Kagay and Caldeira, "A 'Reformed' Electorate? Well at Least a Changed Electorate." Herbert Asher has used the Stokes scheme to interpret presidential elections from 1952 to 1976 in his *Presidential Elections and American Politics* (Homewood, Ill.: Dorsey Press, 1980), revised edition.

[2] See Angus Campbell, Gerald Gurin, and Warren E. Miller, *The Voter Decides* (White Plains, N.Y.: Row, Peterson and Co., 1954); John H. Kessel, *The Goldwater Coalition* (New York: Bobbs-Merrill Company, 1968); Angus Campbell, "Interpreting the Presidential Victory," pp. 256–281, in Milton C. Cummings, Jr. (ed.), *The National Election of 1964* (Washington, D.C.: The Brookings Institution, 1960); and Gerald M. Pomper, *Voters' Choice* (New York: Dodd, Mead, 1975).

scheme of classification can be equally valuable from all points of view. Great specificity in categories may lead one to lose sight of common themes that recur election after election; great generality obscures what respondents actually said. In analyzing the elections of 1964 and 1972 I relate respondents' likes and dislikes to the issues that figured in political commentary and campaign propaganda at the time; the result is a set of forty categories and subcategories for each election. To discuss elections in the terms that voters, journalists, and politicians want to discuss them requires a scheme with something like this degree of elaboration. To learn that "domestic issues" hurt a particular candidate in a particular election, for instance, whets but does not satisfy one's appetite for information; it is considerably more interesting, politically, to learn that the candidate won votes on the issues of social security and medicare but lost them on inflation and civil rights.

Whatever the scheme used to aggregate responses into components, issues, or considerations, it almost certainly will involve debatable judgments and can yield misleading results. Is the comment, "People have confidence in him," one that bears on a candidate's capacity for leadership? Without dogmatism I treat it as such. (As is often true, a misclassification of the response cannot have led me far astray, since it was not a frequent one.) Is "group connections" a good label for the set of responses brought together under that head in the National Election Study codes? The label certainly reflects a common element in those responses, but it also conceals an interesting fact—that most of the comments to which it is applied concern the relationship of the major parties and their candidates to "Big Business," on the one hand, and "the common man" or "the working man," on the other. Faced with these kinds of questions, the surest way to avoid misleading others is to define precisely the sets of responses to which the necessarily ambiguous labels of issues or components apply. I have done so in Appendix II.

As a basis for interpreting elections the Michigan data on voters' likes and dislikes have shortcomings, though fewer than any other data available. The substance of some responses goes unrecorded in the codes except as "other" (e.g., "other domestic issues"). About one-quarter of the respondents in 1972, and one-eighth in 1964, had at least one response relegated to such catchall codes. The import of some responses that are recorded are vague; what a voter meant when he said that a candidate had "too much publicity," for instance, is not readily apparent. A few codes denote responses that are mere statements of preferences (e.g., "I just like him"). It is dubious practice to treat these as considerations in voters' choices; however, excluding them has virtually no effect either on the number of votes one can predict or on the accuracy of predictions.[3] Finally, one cannot be sure how a good many responses relate to the real world of politics. Take, for instance, the statement, "I like Johnson for his stand on medicare." It is possible that some voters who responded in this way thought, incorrectly, that Johnson opposed medicare. If so, it is obviously wrong to attribute their votes to Johnson's actual stand on the issue. It may even be wrong to attribute their votes to Johnson's stand as they perceived it. Of course false beliefs can motivate voting, but they may also be projections—baseless attributions of the voters' own positions to a candidate that the voter favors for other reasons. Projection of this kind would have no motivational significance; it is simply one form of rationalization.

Probably this last shortcoming of the data on voters' likes and dislikes is not great in fact. In cases in which the substance of the response admits of such a judgment, the perceptions involved in most responses are clearly reasonable. Table 4.1 reports the frequency of some matched pairs of responses to the likes-dislikes questions; in each case one pair represents modal, the other nonmodal, perceptions. In the first six panels of the table the modal perceptions are true and the nonmodal responses false, and the latter are very few in number, less than 3 percent of the total. The responses that figure in the remaining panels cannot be so neatly divided into true and

---

[3] Deleting such responses from the data to which the Rule is applied decreases the accuracy of predictions for the 1964 election by 0.6 percent and for the 1972 election by 0.0 percent.

TABLE 4.1

Agreement among Respondents in Perceptions of Parties and Candidates

Panel No.	Survey	Codes	Substance of Comments	No. of Responses	% Nonmodal Responses
1.	1972	0500	McGovern is a (good, typical) Democrat; Nixon is a (good, typical) Republican.	49	
		0501	McGovern is a (good, typical) Republican; Nixon is a (good, typical) Democrat.	2	4
2.	1972	1160	McGovern and the Democrats are against military victory in Vietnam, favor withdrawal, are willing to sacrifice the Thieu-Ky regime.	57	
		1161	McGovern and the Democrats are for military victory in Vietnam and the preservation of the Saigon regime.	2	3
3.	1972	1131	Nixon and the Republicans are for an understanding (thaw, détente, broadening of relations) with Russia.	32	
		1132	Nixon and the Republicans are against an understanding (thaw, détente, broadening of relations) with Russia.	0	0
4.	1972	1126	Nixon and the Republicans are for an understanding (thaw, détente, new relationship) with Red China, recognizing Red China, admitting Red China to the UN.	51	
		1127	Nixon and the Republicans are against an understanding (thaw, détente, new relationship) with Red China, recognizing Red China, admitting Red China to the UN.	0	0

TABLE 4.1 (Continued)

Panel No.	Survey	Codes	Substance of Comments	No. of Responses	% Nonmodal Responses
5.	1972	1173	McGovern and the Democrats are for, Nixon and the Republicans are against, amnesty for draft evaders.	37	
		1174	Nixon and the Republicans are for, McGovern and the Democrats are against, amnesty for draft evaders.	0	0
6.	1972	0992	McGovern and the Democrats are for busing, against neighborhood schools; Nixon and the Republicans are against busing, for neighborhood schools.	29	
		0993	Nixon and the Republicans are for busing, against neighborhood schools; McGovern and the Democrats are against busing, for neighborhood schools.	3	9
7.	1972	0815	McGovern and the Democrats are liberal, too liberal, radical; Nixon and the Republicans are conservative, too conservative, reactionary.	210	
		0816	Nixon and the Republicans are liberal, too liberal, radical; McGovern and the Democrats are conservative, too conservative, reactionary.	15	7

No.	Year	Code	Statement		
8.	1972	1106	Nixon and the Republicans are for, McGovern and the Democrats are against, a strong military position, preparedness, weapons' systems, Pentagon spending, overkill. McGovern and the Democrats are for, Nixon and the Republicans are against, a weaker military position, Pentagon spending cutbacks, no overkill, reduced armed forces.	48	
		1107	McGovern and the Democrats are for, Nixon and the Republicans are against, a strong military position, preparedness, weapons systems, Pentagon spending, overkill. Nixon and the Democrats are for, McGovern and the Republicans are against, a weaker military position, Pentagon spending cutbacks, no overkill, reduced armed forces.	6	11
9.	1972	0932	McGovern and the Democrats are for, Nixon and the Republicans are against, tax reforms; fairer systems; end of loopholes, write-offs, and dodges.	40	
		0933	Nixon and the Republicans are for, McGovern and the Democrats are against, tax reforms; fairer systems; end of loopholes, write-offs, and dodges.	3	7
10.	1972	0805	McGovern and the Democrats are for, Nixon and the Republicans are against, government activity, big government, spending more on domestic needs.	27	
		0806	Nixon and the Republicans are for, McGovern and the Democrats are against, government activity, big government, spending more on domestic needs.	5	16

TABLE 4.1 (Continued)

Panel No.	Survey	Codes	Substance of Comments	No. of Responses	% Nonmodal Responses
11.	1972	0906	McGovern and the Democrats are for, Nixon and the Republicans are against, government aid and activity on welfare and poverty problems.	162	
		0907	Nixon and the Republicans are for, McGovern and the Democrats are against, government aid and activity on welfare and poverty problems.	16	9
12.	1972	0605	Nixon and the Republicans would spend less, too little; Democrats and McGovern would spend more, too much.	51	
		0606	McGovern and the Democrats would spend less. too little; Nixon and the Republicans would spend more, too much.	16	24
13.	1972	0947 0948 1217	McGovern and the Democrats are for, Nixon and the Republicans are against, civil rights, racial justice, desegregation, voting rights, blacks.	33	
		1218	Nixon and the Republicans are for, McGovern and the Democrats are against, civil rights, racial justice, desegregation, voting rights, blacks.	14	30
14.	1972	1233	McGovern and the Democrats are for, Nixon and the Republicans are against, poor people.	84	
		1234	Nixon and the Republicans are for, McGovern and the Democrats are against, poor people.	5	6

15.	1972	1223	McGovern and the Democrats are for, Nixon and the Republicans are against, young people, kids, freaks, hippies.	36	5
		1224	Nixon and the Republicans are for, McGovern and the Democrats are against, young people, kids, freaks, hippies.	2	
16.	1972	1207	McGovern and the Democrats are for, Nixon and the Republicans are against, labor, unions, labor bosses, racketeers.	42	11
		1208	Nixon and the Republicans are for, McGovern and the Democrats are against, labor, unions, labor bosses, racketeers.	5	
17.	1972	1201 1202	Nixon and the Republicans are for, McGovern and the Democrats are against, special interests, privileged people, Big Business, Wall Street, industry, the upper classes, the corporate rich.	257	8
		1209 1210	McGovern and the Democrats are for, Nixon and the Republicans are against, special interests, privileged people, Big Business, Wall Street, industry, the upper classes, the corporate rich.	21	
18.	1972	1206	McGovern and the Democrats are for, Nixon and the Republicans are against, common man, people, little people, working people.	279	11
		1207	Nixon and the Republicans are for, McGovern and the Democrats are against, common man, people, little people, working people.	31	

TABLE 4.1 (Continued)

Panel No.	Survey	Codes	Substance of Comments	No. of Responses	% Nonmodal Responses
19.	1964	5470 5480 6470 6480 7470 7480 8470 8480	Johnson is liberal, too liberal, radical, more liberal than most of his party, more for social welfare and/or government economic activity; will listen to, bring in, liberals. Goldwater is conservative, middle of the road, reactionary, too radical; represents conservative wing of his party; will listen to, bring in, conservatives. Goldwater is liberal, too liberal, radical, more liberal than most of his party, more for social welfare and/or government economic activity; will listen to, bring in, liberals. Johnson is conservative, middle of the road, reactionary, too radical; represents conservative wing of his party; will listen to, bring in, conservatives.	144	3
20.	1964	1410 2410 3410 4410 1420 2420 3420 4420 1670 2670	Johnson and the Democrats are more (too much) for civil rights, are good or better for blacks, are controlled by blacks. Goldwater and the Republicans are less (not enough) for civil rights, are bad for blacks, keep blacks in check.	381	

Note: within panel 19, the "5" and no nonmodal value appears between the two blocks.

Code		Description	Count	
3670	4670	Goldwater and the Republicans are more (too much) for civil rights, are good or better for blacks, are controlled by blacks. Johnson and the Democrats are less (not enough) for civil rights, are bad for blacks, keep blacks in check.	26	6
1770	2770			
3770	4770			
5510	6510			
7510	8510			
5520	6520			
7520	8520			
5770	6770			
7770	8770			

21. 1964

Code		Description	Count	
1120	2121	Johnson and the Democrats would spend more, too much, increase deficit spending, national debt. Goldwater and the Republicans are (too) economy minded, will spend less, balance budget, decrease national debt.	160	7
3120	4121			
1130	2130			
3130	4130			
5080	6081	Goldwater and the Republicans would spend more, too much, increase deficit spending, national debt. Johnson and the Democrats are (too) economy minded, will spend less, balance budget, decrease national debt.	12	
7080	8081			

22. 1964

Code		Description	Count	
1250	2250	Johnson and the Democrats favor, Goldwater and the Republicans oppose, social reform, change, progress.	48	6
3250	4250	Goldwater and the Republicans favor, Johnson and the Democrats oppose, social reform, change, progress.	3	

TABLE 4.1 (Continued)

Panel No.	Survey	Codes	Substance of Comments	No. of Responses	% Nonmodal Responses
23.	1964	1264 2263 3264 4263 5431 6430 7431 8430	Johnson and the Democrats are socialistic, for welfare state. Goldwater and the Republicans would stop socialism, cut down on government activity. Goldwater and the Republicans are socialistic, for welfare state. Johnson and the Democrats would stop socialism, cut down on government activity.	89 1	1
24.	1964	1620 2620 3620 4620 1721 2721 3721 4721 5720 6720 7720 8720	Johnson and the Democrats are (too) good for, help, are controlled by, labor bosses, labor unions, union members. Goldwater and the Republicans are bad for, will keep in check, labor bosses, labor unions, union members. Goldwater and the Republicans are (too) good for, help, are controlled by labor bosses, labor unions, union members. Johnson and the Democrats are bad for, will keep in check, labor bosses, labor unions, union members.	85 1	1

25. 1964 1633 2633 Goldwater and the Republicans are (too) good for,
3633 4633 help, are controlled by Big Business, businessmen,
1731 2731 industry, rich and powerful people, Wall Street.
3733 4731 Johnson and the Democrats are bad for, will keep
in check, Big Business, industry, rich and powerful
people, Wall Street.   146

Johnson and the Democrats are (too) good for,
help, are controlled by Big Business, businessmen,
industry, rich and powerful people, Wall Street.
Goldwater and the Republicans are bad for, will
keep in check, Big Business, industry, rich and
powerful people, Wall Street.   14

26. 1964 1615 2615 Johnson and the Democrats are (too) good for,
3615 4615 help, are controlled by, workers, common people,
1702 2702 the average man. Goldwater and the Republicans
3702 4702 are bad for, will keep in check, workers, common
1713 2713 people, the average man.   593
3713 4713 Goldwater and the Republicans are (too) good for,
5702 6702 help, are controlled by workers, common people,
7702 8702 the average man. Johnson and the Democrats are
5714 6714 bad for, will keep in check, workers, common peo-
7714 8714 ple, the average man.   46

false: Conservative voters, for instance, might reasonably have believed that Nixon was for "big government" (Panel 10) or that he would "spend too much" (Panel 12), and liberals, recalling Lyndon Johnson's efforts to portray himself as a budget cutter, might reasonably have thought that he was "too economy minded" (Panel 21). Even so, such nonmodal responses were infrequent; overwhelmingly (92 percent), responses on the subjects covered in Table 4.1 were of the sort one would expect from people knowledgeable about American politics.

The data reported in Table 4.2 give additional support to the conclusion that, on the issues they raise, respondents to the likes-dislikes questions share the usual perceptions of the positions of the candidates and parties. The table shows the frequency of nonmodal responses to eighteen closed-ended questions for two sets of respondents: (1) all respondents to each question who saw a difference between the parties' or candidates' positions on the issue raised by the question and who voted, and (2) that subset of such respondents who had also volunteered a comment on the same issue (or similar issues) in response to the likes-dislikes questions. The first entry in the right-hand column, for instance, indicates that 16.7 percent of the first group of respondents named the Democrats as the most conservative party in 1964 when asked, "Would you say that either one of the parties is more conservative or more liberal than the other at the national level? Which party is more conservative?"[4] The first entry in the left-hand column shows that 4.3 percent of the second group of respondents—those who had mentioned the liberalism or conservatism of Johnson or Goldwater as something they liked or disliked about them—gave the same response to that question. For the first eight entries of the table the match is very close between the issue raised by the closed-ended question and that suggested by the relevant codes to the likes-dislikes questions. Such exact or nearly exact matches are hard to

_____

[4] If the respondent named no party, the interviewer went on to ask, "Do you think that people generally consider the Democrats or the Republicans more conservative or wouldn't you want to guess about that?"

come by, however. Those involved in the last ten entries are more approximate, usually because coders of the likes-dislikes questions grouped the issue raised by the closed-ended question with other issues.[5]

Table 4.2 shows that nonmodal responses were rare among those respondents who saw a difference between the candidates and parties on an issue *and* who had raised the same or a similar issue in answering the likes-dislikes questions: For the full set of items, 6.6 percent of such respondents' answers were nonmodal, on the average; for the first eight items, just 2.4 percent were. In contrast, among all respondents who saw a difference between the candidates or parties, over 13 percent of the responses were nonmodal, on the average.[6] These results again suggest quite strongly that voters' expressions of their likes and dislikes do not involve idiosyncratic views of political reality and, incidentally, that voters are more knowledgeable about issues that they themselves raise than they are about other issues. The test of these propositions is most exact for entries one to eight of Table 4.2 and are supported by the data for those entries in a striking way. Even the last ten entries, in which the test is not very exact, show that nonmodal responses were less than one-tenth of those drawn from the respondents to the likes-dislikes questions and, in every case but one, that these respondents gave fewer answers that were odd (on their face, at least) than respondents generally.

THE ELECTORAL IMPORTANCE OF ISSUES

The concept *issue* is an ambiguous one, at least as it is used in contemporary political science, history, and journalism. Sometimes, a great deal hangs on a precise definition of the

[5] See the notes to Table 4.2 for a precise indication of the codes matched with particular closed-ended questions.

[6] Note that the closed-ended questions that stimulated this rate of nonmodal response were, with one exception (see Table 4.2), filtered; that is, respondents were invited explicitly to say that they had not thought much about the subject of the question or saw no difference between the candidates or parties on the issue it posed. The proportion of nonmodal responses to unfiltered versions of these same questions would almost certainly be greater, probably considerably greater.

TABLE 4.2

Nonmodal Responses to Selected Closed-ended Questions

Entry	Survey	Subject of Closed-ended Question	% Nonmodal Responses from Respondents to: Likes-Dislikes Questions*	Closed-ended Questions
1.	1964	More conservative party†	4.3	16.7**
2.	1972	Nixon, McGovern positions on liberalism-conservatism scale†	0.0	8.6
3.	1964	Party more likely to want federal government to help local communities provide education	0.0***	19.0
4.	1964	Party more likely to want government to help in getting doctors and medical care at low cost	3.8	8.5
5.	1964	Party more likely to give aid to other countries	2.8	12.4
6.	1972	Nixon, McGovern positions on school busing to achieve integration scale	5.7	19.4
7.	1972	Nixon, McGovern positions on Vietnam withdrawal scale	2.6	4.8
8.	1972	Nixon, McGovern positions on rights of accused scale	0.0	17.9
9.	1964	Party more likely to favor a stronger government in Washington	5.7	15.6
10.	1964	Party more likely to favor the government supporting the right of colored people to go to any hotel or restaurant	3.7	5.5

11.	1972	Nixon, McGovern positions on guaranteed job and living standard scale	7.1	11.7
12.	1972	Nixon, McGovern positions on aid to minority groups scale	10.7	15.9
13.	1964	Party more likely to sit down and talk with leaders of communist countries	11.6	14.7
14.	1964	Party more likely to want government to see to it that Negroes get fair treatment in jobs	9.0	10.2
15.	1964	Party more likely to want the government to see to it that white and Negro children go to the same schools	9.4	10.7
16.	1972	Nixon, McGovern positions on change in tax rate scale	14.8	21.2
17.	1972	Party more in favor of cutting military spending	14.7	15.5
18.	1972	Nixon, McGovern positions on legalization of marijuana scale	12.5	10.7

* The respondents to the likes-dislikes questions were those whose responses were coded as follows in the relevant National Election Study codebook: (1) 470, 480; (2) 815, 816; (3) 310, 593; (4) 330, 594; (5) 540, 550; (6) 991–993; (7) 1160, 1161; (8) 972, 973, 978; (9) 210, 211, 220, 221, 230, 231, 430, 431, 460, 461; (10, 14, 15) 400, 410, 420, 440, 500, 510, 520, 770; (11) 905–907; (12) 946–948, 1217, 1218; (13) 580, 680; (16) 932, 933; (17) 1106, 1107; (18) 982–984.

** This closed-ended question was an unfiltered one; all others were filtered; i.e., respondents were specifically invited to say whether they had thought much about a subject or saw a difference between the parties.

*** Fewer than ten cases.

† The sample size for 1964 was 1126; that for 1972 was 830.

term, as, for instance, in those recent studies of voting which seek to compare the impact of issues on the vote with that of ideology, images, or partisanship.[7] Because the research I report is *not* designed to compare the electoral impact of issues with that of other factors, however, I shall use the term *issue* quite loosely to refer to any point of contention that may offer voters a reason to distinguish between candidates (i.e., that may enter voters' choices as a consideration) or that may give candidates a basis for requesting votes (i.e., that may support an appeal).

If *issue* is not a self-explanatory concept, neither is the term *important,* when applied to an issue. One can call issue X more important than issue Y if

1. X figures as a consideration in the decisions of a greater number of voters than Y;
2. X weighs more heavily than Y in the decisions of those voters for whom both X and Y are considerations;
3. X would yield a greater net advantage in votes than Y to one of the candidates, were it the only issue in the election;
4. the absence of X as an issue would yield a greater net advantage in votes to one of the candidates than the absence of Y, given all the other considerations that are entering into the decisions of voters.

One or more of these criteria—though frequently it is not clear which—underlie most judgments of the relative importance of issues by most analysts. I shall have recourse to all but the second, since the Rule assumes that voters weigh equally all issues salient to them.

On the assumption that voters use the Voter's Decision Rule in deciding how to vote, measuring the importance of particular issues in the other three senses is reasonably

[7] See, for instance, Gregory Markus and Philip Converse, "A Dynamic Simultaneous Equation Model of Electoral Choice," *American Political Science Review* 73 (December 1979), pp. 1055–1071, and, in the same issue of that journal, pp. 1071–1089, Benjamin Page and Calvin C. Jones, "Reciprocal Effects of Policy Preferences, Party Loyalties, and the Vote."

straightforward. In discussing the electoral impact of issues, I shall use four measures of importance—aggregate salience, bias, pull, and marginal impact—defined as follows:

1. *Aggregate salience:* The proportion of a given set of respondents who cite a given issue as something to like or dislike about the major parties and candidates.
2. *Bias:* For a given set of respondents, those who see a given issue as favoring a given candidate or party, as a proportion of those who see that issue as favoring some party or candidate.
3. *Pull:* The proportion of the members of a given set of respondents who see a given issue as favoring a given candidate or party.
4. *Marginal Impact:* The amount by which a given issue increases the proportion of those respondents showing some specified degree of commitment to a candidate or party, given the effects of all other issues on the strength of voters' commitments to that candidate or party.

The importance of an issue is measured in sense (1) by aggregate salience, in sense (3) by bias and pull, and in sense (4) by marginal impact. Among the first three of these measures (when they are expressed as percentages), the following relationship holds for any given issue:

$$\text{Pull} = \frac{\text{aggregate salience} \times \text{bias}}{100}$$

This relationship is only approximate in some of the data I report, because some of the issues I have defined subsume several subissues. For instance, a respondent may like a candidate for his views on taxes but dislike his stand on interest rates. For that respondent, these responses cancel each other when they are combined (as I have done) into one issue, monetary and fiscal policy, and, though they figure in calculating that issue's aggregate salience, they do not in calculating its bias or pull.

It may be helpful to put less formally some of what has just

been said: The *aggregate salience* of an issue tells one how
many voters in a group think it relevant to their choice between candidates. Many voters will think the integrity of the
candidates is relevant to that choice, for instance, while few
will like or dislike candidates for their views on aid to Taiwan.
An issue of very low salience will have a minimal effect on
the outcome of an election, but an issue of high salience
may or may not be important in that regard. It is possible, for
example, that all voters think each of two candidates has
great integrity, thus giving neither an advantage on that
score.

Bias measures the one-sidedness of an issue. If 90 percent of
those who regard an issue as important to their choice think
that that issue favors a given candidate, it has a very high bias
toward that candidate. Such one-sidedness may again mean
much or little for an election's outcome. If an issue has a high
bias but low salience—that is, if those voters who care about it
are overwhelmingly of one view but not many care about it—
most probably it will not greatly affect the candidates' fortunes.

An issue's *pull* tells one the proportion of a group which is
attracted to a candidate by a given issue. In the electorate as a
whole an issue with a pull of 80 toward a given candidate is
one that leads 80 percent of all voters to count that issue in his
favor. An issue with a strong pull is likely to affect the outcome of an election significantly, but it need not do so. It will
not, for example, if all those voters attracted to a candidate by
an issue of strong pull would vote for him even without that
incentive. In the hypothetically extreme case—one in which
all the issues that entered into voters' choices had pulls of 100
toward one of the candidates—no one issue could be said to
determine the election's outcome, since that outcome would
be the same in the absence of any one of them.

The *marginal impact* of an issue tells one the proportion of
all voters which that issue pulls toward, or away from, some
given degree of enthusiasm for a candidate—toward or away
from, say, enthusiasm that is great enough to lead to a vote for
him. Two issues, X and Y, may be equal in aggregate salience,

bias, and pull and yet have a very different marginal impact. To see why they may, let us suppose that X figures in a situation in which many other issues pull most voters very strongly toward a candidate, while Y figures in a situation in which other issues leave most voters uncertain about how to vote. Issue Y, as a tie-breaking consideration for many voters, will have a very large marginal impact. Issue X, because it influences few voters to change their votes, will have a small marginal impact, even though it influences the attitudes of many voters toward the candidates.

To campaign strategists the marginal impact of particular issues, and a good way to measure it, are of obvious interest. Consider these two cases:

1. The aggregate salience of issue X is 85, and its bias toward candidate A is 95. Its aggregate salience among voters with net scores between ±1 is zero.
2. The aggregate salience of issue Y is 85, and its bias toward candidate A is 95. Its aggregate salience among voters with net scores between ±1 is 100, and its bias toward candidate A among the same set of voters is 95.

The marginal impact of issue Y will almost certainly be very high—that is, its presence will almost certainly affect significantly the division of the vote. In contrast, issue X will have no marginal impact on the vote—its presence or absence will not affect any voter's choice between candidates. Thus, in case (1) candidate A's opponent need do nothing so long as the situation remains as specified, but candidate A should most probably try to increase the salience of issue X among weakly committed voters. In case (2) it is candidate A who can stand pat, while his opponent might benefit greatly from an effort to change the opinions of marginal voters on issue Y or from an attempt to divert their attention to other issues.

Computing the aggregate salience, bias, and pull of an issue from data on voters' likes and dislikes of candidates and parties involves only counting and simple arithmetic. Computing an issue's marginal impact on the Democratic (or Republican) candidate's share of the vote is a more involved procedure. For that computation, one must:

1. Compute respondents' net scores, taking into account all the likes and dislikes they cite, and from these scores predict the Democratic (or Republican) candidate's share of the vote.
2. Deleting all responses that bear on issue X, compute anew respondents' net scores and make a second prediction of the vote for the Democratic (or Republican) candidate.
3. Subtract the results obtained at step 1 from those obtained at step 2. This difference, which may be either positive or negative, is the marginal impact of issue X.

This procedure, the reader should note, assumes an *independent* motivating force for each like or dislike cited by a respondent.[8]

AN ALTERNATIVE PROCEDURE

Let us examine another procedure that we might use to assess how important particular considerations are for the outcome of an election. As a first step, we shall consider what might lead voters to vote for or against the candidates—the performance of the economy, for instance, the records of the candidates, various issues of policy, and so on—and then we shall frame questions about these matters and put them to a sample of voters.

If our political intuitions are good and the list of questions is sufficiently long, we can find out in this way what respondents think about many, perhaps even most, of the things that will affect their votes. Still, we are likely to overlook some issues that are important, for we are trying to guess the con-

---

[8] Stokes and his associates estimate the direction and magnitude of the force exerted by particular attitudes (or "components") on the two-party vote in a quite different way than that which I use to estimate marginal impact, but they were attempting to measure essentially the same thing. See Stokes, Campbell, and Miller, "Components of Electoral Decision."

cerns of a very heterogeneous group of people. Moreover, many of our respondents will think many of the subjects raised in our questionnaire irrelevant to their vote. Respondents who give substantive responses to any particular question (that is, all who choose an option other than "no opinion") will fall into three groups, the relative sizes of which will vary with the subject of the question and its wording:

Group 1: Those with an opinion on the subject of the question who regard that opinion as relevant to their choice of candidates;

Group 2: those with an opinion who do not regard it as relevant to their choice; and

Group 3: those with no opinion.

One might suppose that group (3) would be very small or even nonexistent; respondents who have no opinion, after all, can say so. But consider this testimony from Philip Converse, which draws upon his personal experience in interviewing for surveys:

> ... I [was] struck by two facts in particular. One was that very many respondents could not understand that a battery of pure opinion items had no objective "right-wrong" scoring, or that don't know responses were not a confession of the most abject ignorance, to be avoided at all cost. The other was the frequency with which respondents chose a response alternative dutifully but accompanied the choice with side cues (shoulder-shrugging, eye-rolling, giggles, and even *sotto voce* comments) indicating that they were very much out of their element and would pick any alternative haphazardly by way of helping me out.[9]

The number of such pseudo-opinions elicited can be reduced by explicitly inviting respondents to say that they lack knowledge of the issue, that it is of no concern to them, or that they

[9] Philip E. Converse, "Comment: The Status of Nonattitudes," *American Political Science Review* 68 (June 1974), p. 650.

see no difference in the candidates' positions on it; but this tactic does not wholly eliminate electorally meaningless responses of this sort, as Converse's work on the problem of "non-attitudes" argues persuasively.[10]

Because the opinions elicited by our questions will be a mixture of responses from groups (1), (2), and (3), our data in raw form will be of limited value for our purposes. We shall know voters' opinions, to be sure, but not which of these are important to them *as voters,* the only kind of opinion that counts for the interpretation of elections. If, for instance, 45 percent of all respondents say that they favor some policy (a tax cut, aid to Taiwan), 45 percent say that they oppose it, and 10 percent have no opinion, the size of group (1)—the group we care about—could vary from zero to 90 percent, and all of the members of that group could favor the measure or none of them might. For this reason, the next step of our alternative procedure will be to test the association of respondents' opinions with their votes. Intuition suggests that opinions having no bearing on voters' choices—unimportant opinions—should show little or no covariance with such choices; opinions that do figure in voting—important opinions—should covary with it.

Unfortunately, this intuition can lead us astray. Consider, for example, how group (3) respondents—those without a real opinion—are likely to answer this common sort of question: "Which of the candidates—Jones, the Democrat, or Smith, the Republican—will be most effective in handling this country's relations with other nations (or inflation, or the problem of air pollution)?" Having no opinion on the issue posed, some—perhaps most—are likely to name the candidate that they prefer on other grounds. To the extent that they do so, the correlation between voting and answers to the questions will be spuriously strong, and we will be led to believe that

---

[10] See ibid. and two other articles by Converse: "Attitudes and Non-Attitudes: Continuation of a Dialogue," pp. 168–189, in Edward R. Tufte (ed.), *The Quantitative Analysis of Social Problems* (Reading, Mass.: Addison-Wesley, 1970), and "The Nature of Belief Systems in Mass Publics," pp. 206–261, in David E. Apter (ed.), *Ideology and Discontent* (Glencoe: The Free Press, 1964).

opinion on the management of foreign affairs (or inflation, or air pollution) is more important in voters' choices than in fact it is. Indeed, this effect is likely to be perverse: The more of those who in fact have no opinion on the issue posed, the stronger will be the apparent association of responses to voting. The opinions of group (2) respondents on particular issues may also show a spurious correlation with voting, and one that is not a consequence of the kind of question just considered. Those who share opinions that lead them to vote for the same candidate are likely to share other opinions as well, opinions wholly unrelated to their votes. The followers of candidate A might predominantly favor the death penalty, while those of candidate B oppose it, for example, even though that issue was a consideration in the votes of very few on either side.

Even if the responses of the members of groups (2) and (3) should be uncorrelated with their votes, using the strength of the association (however measured) between voting and opinion as an indication of an issue's importance—for that is what our procedure entails—may lead us to misconstrue its electoral significance. Figure 4.1 shows three different ways in which opinion on a particular issue might relate to the strength of voters' commitments to candidates, as measured by net scores. The horizontal axes in the figure give the respondents' net scores, ranging from −20, indicating a very strong commitment to the Republican candidate, to +20, indicating a very strong commitment to the Democratic candidate. The vertical axes give the number of respondents with a given net score who hold a position on the issue; the number holding opinions favoring the Democratic and Republican candidates, respectively, are shown above and below the horizontal axes. Let us assume that (1) we have succeeded in each case in isolating that set of all respondents who see the issue as relevant to voting and have an opinion on it; (2) this set of respondents is the same proportion of the full sample in the three cases; (3) a respondent's opinion on the issue in each case will be one of several influences on his choice of candidates; (4) respondents with net scores between ±4 will divide their votes between the two candidates; and (5) respondents

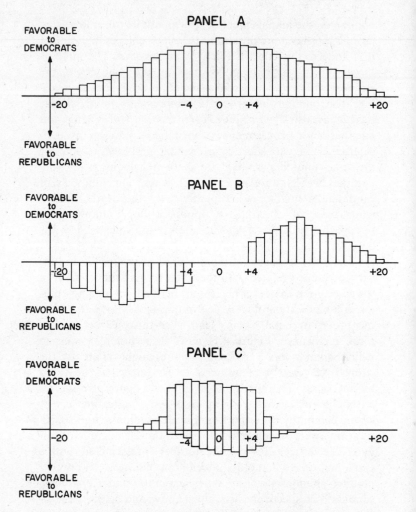

4.1   The Impact of Particular Issues on Electoral Outcomes: Three Cases

with net scores greater than +4 or less than −4 will vote for the Democratic and Republican candidate, respectively.

If we use the strength of the issue's association with voting as a measure of electoral importance, we shall attribute a very different importance to the issues in the three different cases of Figure 4.1, even though (by assumption) each is an actual influence on the voting of those who hold it in all three cases and the same proportion of respondents is involved in all three. Panel A depicts a case in which an issue is pulling all respondents toward a vote for the Democratic candidate, but the covariance of respondents' votes and their opinions is zero. The issue might concern the Republican candidate's part in some scandal or his responsibility for some economic disaster. Panel B depicts a situation in which an issue has high salience for respondents strongly committed to the candidates but not for those who are weakly committed. Opinion on an ideological issue might show a distribution like this one. In this case opinions are perfectly correlated with the vote, though they have little meaning for the outcome of the election, since their marginal impact is zero. To put it another way, this issue is important as a polarizing force but not in deciding which side will prevail. Panel C depicts the opposite situation, in which an issue has high salience only among weakly committed voters; perhaps the controversy over Nancy Reagan's purchase of china for the White House generated a distribution of opinion of this kind. The correlation with voting of the issue of Panel C is likely to be weak, since weakly committed voters are dividing their vote and other issues are also influencing them, but the issue's impact on the election's outcome is likely to be considerable. While all three of these cases are idealized, one cannot assume that similar distributions of opinion will be absent from the real world.

Our alternative procedure thus has serious potential pitfalls. Its crucial difference from the one that I have adopted is its approach to identifying the considerations that enter into voting. For reasons advanced in Chapter 2, I treat respondents' answers to the likes-dislikes questions as those considerations, a procedure that allows me to measure directly their salience, bias, pull, and marginal impact in the sample as a whole or in any part of it. The alternative procedure—which is that employed in a very large proportion of all electoral studies—ignores direct cues from respondents about their concerns, relying instead on the analyst's hunches and a statistical maneuver poorly designed to sort out the different sorts of influence that particular issues may have on electoral outcomes.

DIVIDING THE SAMPLE

A significant additional feature of my analytical procedure is the division of respondents to the 1964 and 1972 surveys into sets; indeed, much of my discussion of the presidential elections in those years proceeds without reference to statistical features of the sample as a whole. These groups of respondents figure in my analysis of both elections:

1. *The winner's core supporters*—that half of the sample most strongly committed to the winning candidate. In any election the voters represented by these respondents are those most responsible, in a double sense, for the winner's victory: They are the voters who most desire his victory *and* who can bring it about by their own action.
2. *The potential opposition majority*—that half of the sample most strongly committed to the losing candidate. This set of respondents represents the voters out of which it would have been easiest for the losing candidate to have fashioned a majority coalition.
3. *The loser's core supporters*—those respondents whose commitment to the losing candidate was as strong as that shown by the winner's core supporters to the winning candidate.
4. *Marginal voters*—that one-fourth of respondents at the intersection of, and equally divided between, the winner's core supporters and the potential opposition majority. The voters represented by these respondents gave the winning candidate the "last" increment of votes he needed to win, "last" in the sense that among

them was the least enthusiastic segment of his core supporters.

In addition, my analysis of the Johnson landslide examines the likes and dislikes of a fifth set of respondents, *weakly committed voters,* the composition of which I shall define later. Note that I take net score as the measure of the strength of respondents' commitments in defining all these sets. Note also that the group of respondents I identify with each set only approximates the set as defined—for instance, the respondents whom I treat as Johnson's core supporters constitute 49.1 percent, not 50 percent, of the sample, and those I treat as marginal voters[11] in 1964 constitute 21 percent, not 25 percent of it. These discrepancies between operational definitions and those I have just set forth are trivial in their analytical consequences, and the leeway they afford greatly simplifies computations of the aggregate salience, bias, and pull of issues in the various sets.

Figure 4.2 shows how I have divided the 1964 sample.

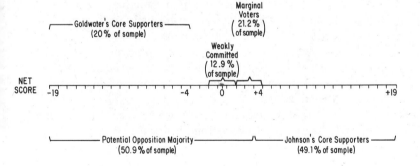

4.2   Analytical Divisions of the 1964 Sample

[11] Practically, I proceeded as follows in identifying marginal voters: I first located by net score the median voter for the winning candidate. I then grouped together the respondents in the immediate neighborhood (as indicated by net scores) of this median voter so that (a) the total group constituted roughly one-quarter of the sample and (b) roughly half the total group had net scores higher, and half scores lower, than the median voter.

CHAPTER FIVE

1964: THE TWICE-OVER
LANDSLIDE

In 1964 many observers regarded the Goldwater campaign as strikingly unorthodox. Republican strategists made the winning of the former Confederate states' 128 electoral votes a premise of their plans to capture the presidency, though Ulysses S. Grant had been the last Republican candidate to carry more than five of these states. Senator Goldwater also promised to sharpen his party's programmatic differences with New Deal and post–New Deal Democracy. For years, conservative Republicans had been urging that course of action on their party as a remedy for its electoral ills. Republican candidates had been defeated in presidential elections after 1936, went the conservative reasoning, largely because the party had failed to offer any genuine alternative to the majority Democrats. "Me-too" campaigns had failed to win liberal support and had lost the support of conservatives, who simply stayed at home on election day. Offered a real choice, proponents of the theory argued, these stay-at-home Republicans would turn out on election day and put a Republican in the White House.

Given this background, much postelection commentary inevitably focused on what had *not* happened on election day. Thus, John Herbers of the *New York Times* observed that "despite Senator Goldwater's strong showing in the Deep South, the results clearly demonstrated that a Presidential candidate can no longer carry the South on the civil rights issue alone,"[1] and the *Times* in a front-page article noted that "Senator Barry Goldwater lost the 1964 election in the vain hope that a huge conservative vote awaited his call."[2] As evi-

[1] Harold Faber (ed), *The Road to the White House* (New York: McGraw-Hill, 1965), p. 275.
[2] Ibid., p. 273.

dence that neither the southern strategy nor hidden conservatives had won the day, the election returns themselves sufficed.

About what *had* happened, one view was dominant: Barry Goldwater lost overwhelmingly because a centrist electorate identified him with a conservative ideology and with conservative positions on issues of public policy. A winning political party, wrote Tom Wicker at the time, "must be hospitable to the most widely differing views and interests. . . . Goldwater was bound to be a weak and divisive national candidate and party leader . . . because he had taken for twelve years in national politics a rigidly 'conservative' position that amounted to a radical rejection of the norms of post–New Deal politics."[3] Walter Lippmann agreed emphatically: "The Johnson majority is indisputable proof that the preponderant mass of the American voters are in the center, inside the two extremes, and that the reason the Democrats win is that Kennedy and Johnson have worked carefully and deliberately to make the Democratic Party represent the center."[4] This explanation of the election's outcome has persisted and doubtless will continue to do so. Though vague, it is an account that conforms perfectly to a longstanding conception of American politics as a game played out along a left-right continuum, with successful candidates planting themselves firmly in the center. To students of politics, Anthony Downs's *Economic Theory of Democracy*[5] had never seemed more relevant to the real world than it did on election night in 1964.

Students of voting also stressed Goldwater's position outside the mainstream of politics as a reason for his defeat,[6] but

[3] Ibid., pp. xiii–xiv.   [4] Washington *Post,* November 5, 1964.
[5] New York: Harper and Brothers, 1957.
[6] Philip E. Converse, Aage R. Clausen, and Warren E. Miller observed that ". . . three prime elements of the 1964 election became intertwined after the manner of a classic script . . . the 'outer' ideological wing of a party captures its nomination, leaving a vacuum toward the center of gravity of national opinion. This vacuum is gleefully filled by the opposing party without any loss of votes from its own side of the spectrum. The outcome, logically and inexorably, is a landslide at the polls." "Electoral Myth and Reality: The 1964 Election," *The American Political Science Review* 59 (June 1965), p. 321.

their analyses of the election developed other themes as well. The fear of nuclear war, Lyndon Johnson's experience and background, the memory of John F. Kennedy, the country's general prosperity, the powers of incumbency, the defection of liberal Republicans, a strongly negative reaction to Goldwater as a candidate, civil rights, social security, health care, welfare, the poverty program, the strength of the Democratic Party and the Republican Party's weakness—all were seen to have played a substantial role in the election. A few analysts, though only a few, ventured opinions on the relative importance of these factors. Louis Harris argued that "peace and a desire not to have three presidents in a year basically determined the outcome."[7] John Kessel concluded that "the power of the federal government was the most influential issue of the campaign."[8]

We can show the impact of these and other factors on voting in 1964 with considerable precision if we make use of the data, concepts, and procedures described in Chapter 4. I shall examine in turn the concerns of the candidates' core supporters, of the potential opposition majority, and of marginal and weakly committed voters. These groups differed markedly in their attitudes as well as in their voting and partisan composition.

LYNDON JOHNSON'S CORE SUPPORTERS

Let us look first at Lyndon Johnson's core supporters. From their net scores, which ranged from +4 to +19, one would expect these respondents to vote for Johnson; 97 percent did so, contributing 73 percent of his total vote. Most were Democrats: Eighty-five percent identified themselves as such, 10

---

[7] *The Anguish of Change* (New York: W. W. Norton and Co., Inc., 1973), p. 251. Stokes has noted that "foreign affairs did intrude on the public's consciousness in the 1964 campaign more than in any election since 1952, but popular references to foreign issues in 1964 still had only about a fourth the frequency of references to domestic issues." See his "Some Dynamic Elements of Contests for the Presidency," p. 21.

[8] *The Goldwater Coalition*, p. 291.

percent identified with the Republican Party,[9] and 5 percent
were independents.

Table 5.1 reports the aggregate salience, bias, and pull of
forty issues and sets of issues among Johnson's core supporters. The table needs some explanation. Within any num-
bered category one set of responses subsumes another if its
label starts farther to the left. Thus, the category of New Deal
issues includes all responses in the following sets: poverty
program; relationships to labor, unions; farm policy; economic issues; social security, the aged, and worker welfare
programs; medical care; ideological stance; and relationship to
Big Business, the common man. In some cases the whole is
greater than the sum of its parts; thus, while *ideological stance*
includes all responses in the sets *liberalism, conservatism* and
extremism, the responses in those two sets do not exhaust
those included in *ideological stance.* In the first four categories
of the table, and in the last, the sets of responses with labels
equidistant from the left-hand margin do not intersect; for example, no response in the set *military preparedness* figures in
the set *foreign aid.* This rule does not hold true for the fifth
and sixth categories, however; for example, some of the same
responses have been included both in the set *quality of stewardship* and in the set *governmental corruption.* These two
labels simply suggest different ways of looking at some of the
things that respondents said. Some (though little) overlapping
also exists between the sets of comments subsumed by issues
in different categories; thus, for example, some responses
that pertain both to *partisanship* and *independence* figure in
both.[10]

A brief statement about several possibly ambiguous labels

---

[9] Here, and throughout, respondents who described themselves as
"strong" Democrats, "not so strong" Democrats, or as independents
leaning toward the Democrats are treated as identifying with the Democratic Party; and respondents who described themselves as "strong" Republicans, "not so strong" Republicans, or as independents leaning toward the Republicans are treated as identifying with the Republican
Party.

[10] Such overlaps are noted in Appendix II.

TABLE 5.1

**The Relative Importance of Issues among
Johnson's Core Supporters**

Considerations	Salience	Dem. Bias	Dem. Pull
1. Foreign Policy	43	90	36
Peace	27	94	24
Military preparedness	4	86	3
Handling of trouble spots			
(e.g. Vietnam, Cuba)	8	70	5
Internationalism	4	71	3
Foreign aid	3	29	1
2. New Deal issues	85	96	79
Economic issues	28	89	24
Government spending	6	41	2
Monetary and fiscal policy	6	88	5
Election's economic impact	19	97	19
Ideological stance	31	80	24
Liberalism, conservatism	21	87	17
Extremism	4	87	4
Relationship to Big Business,			
common man	61	99	60
Poverty program	11	95	10
Farm policy	5	93	5
Social Security, the aged,			
workers' welfare programs	30	97	28
Medical care	15	95	15
Relationship to labor, unions	12	86	10
3. Competence of the candidates	80	99	77
Record, experience	40	99	39
Strength of leadership	14	84	11
Realism	12	98	12
Judgment, stability	25	97	24
4. Candidates' other traits	53	86	41
Integrity, sincerity	22	70	15
Appearance, family	12	76	9
Clarity of positions	21	93	19
Independence	3	59	2

TABLE 5.1 (Continued)

Considerations	Salience	Dem. Bias	Dem. Pull
5. Quality of stewardship	45	80	32
Scandals	4	10	0
Governmental corruption	8	21	2
6. Partisanship	46	93	41
Goldwater Republicanism	17	91	15
Party unity	4	90	3
Conduct of campaign	33	92	28
7. Race-related issues	34	81	27
Relationship to J. F. Kennedy	27	99	27
Vice-presidential candidates	4	91	4

Range of net scores = +4 to +19
Number of respondents = 546
Percent of full sample = 49.1
Percent Democratic = 84.8
Percent voting for Johnson = 96.9

DEFINITIONS:

Salience: The percentage of a group's members who cite a given issue as something to like or dislike about the major parties and/or their candidates.

Dem. Bias: Those in a group who see a given issue as favoring Johnson and/or the Democrats, as a percentage of those who see that issue as favoring one or the other of the major parties and/or their candidates.

Dem. Pull: The percentage of a group's members who see a given issue as favoring Johnson and/or the Democrats.

in Table 5.1 will be useful in interpreting it. *Quality of stewardship* subsumes responses about the integrity, sincerity, trustworthiness, forthrightness, and ideals of the candidates and about scandals and corruption in government. *Goldwater Republicanism* applies to comments about Senator Goldwater's wing of the Republican party and the Senator's relationship to his party, and *independence* to those about the candidates' political autonomy. Comments that a candidate was associated with extremists or insufficiently alert to the

dangers of extremism are treated as pertaining to *extremism.*
Goldwater was attacked on just these grounds by important
leaders in his own party. *New Deal issues,* an important category, subsumes responses that bear on the controversies that
come down to us from the first two administrations of Franklin D. Roosevelt. In substance those controversies are mostly
about social welfare programs and governmental intervention
in the economy; rhetorically they oppose "big government" to
"individualism," "liberalism" to "conservatism," "creeping
socialism" to "galloping reaction," and the interests of the
"common man" or the "working man" to "Wall Street," "Big
Business," and "special interests." Other headings in Table
5.1 should be clear in a rough way; precise definitions for all
categories may be found in Appendix II.

Of the considerations listed in Table 5.1, two sets—New
Deal issues and matters bearing on the competence of the
candidates—were clearly paramount among Johnson's core
supporters. The aggregate salience of these issues was very
high, with 85 percent citing New Deal issues and 80 percent
citing some issue of competence as good or bad points of the
parties or their candidates. The bias of the two sets of issues
toward Johnson was virtually total, and the pull of each toward Johnson far surpassed that of any of the other considerations that figure in the table, as one would expect, given their
high salience and strong bias toward him. Seventy-nine percent of these respondents saw New Deal issues as favoring
Johnson; 77 percent saw issues bearing on competence in the
same light.

The various New Deal issues were not equally helpful to
Johnson. The most salient of these considerations, and the
most biased toward Johnson, was the perception of him and of
the Democratic Party as representing the common man and of
the Republicans as representing Big Business and special interests.[11] This consideration, echoing longstanding Democratic claims to be the party of the many contesting the privi-

---

[11] To avoid cumbersome writing I will sometimes refer to this consideration simply as "the parties' relationship to Big Business."

leges of the few, gave 60 percent of Johnson's core supporters a reason to be for him. Economic issues also earned him substantial support, especially among the bread-and-butter voters concerned about the election's impact on wages, salaries, and income. The Social Security issue (raised by Senator Goldwater in the New Hampshire primary to his later regret) helped Johnson,[12] and to a lesser extent so did the medicare issue. In what was widely described as an ideological contest, less than one-fourth of Johnson's core supporters were attracted to his candidacy for reasons that they phrased explicitly in ideological terms. While there were many comments about the liberalism or conservatism of the candidates, the so-called extremism issue—the charge that Goldwater's conservatism went beyond reasonable and legitimate bounds—did not appear to take with many respondents, at least not in so many words. Moreover, references to governmental spending and to the use of governmental power to achieve economic and social welfare objectives were unfavorable to Johnson, even among his core supporters.

Two sets of responses were most prominent among those which bore on the competence of the two candidates. The first were positive references to Johnson's political experience and his record as president. While Goldwater's record and experience attracted little criticism, praise for them was also rare. The second set of responses were those that assessed the stability, balance, and judgment of the two candidates. Democratic propaganda attacked Senator Goldwater sharply for his alleged lack of these qualities, referring to him or to a vaguely indicated "opponent" as having "more guts than brains" and as someone disposed to deal with problems "with a quick draw and a shot from the hip."[13] These charges found many respondents receptive, helped along somewhat, it is true, by

[12] The reader should note that the National Election Study coders did not distinguish between comments about social security and comments about worker welfare programs. The figures in Table 5.1 (and in the other tables) therefore exaggerate somewhat the role of the social security issue in the campaign.

[13] New York Times, October 13, 1964.

the Senator himself. Among Johnson's core supporters there was no contest on the issue of competence: They saw Lyndon Johnson as someone who had successfully faced the challenge of the presidency and could be relied upon to continue to do so; they saw Barry Goldwater as a risk at best.

The view Johnson's core supporters took of other traits of the two candidates was less one-sided. As the fourth category of Table 5.1 shows, fewer respondents saw these traits as relevant to their vote, and those who did included sizable minorities whose judgments inclined them toward Goldwater. Pro-Johnson bias was lowest in comments on the integrity and sincerity of the candidates and on their independence, and highest in those on the clarity of the candidates' stands. This last result is a bit surprising. Senator Goldwater—who said that he favored selling the Tennessee Valley Authority in a speech in Knoxville, Tennessee, and who went to West Virginia to attack the "phony war on poverty"—persistently presented himself as a man who said what he thought and thought what he said. Moreover, Lyndon Johnson often stated his goals in the vaguest of terms. Consider this statement from one of his speeches:

> The Great Society rests on abundance and liberty for all. It demands an end to poverty and racial injustice. . . . The Great Society is a place where every child can find knowledge to enrich his mind and enlarge his talent. It is a place where leisure is a welcome chance to build and reflect. It is a place where the city of man serves not only the needs of the body . . . but the desire for beauty. . . . It is a place which honors creation for its own sake. . . . But most of all, The Great Society is not a safe harbor, a resting place, a finished objective, a finished work. It is a challenge constantly renewed. . . .[14]

Theodore H. White has described this Great Society speech as "a perception of the nature of America changing. . . . Lyndon

---

[14] As quoted in Theodore H. White, *The Making of the President 1964* (New York: Atheneum, 1965), p. 391.

Johnson's Act of Recognition in the flow of history,"[15] but it was hardly a blueprint for action.

Yet, it would not have been hard to believe Johnson's positions clearer than Goldwater's. Johnson was an incumbent with a record; it would be reasonable to take that record, not his words, as indicating his future policies. Goldwater had modified some of the stands that he had taken before the campaign began,[16] and he attacked big government without saying very precisely how far and how fast he was prepared to go in cutting it down to size. Such an attack was well calculated to create uneasiness among receivers of farm subsidies, unemployment insurance, welfare checks, and other governmental largess.

Some additional features of the data reported in Table 5.1 are worth noting: The campaign as such had considerable salience for Johnson's most committed supporters, while the vice-presidential candidates, Hubert H. Humphrey and William E. Miller, had very little. The effect on these respondents of the Jenkins, Baker, and Estes scandals appears to have been slight, though a large majority of those concerned about corruption in government favored Goldwater and the Republicans on the issue. Partisanship helped Johnson substantially; significant numbers of respondents were attracted to him because he was a Democrat and were repelled by Goldwater's brand of Republicanism. Race-related issues had a strong pro-Johnson bias and gave more than one-fourth of his core supporters a reason to be for him—this in an election in which Democrats had feared, and some Republicans had hoped, that a "white backlash" might play an important role. About the same number of these respondents saw Johnson as John F. Kennedy's political heir and counted that in his favor. Foreign policy issues had an aggregate salience of 43 percent and a strong pro-Johnson bias; of these, the peace issue had by far

[15] Ibid.

[16] An excellent account of Senator Goldwater's modification of some of his precampaign stands is to be found in Benjamin I. Page, *Choices and Echoes in Presidential Elections* (Chicago: University of Chicago Press, 1978), pp. 118–132.

the largest pull. These last results indicate considerable potency for that issue and for the so-called martyr effect arising
out of the assassination of John F. Kennedy; nonetheless,
Louis Harris's observation that the outcome of the 1964 election was determined by the peace issue and "a desire not to
have three presidents in a year" seems a considerable exaggeration.[17]

GOLDWATER'S CORE SUPPORTERS

In most postelection commentary Barry Goldwater's strengths
and Lyndon Johnson's weaknesses received little attention—
landslides bury their victims. Yet some combination of motives led more than 27 million voters to vote for Goldwater,
and it is of substantial interest to know why. The reasons for
their choice become clear when we examine the likes and dislikes of Goldwater's core supporters. Including all respondents with net scores from −4 to −19, this group is a smaller
mirror image of the corresponding group of Johnson adherents not only in that respect but in other ways as well. Each
group gave their favored candidate an overwhelming majority
of their votes—the Johnson adherents, 97 percent; the Goldwater adherents, 95 percent. Each had a strong basis in partisanship; the party affiliation of the favored candidate matched
that of his adherents in over 80 percent of the cases. Each
group, finally, sided with their favored candidate on almost
every issue and to about the same extent: Among Johnson's
core supporters all but four issues had a pro-Johnson bias, and
the mean pro-Johnson bias was 82 percent. Among Goldwater's core supporters (see Table 5.2) all but three issues had
a pro-Goldwater bias, and the mean pro-Goldwater bias was
also 82 percent.

For Goldwater's core supporters, as for Johnson's, New
Deal issues were the most important of those that we have
been examining. For the former group New Deal issues had a
salience of 90 percent, a pro-Goldwater bias of 96 percent,

[17] See footnote 7 above.

and pro-Goldwater pull of 83 percent; for the latter group they had a salience of 85 percent, a pro-Johnson bias of 96 percent, and a pro-Johnson pull of 79 percent. Clearly, New Deal issues polarized the 1964 electorate, although (unhappily for the Republicans) one pole attracted many more voters than the other. Read together, Tables 5.1 and 5.2 show interesting differences in the particular New Deal issues of most concern to strong supporters of the two candidates. Economic issues generally, and government spending and monetary and fiscal policy in particular, had a considerably higher salience for Goldwater's supporters than for Johnson's. So did the ideological stances of the two candidates. The reverse situation—more concern among Johnson's adherents than among Goldwater's—held for social security and worker welfare programs, the relations of the parties to Big Business, and the election's impact on wages, salaries, and income.

Each candidate's average core supporter took a notably different view of the two candidates' qualifications for office. Johnson adherents showed great concern with competence and were almost unanimous in seeing their choice as the better man on that score. They showed considerably less concern and less unanimity about the candidates' other traits. Among Goldwater adherents the situation was almost exactly reversed: The traits not related to competence had a high salience (79 percent) and a pro-Goldwater bias of 98 percent; issues related to competence had considerably less salience (63 percent) and a pro-Goldwater bias of 70 percent. Of those among Goldwater's most committed supporters who were concerned with the judgment and stability of the two candidates, 80 percent thought the issue favored Lyndon Johnson; that fact is surely a token of the weakness of Senator Goldwater's candidacy.

Some other facts of interest show up in Table 5.2. Quality of stewardship was one of Goldwater's best issues among his most committed supporters; the issue had high salience (78 percent) and a bias toward him of 99 percent. Governmental corruption had a salience three and one-half times greater among Goldwater supporters than among Johnson sup-

TABLE 5.2
The Relative Importance of Issues among Goldwater's Core Supporters

Considerations	Salience	Rep. Bias	Rep. Pull
1. Foreign Policy	51	91	43
Peace	18	71	12
Military preparedness	12	96	12
Handling of trouble spots			
(e.g. Vietnam, Cuba)	8	100	8
Internationalism	10	77	8
Foreign aid	7	100	7
2. New Deal issues	90	96	83
Economic issues	38	95	35
Government spending	26	98	26
Monetary and fiscal policy	17	97	16
Election's economic impact	6	62	4
Ideological stance	71	96	67
Liberalism, conservatism	38	91	33
Extremism	4	63*	2
Relationship to Big Business,			
common man	24	66	16
Poverty program	9	74	6
Farm policy	7	93	6
Social Security, the aged,			
workers' welfare programs	10	57	6
Medical care	9	81	8
Relationship to labor, unions	10	87	9
3. Competence of the candidates	63	70	40
Record, experience	16	50	8
Strength of leadership	17	89	15
Realism	6	79	5
Judgment, stability	11	20	2
4. Candidates' other traits	79	98	75
Integrity, sincerity	64	99	64
Appearance, family	14	94	13
Clarity of positions	22	76	16
Independence	14	93	13

TABLE 5.2   (Continued)

Considerations	Salience	Rep. Bias	Rep. Pull
5. Quality of stewardship	78	99	74
Scandals	17	100	17
Governmental corruption	28	100	28
6. Partisanship	47	86	38
Goldwater Republicanism	44	93	39
Party unity	11	17	2
Conduct of campaign	34	70	22
7. Race-related issues	28	86	24
Relationship to J. F. Kennedy	8	88	7
Vice-presidential candidates	5	73	4

Range of net scores = −4 to −19
Number of respondents = 223
Percent of full sample = 20.0
Percent Republican = 80.3
Percent voting for Goldwater = 95.1
* Fewer than ten cases.

DEFINITIONS:
Salience: The percentage of a group's members who cite a given issue as something to like or dislike about the major parties and/or their candidates.
Rep. Bias: Those in a group who see a given issue as favoring Goldwater and/or the Republicans, as a percentage of those who see that issue as favoring one or the other of the major parties and/or their candidates.
Rep. Pull: The percentage of a group's members who see a given issue as favoring Goldwater and/or the Republicans.

porters. Race-related issues polarized the electorate, though to a lesser extent than New Deal issues.[18] Foreign policy issues were more salient for Goldwater's core supporters than for Johnson's and had greater pulling power, though a sizable mi-

[18] The 1964 National Election Study sample included few respondents from the Deep South, so my data may understate the strength of Goldwater's position on race-related issues.

nority of these Goldwater partisans thought that the peace issue favored Johnson.

THE POTENTIAL OPPOSITION MAJORITY

The data just examined show that the two candidates had positions of comparable strength among their core supporters, but this fact tells us very little about the relative strength of the Johnson and Goldwater candidacies among the respondents of the full sample. To make that comparison, it is useful to examine Goldwater's standing with the likeliest recruits to a Goldwater majority, had there been such. This set of respondents, whose attitudes are reported in Table 5.3, equals in size (almost) the set of Johnson's core supporters. For that reason we can compare the salience and pull of issues in Tables 5.1 and 5.3 directly, knowing that equal proportions of the two groups signify roughly equal numbers of respondents.

To examine Table 5.3 is to see that Senator Goldwater had substantial strengths and Lyndon Johnson had substantial weaknesses, despite the election's melancholy outcome from the Senator's point of view. In this half of the sample sixteen issues and sets of issues show a pro-Goldwater pull that equals or exceeds their pro-Johnson pull in the other half. Respondents' attitudes toward the traits of candidates not related to competence, toward the quality of stewardship, and toward corruption in government gave Goldwater such an advantage.[19] Some 36 percent of this group of respondents thought Goldwater to be preferred to Johnson on the grounds of personal integrity and sincerity—that is almost two and one-half times the number who held the contrary opinion in the other half of the sample. However else one may construe the 1964 election, it was not a vote of confidence in Lyndon Johnson's moral leadership.

Goldwater also did relatively well on some New Deal issues and on some issues of foreign policy, as one can see by com-

---

[19] The reader should recall that some of the same responses are treated as referring to all of these issues, as I have defined them. (See Appendix II.)

paring Tables 5.1 and 5.3. His position on economic issues was almost as strong as Johnson's. Among those who referred to the candidates in explicitly ideological terms, Goldwater's stance was preferred by a substantial majority, and his position was preferred by an overwhelming majority of those who raised the issue of government spending.

But Table 5.3 also makes obvious the weaknesses of Goldwater's challenge. In this half of the sample, the pro-Goldwater pull of New Deal issues as a set was much less than their pro-Johnson pull in the other half—33 percentage points less. That disadvantage came from the opposite views on some New Deal issues of the Senator's core supporters, on the one hand, and respondents weakly committed to either candidate, on the other. The bias of issues bearing on competence was also massively against Senator Goldwater; among the respondents concerned about them in the most *pro-Republican* half of the sample, 64 percent saw them as favoring Lyndon Johnson.

Marginal Voters

As a winning candidate's body of supporters swells to a majority, its overall enthusiasm for his candidacy tends to decline. The last recruits to the candidate's cause—the ones who make a winner of him—may hardly prefer him to his opponent, and in their substantive concerns, also, they may differ sharply from the candidate's more enthusiastic followers. To know why most of those who supported a victorious candidate did so, therefore, is not necessarily to know what made him victorious.

This reasoning suggests that we should examine groups of respondents whose enthusiasm for Johnson, as measured by net scores, was relatively weak. Table 5.4 reports the concerns of one such group. Including all respondents with net scores of +2, +3, or +4, this group was situated at the edge of Johnson's core support and cast about 28 percent of the votes that he received. Seventy-two percent of its members were Democrats, 21 percent Republicans. Eighty-seven percent voted for John-

TABLE 5.3

**The Relative Importance of Issues among Respondents
Representative of the Potential Opposition Majority
(1964)**

Considerations	Salience	Rep. Bias	Rep. Pull
1. Foreign Policy	39	69	25
Peace	15	45	7
Military preparedness	8	87	7
Handling of trouble spots			
(e.g. Vietnam, Cuba)	6	91	6
Internationalism	7	80	6
Foreign aid	5	90	5
2. New Deal issues	71	70	46
Economic issues	29	78	22
Government spending	18	96	17
Monetary and fiscal policy	11	79	9
Election's economic impact	7	28	2
Ideological stance	45	88	38
Liberalism, conservatism	25	81	18
Extremism	4	32	1
Relationship to Big Business,			
common man	24	35	8
Poverty program	6	70	4
Farm policy	5	69	4
Social Security, the aged,			
workers' welfare programs	13	31	4
Medical care	7	52	4
Relationship to labor, unions	7	63	4
3. Competence of the candidates	63	36	21
Record, experience	21	21	4
Strength of leadership	12	71	8
Realism	6	49	3
Judgment, stability	15	9	1

TABLE 5.3 (Continued)

Considerations	Salience	Rep. Bias	Rep. Pull
4. Candidates' other traits	58	83	43
Integrity, sincerity	40	92	36
Appearance, family	11	85	9
Clarity of positions	18	52	9
Independence	7	90	7
5. Quality of stewardship	57	86	45
Scandals	11	97	11
Governmental corruption	20	97	18
6. Partisanship	41	63	24
Goldwater Republicanism	29	82	22
Party unity	6	11	1
Conduct of campaign	29	48	12
7. Race-related issues	23	73	16
Relationship to J. F. Kennedy	12	35	4
Vice-presidential candidates	4	62	2

Range of net scores = +3 to −19
Number of respondents = 567
Percent of full sample = 50.9
Percent Republican = 72.3
Percent voting for Goldwater = 61.6

DEFINITIONS:

Salience: The percentage of a group's members who cite a given issue as something to like or dislike about the major parties and/or their candidates.

Rep. Bias: Those in a group who see a given issue as favoring Goldwater and/or the Republicans, as a percentage of those who see that issue as favoring one or the other of the major parties and/or their candidates.

Rep. Pull: The percentage of a group's members who see a given issue as favoring Goldwater and/or the Republicans.

TABLE 5.4

**The Relative Importance of Issues among Voters
at the Margin of Johnson's Core Support**

Considerations	Salience	Dem. Bias	Dem. Pull
1. Foreign Policy	34	74	24
Peace	16	87	14
Military preparedness	3	43*	2
Handling of trouble spots (e.g. Vietnam, Cuba)	6	46	3
Internationalism	5	36	2
Foreign aid	3	25*	1
2. New Deal issues	63	79	48
Economic issues	23	57	13
Government spending	9	14	1
Monetary and fiscal policy	6	46	3
Election's economic impact	11	93	11
Ideological stance	23	53	11
Liberalism, conservatism	14	70	9
Extremism	2	80*	2
Relationship to Big Business, common man	32	92	29
Poverty program	3	43*	1
Farm policy	3	71*	2
Social Security, the aged, workers' welfare programs	15	85	12
Medical care	6	93	6
Relationship to labor, unions	7	50	3
3. Competence of the candidates	74	96	68
Record, experience	34	96	32
Strength of leadership	11	64	7
Realism	9	95	9
Judgment, stability	20	98	20
4. Candidates' other traits	45	66	25
Integrity, sincerity	20	49	9
Appearance, family	11	38	4
Clarity of positions	14	76	11
Independence	3	57*	2

TABLE 5.4   (Continued)

Considerations	Salience	Dem. Bias	Dem. Pull
5. Quality of stewardship	38	59	20
Scandals	5	8	0
Governmental corruption	9	10	1
6. Partisanship	35	84	28
Goldwater Republicanism	13	80	10
Party unity	2	100*	2
Conduct of campaign	29	84	23
7. Race-related issues	22	46	9
Relationship to J. F. Kennedy	19	96	18
Vice-presidential candidates	3	67*	2

Range of net scores = +2 to +4
Number of respondents = 236
Percent of full sample = 21.2
Percent Democratic = 72.0
Percent voting for Johnson = 87.0
* Fewer than ten cases.

DEFINITIONS:

Salience: The percentage of a group's members who cite a given issue as something to like or dislike about the major parties and/or their candidates.

Dem. Bias: Those in a group who see a given issue as favoring Johnson and/or the Democrats, as a percentage of those who see that issue as favoring one or the other of the major parties and/or their candidates.

Dem. Pull: The percentage of a group's members who see a given issue as favoring Johnson and/or the Democrats.

son—a 10 percentage point drop from the share of the vote that he received among his core supporters.

There were other sharp differences between this group of marginal voters and Johnson's core supporters. New Deal issues emerge as much less important; from Table 5.1 to Table 5.4 the salience of those issues drops 22 points, their pro-Johnson bias 17. Concern about the competence of the candidates has become relatively much more important; with a drop in salience of only 6 percentage points, this set of issues has a far greater pull than New Deal issues among these respondents. Among Johnson's core supporters a large majority of those concerned with race-related issues favored Johnson's position. In this marginal group the pro-Johnson bias of race-related issues drops 35 percentage points, and a majority favor Goldwater's position. The direction of bias on the issue of integrity is also reversed. Criticism of Johnson as a "politician," as "lacking in integrity," and as associated with "immorality in government" was not limited to his strongest opponents; the incidence of these pejorative judgments was also substantial among marginal voters.

A look at a second group of marginal voters, those with net scores between ± 1, is also instructive (see Table 5.5). The set of respondents just discussed was at the margin of Johnson's *majority;* this new set was at the margin of his *landslide majority* and was weakly committed to both candidates. Compromising 13 percent of the sample, the group cast a three-to-two vote for Johnson. About 12 percent of its members were independents, and the rest were evenly divided between Democrats and Republicans.

Note these features of Table 5.5: The bias column is much less favorable to Johnson than that in Table 5.4. From Table 5.4 to Table 5.5 bias toward Johnson declines on thirty-three of the forty considerations, and five of the exceptions involve small numbers of cases. More than half of the issues now have a pro-Goldwater bias, and there is a tie on two more. Something interesting also happens in the salience column. Among these respondents one-half of the issues examined have an aggregate salience *greater* than they had in the group with net scores from +2 to +4, and ten have a salience greater than they had among Johnson's core supporters. For the most part this heightened salience came on issues favoring Goldwater and the Republicans, as one might expect.

Nonetheless, Johnson won a comfortable majority of the votes of these weakly committed voters, and Table 5.5 suggests the reason. New Deal issues and the competence of the candidates were their most salient concerns. Both sets of issues had a pro-Johnson bias, the latter a very strong one. Sizable

TABLE 5.5

**The Relative Importance of Issues among
Weakly Committed Voters (1964)**

Considerations	Salience	Dem. Bias	Dem. Pull
1. Foreign policy	28	40	10
Peace	13	81	9
Military preparedness	8	27	2
Handling of trouble spots			
(e.g. Vietnam, Cuba)	6	14*	1
Internationalism	4	0*	0
Foreign aid	6	13*	1
2. New Deal issues	54	55	26
Economic issues	22	39	8
Government spending	13	0	0
Monetary and fiscal policy	8	67	6
Election's economic impact	4	100*	4
Ideological stance	29	22	6
Liberalism, conservatism	19	36	6
Extremism	5	86*	4
Relationship to Big Business,			
common man	22	87	19
Poverty program	4	40*	1
Farm policy	5	57*	3
Social Security, the aged,			
workers' welfare programs	13	78	10
Medical care	7	70	5
Relationship to labor, unions	1	100*	1
3. Competence of the candidates	55	79	40
Record, experience	22	86	17
Strength of leadership	7	20	1
Realism	4	50*	2
Judgment, stability	15	96	15
4. Candidates' other traits	43	36	11
Integrity, sincerity	24	17	4
Appearance, family	9	27	2
Clarity of positions	19	84	15
Independence	4	17*	1

TABLE 5.5   (Continued)

Considerations	Salience	Dem. Bias	Dem. Pull
5. Quality of stewardship	42	32	10
Scandals	6	11*	1
Governmental corruption	12	8	1
6. Partisanship	38	49	17
Goldwater Republicanism	23	24	5
Party unity	4	100*	4
Conduct of campaign	21	73	11
7. Race-related issues	17	38	6
Relationship to J. F. Kennedy	11	80	8
Vice-presidential candidates	4	50*	2

Range of net scores = + 1 to − 1
Number of respondents = 144
Percent of full sample = 12.9
Percent Democratic = 44.1
Percent voting for Johnson = 60.4
* Fewer than ten cases.

DEFINITIONS:
Salience: The percentage of a group's members who cite a given issue as something to like or dislike about the major parties and/or their candidates.
Dem. Bias: Those in a group who see a given issue as favoring Johnson and/or the Democrats, as a percentage of those who see that issue as favoring one or the other of the major parties and/or their candidates.
Dem. Pull: The percentage of a group's members who see a given issue as favoring Johnson and/or the Democrats.

numbers of respondents also showed concern about peace, the clarity of the candidates' positions, and the conduct of the campaign, all of which issues worked for Johnson.

Senator Goldwater's greatest appeal was to those concerned with honesty, openness, and integrity in government—with what I have called the quality of stewardship—and he owed a good deal of this advantage to those who rated his personal honesty and integrity above Johnson's. Goldwater was helped also by economic and foreign policy issues and by his conservative Republicanism. From the evidence of Table 5.5 it would be wrong to conclude, as some did, that these were the issues that put the last bit of icing on the Johnson cake.

THE MARGINAL IMPACT OF ISSUES

By examining the likes and dislikes of marginal voters, as we just have, one can assess roughly the marginal impact of issues—that is, how much they are adding to, or subtracting from, the winner's support, given the impact of all other issues on voters' preferences. Another approach to the same kind of assessment is the simulation procedure described in Chapter 4.

Table 5.6 reports the estimates of marginal impact at two margins, +4 and +0, that were produced by that procedure. The first of these margins was critical for membership in the set of Johnson's core supporters, the second for the respondent's vote.

The table has few (if any) surprises, given what we already know about the attitudes of marginal voters. New Deal issues and issues relating to the competence of candidates were clearly most important at the margin of +4, with the former somewhat more important than the latter. At the margin critical for voting the potency of both sets of issues was much less, but issues of competence had the larger impact.[20] Other issues did not benefit Johnson greatly at that margin: If one takes seriously the small differences in the estimated marginal impact of other issues, Johnson's next best appeals were the clar-

---

[20] Note that the figures for the marginal impact of the component parts of an issue will not necessarily sum to that for the issue of which they are components. That some issues subsume more likes and dislikes than those subsumed by their components taken together is one reason for this nonadditivity, but not the only one. An issue or subissue will show a marginal impact only if the deletion of the likes and dislikes it involves moves at least one voter's net score across the margin at which impact is being measured. Thus, the marginal impact of each of two components may be zero, while that for the two taken together is nonzero.

TABLE 5.6

The Marginal Impact of Issues on Support for Johnson

Considerations	Changes in the Proportion of the Sample Supporting Johnson with Net Scores That Were:	
	$\geq +4$	$\geq +0$
1. Foreign Policy	− 1.5	+ 0.1
Peace	− 1.2	− 0.2
Military preparedness	0.0	+ 0.1
Handling of trouble spots		
(e.g. Vietnam, Cuba)	− 0.1	0.0
Internationalism	+ 0.3	+ 0.3
Foreign aid	+ 0.1	0.0
2. New Deal issues	−11.5	− 0.8
Economic issues	− 0.9	+ 0.3
Government spending	+ 0.6	+ 0.6
Monetary and fiscal policy	− 0.1	+ 0.1
Election's economic impact	− 1.5	− 0.4
Ideological stance	− 0.6	+ 0.9
Liberalism, conservatism	− 1.3	0.0
Extremism	0.0	− 0.2
Relationship to Big Business,		
common man	− 5.1	− 0.9
Poverty program	+ 0.1	+ 0.3
Farm policy	− 0.3	0.0
Social Security, the aged,		
workers' welfare programs	− 1.4	− 0.3
Medical care	− 0.4	− 0.2
Relationship to labor, unions	− 0.2	0.0
3. Competence of the candidates	− 7.8	− 1.9
Record, experience	− 3.7	− 0.9
Strength of leadership	− 0.6	0.0
Realism	− 0.8	0.0
Judgment, stability	− 2.0	− 0.8

TABLE 5.6   (Continued)

| Considerations | Changes in the Proportion of the Sample Supporting Johnson with Net Scores That Were: | |
	$\geq + 4$	$\geq + 0$
4. Candidates' other traits	− 3.1	0.0
Integrity, sincerity	0.0	+ 1.0
Appearance, family	+ 0.1	+ 0.4
Clarity of positions	− 0.9	− 0.5
Independence	− 0.4	+ 0.2
5. Quality of stewardship	− 0.9	+ 1.1
Scandals	+ 0.5	+ 0.1
Governmental corruption	+ 0.7	+ 0.1
6. Partisanship	− 3.5	+ 0.3
Goldwater Republicanism	− 1.0	+ 0.6
Party unity	− 0.2	0.0
Conduct of campaign	− 2.1	− 0.2
7. Race-related issues	− 0.3	+ 0.4
Relationship to J. F. Kennedy	− 2.0	− 0.6
Vice-presidential candidates	− 0.1	0.0

Marginal impact: The amount by which a particular issue increases or decreases the proportion of voters showing some specified degree of commitment to a candidate, given the effects of all other issues on strength of voters' commitments to that candidate. In this table such increases and decreases are expressed as percentages of the full sample, and degrees of commitment are measured by net scores. Negative signs indicate a marginal impact favorable to Johnson and positive signs a marginal impact favorable to Goldwater.

ity of his positions and his relationship to John F. Kennedy. Two related issues—the honesty and integrity of the candidates and the quality of stewardship—were Goldwater's best ones, and the sign of the estimates for governmental spending at both margins suggests that the Senator was right in stressing that issue.

Some Concluding Observations

The preceding analysis should make one cautious about attributing the outcome of the election of 1964, or any other election, to the influence of one or even several issues. Many issues contributed in some degree and in different ways to Lyndon Johnson's landslide. Nonetheless, two sets of issues were predominant: Lyndon Johnson won twice in 1964, once on New Deal issues and once on issues of competence. Of these two sets of issues, New Deal issues were somewhat more important in giving him a strong base of support, issues of competence in bringing to his side voters who otherwise were not strongly attracted either to him or to his opponent. The view that the electorate of 1964 endorsed "a candidate and a party who were in the most direct sense heirs of F.D.R. and the New Deal tradition"[21] is rightly a major theme in the story of that election, but what Philip Converse and his associates called the "phenomenally unfavorable" Goldwater image[22] is a second theme that deserves equal if not greater emphasis.

---

[21] Tom Wicker, p. ix, in Faber, *The Road to the White House.*

[22] Converse, Clausen, and Miller, "Electoral Myth and Reality," p. 330.

CHAPTER SIX
1972: A CLOSE LANDSLIDE

Even before the votes were counted in 1972, Richard Nixon was considering how he might use the lopsided victory that he expected. A landslide and the mandate it implied, he told Theodore H. White, would strengthen his hand in foreign affairs: "If we can win and win well, we can talk to China with great authority, to the Soviet Union, to Japan."[1] To Congress, "he [Nixon] was going to say . . . the country has spoken, and put out his own views on welfare, on a program of fiscal responsibility, on other matters."[2]

It was not long before Nixon was invoking his landslide for a very different purpose. As new details of the Watergate scandals came into public view, his authority began to dissolve, and he began to look for ways to restore it. In a memorandum of July 25, 1973, one of his aides, Patrick J. Buchanan, suggested a tactic: Public attention should be diverted "from a question of whether the President 'knew' of the cover-up, where 70 percent of the nation is against us—to a question of whom do you wish to govern this nation—the President or the men who would destroy him?" The President should accuse his opposition of "seeking to destroy the democratic mandate of 1972."[3] Nixon made that charge—not for the last time—in an address to the nation on August 15, 1973:

> Last November, the American people were given the clearest choice of this century. Your votes were a mandate, which I accepted, to complete the initiatives we began in my first term and to fulfill the promises I made for my second term.

[1] Theodore H. White, *The Making of the President 1972* (New York: Atheneum, 1973), p. 302.

[2] Ibid.

[3] As quoted by Jules Witcover, Washington *Post*, July 24, 1974.

This Administration was elected to control inflation, to reduce the power and size of government, to cut the cost of government so that you can cut the cost of living, to preserve and defend those fundamental values that have made America great, to keep the nation's military strength second to none, to achieve peace with honor in Southeast Asia and to bring home our prisoners of war, and to build a new prosperity, without inflation and without war, to create a structure of peace in the world that would endure long after we are gone. . . .

If you share my belief in these goals—if you want the mandate you gave this Administration to be carried out—then I ask your help to insure that those who would exploit Watergate in order to keep us from doing what we were elected to do will not succeed.[4]

Others found different reasons for recalling the election of 1972. Democratic factions fried their fish in the ashes of their party's defeat, just as Republicans had after their great defeat in 1964. In early January of 1973 Ben J. Wattenberg advanced this view of the election, popular among party regulars:

I would say that what happened substantively in this election was that there was the equivalent of a referendum in this country. It was a referendum on the so-called cultural revolution that has been going on allegedly for four or five years in this country. It involved many, many facets—busing and defense and welfare and all sorts of things—and a perception of whether this country was doing pretty well or teetering on the brink of failure. If there was going to be an election on something in this country, this was a pretty good thing to have an election on. And the American people voted no on what the whole "new politics" movement was about.[5]

[4] Washington *Post,* August 16, 1973.
[5] Ernest R. May and Janet Fraser (eds.), *Campaign '72: The Managers Speak* (Cambridge: Harvard University Press, 1973), p. 233.

On the same occasion Gary W. Hart, McGovern's national campaign director in 1972, advanced a quite different view:

> I'll go to my grave thinking that this election was decided on the issue of who was competent, who had those characteristics of leadership that people generally think should be in the White House.... I don't think the American people ever got to the substantive issues themselves. They judged by what seemed to be the confusion around McGovern and decided not to take a chance on putting him in the White House.[6]

McGovern himself interpreted the election in much the same way, attributing his defeat to voters' rejection of what "they perceived to be a confusion and uncertainty of leadership."[7] He listed among his mistakes the inadequate preparation of his welfare proposals, the disorganization and disputatiousness of his staff, the selection of Senator Thomas Eagleton as his running mate, and his delivery of his acceptance speech to a sleeping nation at 3:00 a.m. This apology carried with it a denial that the 1972 Democratic campaign had been defeated on the issues, and McGovern urged Democrats to continue to work for tax reform, control of weapons, and the elimination of the oil depletion allowance.[8]

One could dismiss these various accounts of the Nixon landslide as dictated by political interest, and doubtless many observers saw what they wanted to see in that event. When one confronts such accounts with evidence, however, some look a good deal better than others.[9]

[6] Ibid., pp. 231–232.

[7] *New York Times*, October 26, 1975.

[8] Ibid.

[9] My discussion of the Johnson landslide focused attention on the attitudes and behavior of particular groups of voters; my discussion of the 1972 election will focus on particular issues and their impact on its outcome. Both of these ways of thinking about elections illuminate their meaning, and I vary the organization of Chapters 5 and 6 to demonstrate that fact. Each chapter's tables include all the data needed for taking either approach.

PERCEPTIONS OF THE CANDIDATES

Table 6.1 reports the distribution of attitudes on forty issues and sets of issues that figured in the 1972 election.[10] Those relating to the competence of the candidates were by far the most important in giving Nixon his landslide. Issues of competence gave three-quarters of his core supporters[11] a reason to support him and showed both high salience (53 percent) and an overwhelmingly pro-Nixon bias (94 percent) among respondents at the margin of his majority. Even among McGovern's core supporters, comments on competence had a strong (58 percent) bias toward Nixon. The figure for marginal impact in Table 6.1 suggests that this set of issues added over 6 percentage points to the share of the vote that other issues would have given Nixon. The extent of McGovern's disadvantage is startling: In the half of the sample most favorable to him only 25 percent of those for whom competence-related issues were salient thought those issues favored him, a figure 11 percentage points below the comparable one for Barry Goldwater in 1964.

Note also that experience and achievements in government favored Nixon more heavily even than Johnson.[12] So did the stronger leadership expected of him, although this advantage mostly reflected criticism of McGovern for weakness, vacillation, and indecisiveness, not praise of Nixon. The candidates' realism was a less frequent theme than either their experience

[10] Appendix II lists the remarks of respondents that I have treated as pertaining to each issue or set of issues.

[11] Nixon's core supporters, like Johnson's, comprise that half of the sample with net scores most favorable to him. Note, however, that Nixon's core supporters supported him less strongly, on the average, than their counterparts supported Johnson.

[12] The overwhelming one-sidedness with which respondents counted "record and experience" for Nixon and Johnson suggests one source of an incumbent's advantage. Though both Goldwater and McGovern had held high office for many years, few voters spoke positively of either's record or experience, and those few were equaled or exceeded in number by those who thought the two challengers inexperienced. It is as if voters regarded prior service as president as the only highly relevant experience for being president.

TABLE 6.1

The Relative Importance of Issues in the 1972 Election

Considerations	Nixon Core S (%)	RB (%)	RP (%)	Marginal Voters S (%)	RB (%)	RP (%)	McGovern Core S (%)	DB (%)	DP (%)	Potential Opposition Majority S (%)	DB (%)	DP (%)	Marginal Impact
Competence of the candidates	80	97	76	53	94	45	41	42	13	43	25	9	− 6.4
Record, experience	47	98	46	27	97	26	12	31	3	16	14	2	− 2.8
Strength of leadership	30	96	29	21	92	19	17	24	4	18	14	2	− 1.6
Realism	18	100	18	11	96	11	7	44	3	8	25	2	− 1.0
Candidates' other traits	51	89	42	34	57	18	56	96	52	45	84	37	− 1.4
Integrity, sincerity	33	85	28	22	53	11	49	98	47	37	87	32	− 0.8
Appearance, family	8	73	5	4	56*	2	4	70	3	4	67	2	0.0
Independence	3	67	2	3	50*	1	1	100	0	2	57	1	− 0.1
Vietnam War, peace	60	93	53	41	69	27	56	87	46	49	70	33	− 2.1
Foreign policy	33	88	28	18	79	14	28	48	13	23	38	9	− 1.7
Relations with Red China	9	87	8	7	88	6	9	38	3	8	25	2	− 0.5
Relations with the U.S.S.R.	7	79	5	4	89*	3	3	25	1	3	14	0	− 0.2
Military preparedness	10	93	9	5	73	3	8	61	5	6	52	3	− 0.3
Internationalism	7	72	5	4	56	2	4	44	2	3	36	1	− 0.3

TABLE 6.1 (Continued)

The Relative Importance of Issues in the 1972 Election

Considerations	Nixon Core			Marginal Voters			McGovern Core			Potential Opposition Majority			Marginal Impact
	S (%)	RB (%)	RP (%)	S (%)	RB (%)	RP (%)	S (%)	DB (%)	DP (%)	S (%)	DB (%)	DP (%)	
New Deal issues	73	79	53	57	24	11	90	97	84	76	93	66	+ 4.9
Economic issues	40	78	30	32	35	8	48	91	39	39	84	30	+ 0.5
Government spending	9	83	7	5	86*	3	5	50	3	4	44	2	- 0.2
Election's economic impact	18	71	12	15	21	3	34	96	31	26	92	23	+ 0.4
Monetary and fiscal policy	17	74	12	13	33	4	22	91	20	19	85	16	+ 0.5
Ideological stance	38	90	32	20	53	9	29	74	21	25	67	16	- 0.8
Liberalism, conservatism	28	94	25	14	70	9	15	56	8	14	46	6	- 0.7
Welfare	29	93	27	16	84	13	21	61	12	17	52	9	- 0.8
Social Security, the aged, workers' welfare programs	8	65	5	7	38	3	13	97	12	11	86	9	+ 0.1
Relationship to labor, unions	5	67	3	6	15	1	8	63	5	7	73	5	+ 0.4
Relationship to Big Business, common man	27	29	8	36	5	2	68	99	67	55	98	53	+ 3.2
Farm policy	2	78*	2	3	17*	0	2	100*	2	2	100*	2	+ 0.2
The Social Issue	27	90	24	17	63	10	25	77	18	22	68	14	- 0.9
Law and order	4	88	4	0	0*	0	7	69	5	4	69	3	0.0
"Amnesty, acid, abortion"	9	100	9	3	86	3	7	47	3	6	38	2	- 0.2
Youth-related issues	14	95	13	8	61	5	11	54	5	10	54	5	- 0.1
Race-related issues	11	86	9	7	69	7	10	91	9	9	72	6	- 0.8

Governmental corruption	8	23	2	5	8	0	15	100	15	11	98	10	2	+ 0.2
Watergate affair	4	13	1	3	13*	0	8	100	8	7	96	6		+ 0.2

	−2 to −20			−2 to +1			+2 to +20			−1 to +20			−20 to +20
Conventions, Eagleton affair	10	90	9	8	95	8	13	22	3	11	15	2	− 1.2
Eagleton affair	7	100	7	7	100	7	9	14	1	9	9	1	− 1.2
Conduct of campaign	19	95	17	12	77	8	12	60	6	11	48	5	− 0.4
Partisanship	17	68	11	14	31	4	27	84	21	21	80	16	+ 0.4
Party unity	4	100	3	4	89	3	6	21	1	5	18	1	− 0.4
Vice-presidential candidates	4	67*	2	1	67*	1	2	100	2	1	83	1	− 0.1

Range of net scores	− 2 to − 20	− 2 to + 1	+ 2 to + 20	− 1 to + 20	− 20 to + 20
Number of respondents	416	239	241	414	830
% full sample of voters	50.1	28.8	29.0	49.9	100.0
% voting for Nixon	93	66	16	35	64.5

· S = Aggregate Salience   DB = Democratic Bias
RB = Republican Bias   DP = Democratic Pull
RP = Republican Pull

DEFINITIONS:

Salience: The percentage of a group's members who cite a given issue as something to like or dislike about the major parties and/or their candidates.

Bias: Those in a group who see a given issue as favoring a given candidate and/or his party, as a percentage of those who see that issue as favoring one or the other of the major parties and/or their candidates.

Pull: The percentage of a group's members who see a given issue as favoring a given candidate and/or his party.

Marginal impact: The amount by which a particular issue increases or decreases the proportion of voters showing some specified degree of commitment to a given candidate, given the effects of all other issues on strength of commitment to that candidate. In this table the figures for marginal impact show the percentage-point changes produced by each issue in the proportion of the sample with net scores of − 0 or less. Negative signs indicate issues favorable to Nixon; positive signs, issues favorable to McGovern.

* Fewer than 10 cases.

or qualities of leadership, but of the 18 percent of Nixon's core supporters who voiced opinions on the matter, *all* saw the issue as favoring him.

Voters' assessments of the two candidates' other qualities and qualifications were strongly polarized and in that sense more balanced. Among his core supporters Nixon was favored by large majorities of those concerned about integrity and sincerity, the independence of the candidates, their appearance and families, and other personal qualities. McGovern stood nearly as well with respondents in the other half of the sample and (except for appearance and family) considerably better among his own core supporters. Among marginal voters this set of issues had a quite modest Nixon bias; 47 percent of those concerned about the issue of integrity saw it as counting for the challenger, and the marginal impact of the whole set of issues, though small, was pro-Nixon.

An interesting pattern in respondents' views of incumbent and challenger in 1964 repeats itself in 1972: In the half of the sample defined as Nixon's core supporters, both the salience and pro-Nixon bias of issues of competence are high; in the other half of the sample the bias of these issues remains pro-Nixon (though it declines), but their salience drops 37 percentage points. What happens with the integrity issue is quite different: Among Nixon's core supporters the issue's salience is relatively low, while its pro-Nixon bias is high; among respondents' representative of the potential opposition majority, this bias drops over 70 percentage points while the salience of the issue increases. This pattern and its counterpart in 1964 could mean that many respondents were suppressing doubts—those for the incumbents, doubts about integrity; those for the challengers, doubts about competence. Another explanation fits the facts equally well, however: Voters more concerned with integrity than competence tended to favor Goldwater and McGovern; those who cared more about competence than character tended to favor Richard Nixon and Lyndon Johnson.

That voters' evaluations of the candidates in 1972 were the most important factor in the outcome of the 1972 election and that they worked strongly for Nixon has been reported by a number of scholarly analysts.[13] The findings just reported show what those evaluations involved. Collectively, voters did not see Nixon simply as the all-round better man. It was issues related to the competence of the two candidates—experience, record in public life, strength of leadership, realism—that gave him such a decisive advantage.[14]

THE VIETNAM WAR AND ISSUES OF FOREIGN POLICY

Analysts of the 1972 presidential election have also seen the Vietnam War as an issue that worked strongly for Nixon.[15] My results support that conclusion.

[13] See Pomper, *Voters' Choice*, p. 149; Kagay and Caldeira, "A 'Reformed' Electorate? Well at Least a Changed Electorate"; Samuel Popkin, John W. Gorman, Charles Phillips, and Jeffrey Smith, "Comment: What Have You Done for Me Lately? Toward an Investment Theory of Voting," *American Political Science Review* 70 (September 1976), p. 799; David E. RePass, "Comment: Political Methodologies in Disarray: Some Alternative Interpretations of the 1972 Election," *American Political Science Review* 70 (September 1976), p. 816; Arthur H. Miller and Warren E. Miller, "Ideology in the 1972 Election: Myth or Reality—A Rejoinder," *American Political Science Review* 70 (September 1976), p. 833.

[14] This point is argued strongly by Popkin et al., "Comment: What Have You Done for Me Lately?" though they attach somewhat greater importance to perceptions of McGovern's incompetence than my data indicate. Voters' positive assessments of Nixon's experience in office also helped him greatly and might well have done so against any challenger. Miller and Miller, "Ideology in the 1972 Election," also cite data showing the importance of voters' estimates of ability, experience, decisiveness, stability, and responsibility in their evaluations of McGovern and Nixon.

[15] See Pomper, *Voters' Choice*, p. 160; Arthur H. Miller, Warren E. Miller, Alden S. Raine, and Thad A. Brown, "A Majority Party in Disarray: Policy Polarization in the 1972 Election," *American Political Science Review* 70 (September 1976), pp. 763, 769; Frederick T. Steeper and Robert M. Teeter, "Comment on 'A Majority Party in Disarray,'" *American Political Science Review* 70 (September 1976), p. 806. However, David RePass, "Comment: Political Methodologies in Disarray," saw the impact of the Vietnam issue as small, and William H. Flanigan and Nancy H. Zingale have concluded that "among all the issues of the campaign, only Vietnam appears to have benefited McGovern." See their *Political Behavior of the American Electorate,* 3d edition (Boston: Allyn, Bacon, Inc., 1975), p. 139.

The war polarized the electorate. Fifty-three percent of Nixon's core supporters thought the issue favored him (see Table 6.1), giving it a pro-Nixon pull in that group second only to that of issues of competence. In the other half of the sample, among respondents representative of the potential opposition majority and among McGovern's core supporters, the issue had a high (70 percent and 87 percent) pro-McGovern bias and a substantial pro-McGovern pull. Among marginal voters, the war ranked next to competence in its ability to attract adherents to the Nixon cause, and it seems to have added a little more than 2 percentage points to Nixon's margin of victory.[16]

Frederick T. Steeper and Robert M. Teeter, commenting on the role of the War issue in 1972, have argued that

> The impression . . . that Nixon won a landslide victory based on a coalition of voters who favored an escalation of the war is directly contrary to what MOR [Market Opinion Research] was continually finding throughout the election year . . . we consistently found Nixon's biggest asset was that a clear plurality of voters perceived him as successfully *de-escalating* the war.[17]

An examination of the coded responses supports this view. Only a few respondents declared themselves for Nixon because they thought he would fight through to a military victory. Over seven times as many thought that Nixon's policies offered a better chance for peace than McGovern's, and nearly twice as many thought that Nixon stood *against* a policy of military victory. Among voters, to be pro-Nixon on the war was not to be prowar.

---

[16] Though less, this assessment of the marginal impact of the issue is very close to that which Pomper derived from a regression analysis of the same data. See Pomper, *Voters' Choice,* p. 160.

[17] "Comment on 'A Majority Party in Disarray,' " p. 806. Market Opinion Research was one of the research organizations that surveyed voters for the Nixon campaign.

Foreign policy issues other than the Vietnam War were not polarizing in 1972. As Table 6.1 shows, they had a pro-Nixon bias across the board. Their salience was modest, reaching a high of 33 percent among Nixon's core supporters and a low of 18 percent among marginal voters. This set of issues seems to have added somewhat less than 2 percentage points to Nixon's share of the vote.[18]

Table 6.1 suggests some components of Nixon's foreign policy advantage. Among those concerned with the issue of military preparedness, approval of McGovern's position (or what was seen as his position) barely exceeded 50 percent in the most Democratic half of the sample. And Nixon's summitry was popular—those concerned about relations with Red China and the Soviet Union largely approved Nixon's handling of them. Indeed, the issue of relations with the Soviet Union had a smaller pro-Nixon bias (79 percent) among Nixon's core supporters than it did in the other half of the sample (86 percent).

NEW DEAL ISSUES

A large proportion of Nixon's core supporters (73 percent) were concerned about New Deal issues—fewer, but not many fewer, than were concerned about issues relating to competence—and the pro-Nixon pull of these issues in that group equaled that of the war (or peace) issue (see Table 6.1). New Deal issues must therefore be counted as a major influence in shaping the Nixon coalition.

Two other features of their role, however, are perhaps more interesting. One was the strength that New Deal issues lent McGovern's candidacy. Among McGovern's core supporters their salience was a phenomenal 90 percent, and their pro-McGovern bias was almost total (97 percent). In the most pro-McGovern half of the sample, 66 percent of the respondents favored McGovern's position on these issues, a considerably better showing than Nixon made in the other half (53

[18] In this instance Pomper's estimate of marginal impact is a little less than mine.

percent). McGovern also did much better than Nixon among
marginal voters. The estimate of marginal impact in Table 6.1
suggests that this set of issues added almost 5 percentage
points to *McGovern's* share of the vote.

The similarity in detail of the role of New Deal issues in
1972 and 1964 is also striking. Their aggregate salience in the
two elections was 78 percent and 75 percent, respectively.
When one splits each of the samples into pro-Republican and
pro-Democratic halves[19] and compares the bias and pull of
issues in the two halves, one is again struck by how alike the
distribution of attitudes was. In 1972 the salience of the election's economic impact, monetary and fiscal policy, the relationship of the candidates and parties to trade unions and to
Big Business, and of New Deal issues as a set, was greater in
the Democratic half of the sample, while economic issues,
government spending, and the ideological stance of the parties
and candidates were more salient in the Republican half. The
same was true in 1964, except that monetary and fiscal policy
was more salient in the Republican half of the sample in that
year.[20] In both elections, when an issue had greater salience in
one party's half of the sample, that party also enjoyed an advantage in pull on that issue.[21] Economic issues were the one
exception to this rule. Given these facts it would be hard to
conclude that the New Deal coalition broke up in 1972. Instead, the traditional New Deal issues were highly salient and
worked for McGovern in much the same way that they had
worked for Lyndon Johnson eight years before.[22]

---

[19] That is, into core supporters of the winners, on the one hand, and
respondents representative of the potential opposition majority, on the
other.

[20] Compare the relevant entries in Table 6.1 with those in Tables 5.1
and 5.5 above.

[21] That is, if an issue had greater salience in the Democratic side of the
sample, its pro-Democratic pull in that half of the sample was greater
than its pro-Republican pull in the other half.

[22] Except for ideological issues and, to a lesser extent, welfare, relatively little attention has been given the role of New Deal issues in the
1972 election. Steeper and Teeter have argued that Nixon's greatest vul-
nerability was on economic issues. (See "Comment on 'A Majority Party

THE SOCIAL ISSUE

In their book, *The Real Majority,* first published in 1970, Richard M. Scammon and Ben J. Wattenberg argued that a new "Voting Issue" had found its way into American politics, "an issue so powerful that it may rival bimetallism and depression in American political history, an issue powerful enough that under certain circumstances it can compete in political potency with the older economic issues."[23] The book gave Barry Goldwater credit for being the first major-party presidential candidate to "touch the raw nerve ending of the Social Issue," as Scammon and Wattenberg called it, when in the 1964 campaign he decried "violence in the streets, corruption in our highest offices, aimlessness among our youth, anxiety among our elderly," and "the growing menace to personal safety, to life, to limb and property, in homes, in churches, on the playgrounds and places of business, particularly in our great cities."[24] The book's final chapter had a warning for Democrats: To be seen as soft on the Social Issue would be to commit political suicide.

The McGovern campaign was widely seen as having ignored this well-publicized warning, and some saw that fact as a major reason for the campaign's failure. Writing soon after the election, Jeane Kirkpatrick declared the result to have revealed "that the Presidential election of 1972 had become a cultural class struggle with Richard Nixon cast as leader of the

---

in Disarray,' " p. 807.) Pomper noted both the relatively high salience of economic and welfare issues in 1972 and the tendency of the electorate to believe such problems are better handled by the Democrats (*Voters' Choice,* pp. 144–145). At one point in his analysis of the election Pomper observes that the Democratic Party "is liked because it is good for the 'common man' or 'the working people,' because it opposes the interests of 'big business,' and because of its association with popular policies such as social security and economic prosperity. The positive qualities ascribed to the party clearly date to the times of the Great Depression and the New Deal" (*Voters' Choice,* p. 148).

[23] New York: Coward-McCann, Inc., 1970, p. 40.

[24] Ibid., p. 37. The phrases quoted from Goldwater are from his acceptance speech to the 1964 Republican National Convention.

masses and George McGovern as the spokesman of an em-
battled revolutionary elite. This . . . was a strange situation . . .
and it led, for the first time in American history, to a landslide
defeat for the majority party."[25] What was the struggle about?
In her words, " 'the streets of Chicago,' Mayor Daley, hard-
hats, hippies, Hubert Humphrey, quotas, pot, draft resistance,
university disorders, the Vietnam spring, Forest Hills, com-
munity control, Richard Nixon, the flag, Archie Bunker, the
American Dream. Everyone knows these code words: they
define the sides and the stakes in a struggle over individual
morality and national purpose."[26]

Except for a nod toward "polls and observation," Kirkpatrick argued her case without resort to data. When data
were considered, the meaning of the election became rather
more ambiguous. Miller, Miller, Raine, and Brown found that
responses to questions about amnesty for draft dodgers and
deserters, the use of marijuana, and campus unrest were
strongly related to the vote in bivariate analyses with party
identification held constant, and that responses to questions
about aid to minorities and school integration were somewhat
less strongly related.[27] The meaning of these results were cast
into some doubt, however, by multivariate analysis. When indices of opinion on social and cultural issues were regressed
on the vote—together with measures of party identification
and of attitudes toward the candidates, the war, and economic
issues—the independent effect of social issues was quite modest and that for cultural issues nonexistent.[28]

To ascertain the role of the Social Issue in the 1972 election
is a necessarily uncertain enterprise, since Scammon and
Wattenberg failed to define the issue once and for all. At various points in their book, all of the following concerns are an-
nexed to it: street violence, governmental corruption, youthful
aimlessness, racial integration, civil rights, crime, lawlessness,
urban riots, pornography, permissive sexual codes, protest

[25] Jeane Kirkpatrick, "The Revolt of the Masses," *Commentary* (February 1973), p. 58.
[26] Ibid., p. 60.
[27] "A Majority Party in Disarray," pp. 761–764.
[28] See ibid., unabridged version.

against the Vietnam War, drug use, student activism, campus disruptions, the generation gap, the hippie lifestyle, welfare handouts, confrontation politics, muggers and rapists, and gay culture.[29] A multitude of sins, truly. The definition I have used treats comments on any of these subjects except welfare as pertaining to the Social Issue.[30] Since controversy about welfare policies and programs dates at least from the New Deal period, it seems reasonable to treat it as a New Deal issue.

Thus defined, the role of the Social Issue in the 1972 election seems to have been relatively small. A little less than one-fourth of Nixon's core supporters saw in it a reason to prefer Nixon (see Table 6.1). The Social Issue had a pro-McGovern bias among respondents representative of the potential opposition majority and among McGovern's core supporters, though it was not so high as the pro-Nixon bias of the issue in the most pro-Nixon half of the sample. Among marginal voters the Social Issue had a salience of 17 percent and a pro-Nixon bias of 63 percent, and it appears to have added about one percentage point to Nixon's share of the vote.

Of the various components of the issue, youth-related issues had the greatest pro-Nixon pull among Nixon's core supporters (13 percent); in the other half of the sample race-related issues had the greatest pro-McGovern pull. Law-and-order questions and "amnesty, acid, abortion"[31] had quite a low salience in all groups (from none to 9 percent). None of

[29] *The Real Majority,* pp. 37–38, 42, 44–45, 282, 285, 295–297, 301.

[30] I should say, "would treat," since no responses were coded on some of these subjects. Appendix II shows the responses that I have treated as relating to the Social Issue. The reader will note that other issues subsume some of the same responses and that the sets of responses subsumed by the components of the Social Issue also intersect. I allowed this intersection so that my definition of the Social Issue and its components would conform as closely as possible to that implied by Scammon and Wattenberg, thus fairly testing their thesis about the Social Issue's importance. Responses subsumed under two different issues contribute equally, of course, to the salience, bias, pull, and marginal impact of each. Their *joint* importance will be inflated relative to other issues, however, and Table 6.1 must be interpreted with that fact in mind.

[31] The "acid" of this phrase refers, of course, to drugs. The phrase itself has been credited by some to former Senator Hugh Scott of Pennsylvania.

the marginal respondents was concerned about law-and-order issues; the bias of youth-related issues ("kidlash" in the Scammon and Wattenberg lexicon) in the same group was fairly strongly pro-Nixon. The marginal impact of all these elements of the Social Issue except racial questions appears to have been near zero.[32]

If one treats the welfare issue as a component of the Social Issue, the results change considerably. *This* Social Issue has a marginal impact in Nixon's favor more than double that shown in Table 6.1. All that this exercise shows, however, is that the welfare issue had about as great an influence on the vote in 1972 as all the other components of the Social Issue combined. Since both welfare and race relations have been issues in American politics for a very long time, the *new* components of the Social Issue clearly played a quite limited role in Nixon's landslide.

Other studies do not challenge this conclusion seriously. On methodological grounds the findings of the multivariate analysis done by Miller and his associates, which showed a quite restricted influence for the social issue,[33] deserve more credence than those from bivariate analyses.[34] It is hard to believe, for instance, that campus demonstrations were a major issue in the 1972 election when only two of 830 respondents—0.2 per cent of the sample—volunteered comments on the subject in stating their likes and dislikes of the candidates and their parties. It is possible that some of the influence of the Social Issue was masked in other comments; respondents who

[32] Pomper, working from the same data but defining "the Social Issue" somewhat differently (and, on the whole, more narrowly) than I, reached the same conclusion (see *Voters' Choice,* pp. 160–161).

[33] Defined in their study as involving ways to deal with urban unrest and urban problems, aid to minorities, protection of civil liberties in criminal cases, and ways to deal with student demonstrations ("A Majority Party in Disarray," pp. 777–778).

[34] Or those from multivariate analyses from which important variables have been excluded. The multivariate analyses just referred to included as independent variables attitudes toward each of the candidates and an index of their ideological affinity to the voter; some other multivariate analyses done by Miller and his associates did not.

found McGovern "too liberal" or "too radical" may have based that judgment on their perceptions of his stand on law-and-order issues or on student demonstrations. Even if one coded all such comments as comments on the Social Issue, however, it would hardly qualify as *the* voting issue of 1972.

EVENTS

On June 17, 1972, five men, one of them the director of security for the Nixon campaign committee, were caught planting eavesdropping devices in the headquarters of the Democratic National Committee in the Watergate complex in Washington. By September 15 two former White House aides had been indicted for their part in the incident.

On July 25, Senator Thomas F. Eagleton, the Democratic vice-presidential candidate, told a press conference that he had been hospitalized on three occasions for nervous exhaustion and fatigue and that his treatment had involved both psychiatric counseling and electroshock therapy. At the same press conference Senator McGovern said that Eagleton remained his choice for vice-president. Later, McGovern said that he stood "a thousand percent" behind Eagleton, and still later—six days—he announced that he and Eagleton had reached a joint decision that the latter should resign from the Democratic ticket.

Though the first of these celebrated incidents eventually cost Richard Nixon the presidency, during the campaign it was not thought likely to influence many votes. The data confirm that judgment. In stating their likes and dislikes of the candidates and parties, only 5 percent of the respondents of the full sample mentioned Watergate. Its salience was higher than that among McGovern's core supporters and among respondents representative of the potential opposition majority, lower among Nixon's core supporters, and lowest—3 percent—among marginal voters (see Table 6.1). The bias of the Watergate issue was heavily anti-Nixon in all these groups, but that was not enough to give it any appreciable marginal impact. The salience of corruption as an issue, which might have been fed by other activities of the Nixon administration as well as by Watergate, reached 10 percent in the full sample and 5 percent among marginal respondents but had no greater marginal impact than Watergate alone.

In contrast, the Eagleton affair appears to have affected the vote appreciably. The salience of the issue ranged from 9 percent among McGovern's core supporters to 7 percent among marginal voters,[35] and the issue's pro-Nixon bias ranged from 100 percent among Nixon's core supporters and marginal voters to 86 percent among McGovern's core supporters. The affair's marginal impact, measured by simulation, was a little over one percentage point in Nixon's favor.

This result, based as it is on explicit references to Eagleton and the handling of the Eagleton affair, may understate its impact. Some respondents may have expressed their views of the affair in adverse judgments about the conduct of the McGovern campaign, another issue that counted heavily against the Democratic candidate among the 12 percent of marginal respondents for whom it was salient. Moreover, the Eagleton affair is a likely source of judgments that McGovern was weak and vacillating and a man who did not keep his promises. In the full sample, some 20 percent of the respondents expressed the first of these views and about 10 percent the second. That is about two and one-half times the number of respondents who said that McGovern (or the Democratic Party) was "too liberal."

SOME COMBINED EFFECTS

As a final maneuver in assessing the influence of various issues and appeals on the outcome of the 1972 election, we can measure the marginal impact of some of them in combination. Table 6.2 reports the results of three such efforts. The issues (or issue-sets) involved are the competence of the candidates,

---

[35] Popkin and his associates have reported that a survey of the electorate in September found one of every ten voters critical of McGovern's handling of the Eagleton affair ("Comment: What Have You Done for Me Lately?" p. 801).

TABLE 6.2

**Selected Sets of Considerations and
Their Marginal Impact on the Vote**

Considerations	Marginal Impact
Competence of candidates	− 6.4
Competence of candidates + Vietnam War, peace	− 8.0
Competence of candidates + Vietnam War, peace + Eagleton affair	− 8.5
Competence of candidates + Vietnam War, peace + Eagleton affair + Foreign policy	− 10.9

NOTE: The figures for marginal impact show the percentage-point change produced by each issue in the proportion of the sample with net scores of − 0 or less. The negative signs indicate a marginal impact favorable to Nixon.

the Vietnam War, the Eagleton affair, and foreign policy. As the table shows, issues of competence and the Vietnam War together added about 8 percentage points to Nixon's share of the vote. All four issues added 11 percentage points. To account for the landslide proportions of Nixon's victory, there is no need to invoke ideology, the welfare issue, or the Social Issue. The war issue and Nixon's handling of foreign policy put McGovern at a distinct disadvantage; the Eagleton affair and questions about his competence put him out of contention.

CAMPAIGN STRATEGIES

With those four issues working against him a McGovern victory was doubtless never in the cards, but he compounded his problems by playing his hand with little or no finesse. The precampaign situation was by no means wholly favorable to Nixon's reelection bid. As 1972 opened Democrats outnumbered Republicans in the electorate by about 1.8 to 1.[36] In

---

[36] *Gallup Opinion Index, Report No. 79* (January 1972), p. 2.

August a Harris survey found less than majority support for
Nixon's handling of the Vietnam War and of the problems of
crime, unemployment, race, taxes, spending, and living
costs.[37] Nixon himself was, in the words of Peter H. Dailey,
"perceived as rather cold and as having a lack of frankness."[38]

As an exercise in electoral politics, the propaganda strategy
that the Nixon campaign designed to meet this situation is
hard to fault. Nixon's candidacy was kept free of Republican
trappings; said Dailey, "We very definitely did not want
Nixon to be perceived as the Republican candidate for President, but as Richard Nixon running for re-election or the
President running for re-election."[39] The election was defined
as a choice between "the President" and "the challenger, the
candidate, George McGovern."[40] Some effort was made to
make Nixon appear a shy man rather than a cold one, but the
chief emphasis in the campaign's presentation of him was on
"the professionalism, the toughness, the competence in office"
and on identifying him "as a person who was moving for
change."[41] Positive advertising showed Nixon in Peking and
Moscow. Negative advertising, distributed under the aegis of
Democrats for Nixon, attacked McGovern's welfare plan, his
position on defense spending, and his credibility.

The propaganda strategy for the McGovern campaign was
not so clearly articulated as the Nixon strategy, nor was it im-
plemented in so orderly a way.[42] In his acceptance speech

[37] *The Harris Survey Yearbook of Public Opinion, 1972* (New York:
Louis Harris and Associates, 1976), p. 9. Peter Dailey, head of the November group that handled advertising for the Nixon campaign, told the
participants of a postelection conference at Harvard University that "the
research we looked at in January . . . showed us that on the issues we
were in a relatively bad position; and it also showed a general dissatisfaction among the electorate with the direction of the country." May and
Fraser, *Campaign '72,* p. 196.

[38] May and Fraser, *Campaign '72,* p. 197. This judgment was based on
research done for the Nixon campaign.

[39] Ibid., p. 223.

[40] Ibid., p.244.

[41] Ibid., pp. 196–197.

[42] Charles Guggenheim, chief consultant on media to the McGovern
campaign, has observed, ". . . you're only capable of carrying out grand
strategies when you have the money in hand. . . . Our money was coming

McGovern said that Nixon was "the fundamental issue of this campaign." He called for an end to the war, and for honesty and integrity in government, an alert national defense, a job for every American, an end to the "hopeless welfare mess," an end to economic controls that let "profits soar and wages be depressed," a fairer tax system, national health insurance, and stricter enforcement of the drug laws.[43]

The campaign developed these themes very unequally. Charles Guggenheim's media program did *not* make Nixon the issue: in his words, "You can . . . use the media to accentuate the negative—to go after Richard Nixon and make people know in more vivid terms why they dislike the man; or you can take George McGovern and make him a viable alternative. We chose to make George McGovern a viable alternative."[44] Guggenheim's spot announcements and five-minute trailers showed McGovern listening sympathetically to ordinary citizens and saying what he thought should be done about their problems. In the last three weeks of the campaign McGovern's speeches increasingly featured attacks on Nixon, but only in the last week did some negative spot announcements by Tony Schwartz run on network television. The extent to which anti-Nixon material should be used was a source of considerable controversy in the McGovern campaign, with Lawrence O'Brien and Frank Mankiewicz in favor, and Guggenheim and Gary Hart against.[45] Hart argued: "Everyone knew Nixon well enough; they didn't need to be reminded. Our job was to reveal the true McGovern, a leader who offered hope and promise, who was constructive, not destruc-

---

in literally on a day-to-day basis" (ibid., p. 202). In his book on the McGovern campaign, Gary Hart told of a discussion with an unhappy Lawrence O'Brien: "Larry couldn't figure out how decisions were made on the issues, on what McGovern was saying. I laughed a little bitterly . . . I assured Larry that many of those working on speeches, position papers, and new statements . . . felt only passingly obligated, if at all, to notify the campaign management of what they were up to." *Right from the Start* (New York: Quadrangle, 1973), p. 283.

[43] *New York Times*, July 14, 1972.

[44] May and Fraser, *Campaign '72*, p. 204.

[45] Hart, *Right from the Start*, p. 292.

tive. The negative stuff ran counter to the basic McGovern character."[46]

Of the issues that McGovern broached in his acceptance speech, Vietnam was given most attention. McGovern gave five televised "fireside chats" in October and early November. Three of these, including the last two before election day, were devoted to the Vietnam War; economic issues were featured in one and the corruption issue in one. Twelve telethons were broadcast locally in twelve large cities. These programs, cast in question-and-answer format, found McGovern frequently explaining his position on amnesty, marijuana, and abortion.

Although no one can prove what strategy would have reduced McGovern's margin of defeat, I shall hazard a guess. First of all, in the manner of John F. Kennedy, he should have attempted to define the choice for voters as one between Richard Nixon, the Republican candidate, and himself, the Democratic candidate. This identification was one that the Nixon campaign wanted to avoid for good reason: Partisanship worked for McGovern in 1972,[47] and it probably could have been made to work for him more strongly than it did. The salience of references to the candidates' partisanship was lower in 1972 by 9 percentage points than it was in 1964, when neither Johnson nor Goldwater called attention to their party labels.[48] In the data we have been examining, favorable references to Johnson as a good party man were more than two and one-half times as numerous as such references to McGovern.

Second, McGovern should have given greater prominence to economic issues than he did. This view is one that was shared by Nixon strategists:

    ... Nixon's real vulnerability was the economy. ...
    Typically, MOR's [Market Opinion Research's] issue

[46] Ibid., p. 313.
[47] See Table 6.1.
[48] See Stanley Kelley, Jr., "The Presidental Campaign," pp. 58–60, in Cummings, *The National Election of 1964.*

handling ratings taken on Nixon showed "foreign policy" and "the Vietnam War" to be his strongest issue areas and "unemployment" and "inflation" to be his weakest issues with the voters. . . . McGovern's "principal error" . . . was . . . his emphasizing the Vietnam War rather than economic problems as the issue upon which voters should base their voting decision. The Nixon strategists could not have been happier.[49]

Table 6.1 also shows McGovern's advantages on economic issues among marginal voters to have been considerable, and as the Democratic candidate he would have had almost automatic credibility among many voters as a spokesman for the economic interests of the working man.

Third, the McGovern campaign should have gone negative against Nixon earlier and differently. Among a large minority of marginal voters integrity and sincerity were issues that favored McGovern, and it seems likely that they could have been given greater salience and a greater anti-Nixon bias. Gary Hart notwithstanding, it is almost certain that everyone did *not* know Nixon well enough to make negative materials unnecessary in an electorate that included some millions of first voters. Nor would it have been necessary or desirable for McGovern himself to attack Nixon personally—probably he did too much of that as it was. If a "Democrats for Nixon" organization was possible, however, so was a "Republicans for McGovern" committee; its membership might have included few prominent Republicans, but their absence would have mattered little.

Finally, the McGovern campaign could have handled the war issue differently, though that issue could not have been ignored, given the history of McGovern's candidacy. McGovern's speeches on the war had a strident moralism that I doubt won votes among those troubled by the war but not part of the antiwar movement. His best stance, perhaps, would have been to illustrate in concrete terms the war's great costs and to as-

[49] Steeper and Teeter, "Comment on 'A Majority Party in Disarray,'" p. 807.

sert strongly the need to end it and so to move beyond it. He could then quote the Nixon of 1968 against himself (as he did) that ending the war should not be entrusted to an administration that had had four years to do so and had failed.

CONTINUITY AND DISCONTINUITY

Speculation that a "critical" or "realigning" election has occurred is the almost inevitable accompaniment of any outsized victory for a minority party. Claims of such a status for Nixon's landslide became rare rather quickly, but some observers began later to point to it as an important milestone on the road to 1980. The *National Review,* for instance, represented Reagan's victory in 1980 as the culmination of an anti-liberal revolution that "really got rolling in 1968, when George Wallace and Richard Nixon between them put together a 60 to 40 landslide against the liberal candidate, Hubert Humphrey,"[50] and "reached into all sections of the country when Nixon achieved his 49-state trouncing of George McGovern."[51] Jimmy Carter, in this view, was an "aberration, historically considered,"[52] whose presidency was made possible by the Watergate scandals.

What we have learned about the issues underlying Nixon's victory gives little support to this view. His advantage on issues relating to competence—clearly the most important ingredient of the landslide—was not something that he could bequeath to other Republican or conservative candidates. The same is true for the war issue; though a clear and sizable majority of the many voters concerned about the Vietnam War preferred Nixon's way out of it to McGovern's, by 1976 Vietnam was no longer an issue. The benefit Nixon derived from his handling of foreign policy was not readily transferable; presidents may become locked into positions on issues of foreign policy, but parties rarely do. The Eagleton affair was a wholly transient matter, and the voters' disdain for Senator McGovern's welfare proposals, which he himself called "inad-

[50] *National Review* (November 28, 1980), p. 1434.
[51] Ibid.
[52] Ibid., p. 1435.

TABLE 6.3

New Deal Issues in the Johnson and Nixon Landslides

Considerations	Aggregate Salience		Republican Bias	
	1964	1972	1964	1972
New Deal issues	78	75	34	42
Economic issues	29	40	46	48
Government spending	12	7	87	75
Monetary and fiscal policy	9	15	56	43
Election's economic impact	13	22	9	34
Ideological stance	38	31	61	67
Liberalism, conservatism	23	21	50	81
Relationship to Big Business, common man	42	41	11	11
Poverty program, welfare	8	23	27	77
Social security, the aged, workers' welfare programs	21	9	12	36
Farm policy	5	2	38	39
Relationship to labor, unions	9	6	32	45

For 1964, N = 1,113
For 1972, N = 830

equately prepared," was partly so. The Social Issue yielded only a middling advantage to Nixon, and, while ideology and race-related issues worked for him, they had worked just as strongly for Goldwater. On New Deal issues, the Republicans remained at a considerable disadvantage. If the 1972 election had been determined by New Deal issues alone, the Republicans would have lost badly.

For assigning that election a place in history, this last fact is of critical importance. New Deal issues have been the principal theater of partisan warfare since the 1930's. If a fundamental realignment occurred between 1964 and 1972, it should manifest itself in reduced salience for this set of issues, a marked change in their bias, or a looser relationship between them and the party affiliations of voters. In fact, as Table 6.3 shows, the salience of New Deal issues changed very little between the two elections. Their pro-Democratic bias

TABLE 6.4

Party Identification and Net Scores on New Deal Issues

Net Score on New Deal Issues	% Democratic Identification		% Republican Identification	
	1964	1972	1964	1972
− 6	0.0	0.0	100.0	100.0
− 5	4.2	14.3	95.8	85.7
− 4	10.0	15.4	86.7	84.6
− 3	23.9	12.5	65.2	85.4
− 2	19.2	28.8	76.9	63.5
− 1	32.5	25.0	63.9	62.5
0	52.9	44.5	35.4	43.0
+ 1	77.9	65.1	18.6	24.5
+ 2	80.7	83.3	14.3	13.6
+ 3	86.9	84.7	11.1	10.2
+ 4	91.5	75.0	5.1	19.4
+ 5	97.4	88.0	0.0	4.0
+ 6	89.8	91.7	5.1	5.6

For 1964, N = 1,113
For 1972, N =   830

was smaller in 1972, but, with a Republican candidate whose stance on these issues was more moderate than Goldwater's, some such improvement was surely to be expected.

Moreover, New Deal issues continued to be strongly associated with party affiliation in 1972. (See Tables 6.4 and 6.5). The left-hand column of Table 6.4 displays the range of net scores generated when one applies the Voter's Decision Rule to those likes and dislikes of parties and candidates which were related to New Deal issues and those issues only; the other columns show the percentages of respondents with a given score (call it a New Deal Score) who identified themselves as Democrats or Republicans in 1964 and 1972. In both years the relationship between New Deal issues and party identification is abundantly evident: Changes in the value of New Deal scores bring sharp changes in the probability of Republican and Democratic affiliation. The relationship was

TABLE 6.5

**Inconsistency between Partisan Identification and
Net Scores on New Deal Issues**

Identification	% of Identifiers with Inconsistent Scores	
	1964	*1972*
Strong Democrats	2.8	7.4
Weak Democrats	12.6	15.4
Independent Democrats	16.7	7.6
All Democrats	8.5	11.6
Strong Republicans	9.7	11.2
Weak Republicans	23.8	14.3
Independent Republicans	19.1	20.6
All Republicans	17.6	15.1
All Partisans	11.7	13.2

NOTE: Inconsistent scores are positive for Republican identifiers, negative for Democratic identifiers.
    For 1964, N = 1,113
    For 1972, N =   830

looser in 1972 but not much looser, as Table 6.5 demonstrates. That table shows how many respondents had a party affiliation inconsistent with their New Deal scores (that is, a Republican identification and a positive score, or vice-versa.) In 1964, 12 percent of all partisans showed such inconsistency; in 1972, 13 percent did.

To sum up: In Nixon's landslide the issues central to the New Deal party system remained highly salient and strongly biased toward the Democrats, and the issues that produced the landslide were largely nonpartisan in their implications for the future. *Sic transit gloria mundi.*

CHAPTER SEVEN

LANDSLIDES AND MANDATES

A recurrent feature of the interpretation of elections—particularly of landslides—is the search for mandates. Both the politicians and the press look for mandates, find them, and invoke them in debates of governmental policy. Willy-nilly, the theory of electoral mandates has become part of American constitutional doctrine, albeit an oddly casual part. Those who find mandates hardly ever say how they did so, and those who claim to be acting in obedience to mandates rarely see any need to justify such obedience.

THE THEORY OF ELECTORAL MANDATES

The theory of electoral mandates has never loomed so large in American politics as it has in that of Great Britain.[1] Nonetheless, relying on the dicta of presidents and guided by analogies to the British case, one can piece together a coherent statement of the theory.

Its first element is the belief that elections carry messages about problems, policies, and programs—messages plain to all and specific enough to be directive. The confidence with which presidents have announced mandates implies such a belief, however murky the grounds for it may be. President Eisenhower seems to have assumed that voters for the winning side actively endorse the individual pledges of the victorious party's platform: ". . . the Republican Platform of 1956 . . . was unanimously adopted by the National Convention. It was then overwhelmingly endorsed by the country's voters— by a margin of almost ten million votes. On the pledges of that Platform, your Administration was returned for another four

---

[1] A comprehensive history of the evolution of the doctrine of the mandate in Great Britain may be found in Cecil S. Emden, *The People and the Constitution,* 2d edition (Oxford: Oxford University Press, 1956).

years."[2] Coolidge suggested that voters endorse at least "the broad general principles" of the party platform.[3]

Second, the theory holds that certain of these messages must be treated as authoritative commands, commands either to the victorious candidate or to the candidate and his party. In his state of the union address in 1965 Lyndon Johnson claimed to be responding to a mandate directed to him, personally: "With the Soviet Union we seek peaceful understanding that can lessen the danger to freedom. Last fall I asked the American people to choose that course. I will carry forward their command."[4] Herbert Hoover, the only recent president who both came into office and went out of it on a landslide, emphasized the partisan significance of mandates:

> In our form of democracy the expression of the popular will can be effected only through the instrumentality of political parties. We maintain party government not to promote intolerant partisanship but because opportunity must be given for the expression of the popular will, and organization provided for the execution of its mandates. . . . It follows that the Government both in the executive and the legislative branches must carry out in good faith the platform upon which the party was intrusted with power.[5]

Hoover's words echoed those of Coolidge, who in his inaugural address had also argued, "When the country has bestowed its confidence on a party by making it a majority in the Congress, it has a right to expect such unity of action as will make the party majority an effective instrument of government."[6]

[2] *Public Papers of the Presidents of the United States: Dwight D. Eisenhower,* vol. 1957 (Washington, D.C.: United States Government Printing Office, 1958), p. 454.

[3] *A Compilation of the Messages and Papers of the Presidents,* vol. xviii (New York: Bureau of National Literature, Inc.), p. 9485.

[4] *New York Times,* January 5, 1965.

[5] William Starr Myers (ed.), *The State Papers and Other Public Writings of Herbert Hoover,* vol. 1 (New York: Doubleday, Doran and Co., 1934), p. 10.

[6] *A Compilation of the Messages and Papers of the Presidents,* vol. xviii, p. 9485.

To qualify as mandates, messages about policies and programs must reflect the *stable* views both of individual voters and of the electorate. Warren G. Harding invoked the "deliberate, intelligent, dependable popular will of America" when, in his inaugural address, he pledged "an administration wherein all the agencies of Government are called to serve and ever promote an understanding of Government purely as an expression of the popular will."[7] Theodore Roosevelt avowed the futility of efforts "to thwart the determination of the great body of our citizens," but spoke of the duty of public officials to "resist and defy a gust of popular passion."[8] Both men implied that lightly held or wavering opinions should not count toward mandates.

In the electorate as a whole, the numbers of those for or against a policy or program matter. To suggest that a mandate exists for a particular policy is to suggest that more than a bare majority of those voting are agreed upon it. The common view holds that landslide victories are more likely to involve mandates than are narrow ones, and presidents who claim mandates frequently cite the size of the majorities that put them in office. Franklin D. Roosevelt, for instance, in a 1937 fireside chat on his plan to reorganize the judiciary, charged the Supreme Court with "acting not as a judicial body, but as a policy-making body" which had frustrated "compliance with a popular mandate issued by overwhelming majorities in the elections of 1932, 1934, and 1936."[9]

The final element of the theory is a negative imperative: Governments should not undertake major innovations in policy or procedure, except in emergencies, unless the electorate has had an opportunity to consider them in an election and thus to express its views. Woodrow Wilson invoked this aspect

[7] Ibid., vol. xvii, p. 8924.

[8] Ibid., vol. xiv, p. 7190. Roosevelt was discussing the use of injunctions in labor disputes and advocating limitations on their use.

[9] See *The Public Papers and Addresses of Franklin D. Roosevelt: The Constitution Prevails* (New York: The Macmillan Co., 1941), pp. 123–126.

of the theory in his veto of an immigration bill in 1915. In his words,

> If the people of this country have made up their minds to limit the number of immigrants by arbitrary tests and so reverse the policy of all the generations of Americans that have gone before them, it is their right to do so. I am their servant and have no license to stand in their way. But I do not believe that they have. I respectfully submit that no one can quote their mandate to that effect.[10]

CRITICISMS OF THE THEORY OF MANDATES

The theory of electoral mandates has found few defenders outside the political arena. The most frequent targets of criticism are the theory's imperatives—that officials and parties should do what the electorate wants them to do and that they should not act on major issues which voters, as voters, have had no opportunity to consider.

A fundamental objection of this sort is identified with Edmund Burke, specifically with his address to the electors of Bristol.[11] A representative, Burke argued, should always prefer his constituents' interests to his own,

> but his unbiased opinion, his mature judgment, his enlightened conscience, he ought not to sacrifice to you, to any man, or to any set of men living. . . . Your representative owes you, not his industry only, but his judgment; and he betrays, instead of serving you, if he sacrifices it to your opinion.[12]

[10] Albert Shaw (ed.), *The Messages and Papers of Woodrow Wilson*, vol. I (New York: The Review of Reviews Corporation, 1924), p. 96.

[11] At other times Burke saw popular opinion as more authoritative than he described it in his famous address. See Emden, *The People and the Constitution*, pp. 51–53.

[12] "Speech to the Electors of Bristol," *The Writings and Speeches of the Right Honourable Edmund Burke*, vol. 2, Beaconsfield Edition No. 166 (Boston: Little, Brown and Co., 1901), p. 95. The words Burke used to sugarcoat his famous statement also deserve quotation: "Certainly, Gentlemen, it ought to be the happiness and the glory of a representative to

This argument has two premises: (1) That the representative is usually better situated than those who elect him to judge how well a policy will serve his constituents' interests (or the nation's, a complication on which I shall reserve comment for the moment); and (2) that the representative will in fact act in his constituents' interest, once he has correctly determined what it is. Grant these premises and the conclusion seems to follow easily: In cases in which the opinions of the constituency and the representative conflict, it is in the interest of the constituency to defer to the representative and the obligation of the representative to follow his own best judgment.

Since Burke addressed his argument to voters, one may fairly ask whether they should be persuaded by it and what its force should be if they are not. At least some voters are likely to find Burke's first premise unacceptable. People commonly believe that they are the best judges of their own interests and that expertise counts for little in assessing the merits of some policies, for instance, those which raise mainly moral issues. Moreover, even those voters who grant their representative's greater competence in evaluating public policy will not necessarily defer to his views, nor should they. Because no representative has a monopoly on informed judgment, a voter may reasonably look elsewhere for leadership—in our system of government, to other representatives, perhaps, or to leaders of interest groups.

One would expect Burke's second premise to be widely doubted, and it has been. In the period from 1964 to 1978 (see Table 7.1), from one-third to two-thirds of American voters believed that their government was run by "a few big interests looking out for themselves," and from one-third to over 40 percent believed that "quite a few of the people running the

---

live in the strictest union, the closest correspondence, and the most unreserved communication with his constituents. Their wishes ought to have great weight with him; their opinions high respect; their business unremitted attention. . . . To deliver an opinion is the right of all men; that of constituents is a weighty and respectable opinion, which a representative ought always to rejoice to hear, and which he ought always most seriously to consider."

TABLE 7.1
Doubt about the Integrity of Government in Elections, 1964-1978

Question: "Would you say the government is pretty much run by a few big interests looking out for themselves or that it is run for the benefit of all the people?"

Responses:	Run by Big Interests	Don't Know
1964	29%	8%
1966	33	14
1968	40	9
1970	50	9
1972	53	9
1974	66	9
1976	66	10
1978	67	9

Question: "Do you think that quite a few of the people running the government are a little crooked, not very many are, or do you think hardly any of them are crooked at all?"

Responses:	Quite a Few	Don't Know
1964	29%	4%
1968	25	4
1970	32	3
1972	36	4
1974	45	3
1976	42	5
1978	40	6

SOURCE: Warren E. Miller, Arthur H. Miller, and Edward J. Schneider, *American National Election Studies Data Sourcebook, 1952-1978* (Cambridge: Harvard University Press, 1980), pp. 257, 259.

government" were "a little crooked." Such views may be wrong, but they are not irrational. From too many actual incidents, voters know that some representatives betray their constituents' interests and do so for a long time without being caught. Voters are aware also that all representatives have motives, means, and opportunities for such betrayals. Must a voter defer to the judgment of a representative whose probity he doubts? Clearly not, if there is anyone else whose judgment the voter values as much and in whose integrity he has greater faith.

A society in which constituents, for good or bad reasons, in fact deferred to their representatives' judgment would avoid many sticky problems of government. When constituents cannot be relied upon for such deference, however, the ethically correct course of action for an honest representative is less simple than Burke suggested. Though opposed in general to mandates, John Stuart Mill argued that electoral opinion should control governmental action when that opinion involves deeply held beliefs, "even though these may be in some points erroneous."[13] The reason he gave for this conclusion was a reason of state: "A people cannot be well governed in opposition to their primary notions of right."[14] One can extend Mill's argument in two ways. First of all, even if no "primary notions of right" are involved, governmental policies that offend an electoral majority invite resistance fatal to their success and subversive of governmental authority. In modern states, particularly, the achievement of governmental objectives is frequently dependent on their popularity. Second, to disobey electoral mandates frequently and routinely in democratic states would risk the alienation of voters from the regime, no matter what the content of such mandates. To most voters democracy implies the normal acquiescence of government in the will of the majority, and a government which repeatedly fails to satisfy that expectation calls sharply into question its right to govern. Constituents have an interest in the survival of a democratic regime, in orderly government, and in the successful implementation of policy, and, when constituents cannot be expected to defer to the representative, these interests may require the representative to defer to his constituents.

[13] Mill, *Considerations on Representative Government,* p. 243. For an excellent discussion of Mill's view of mandates, see Dennis F. Thompson, *John Stuart Mill and Representative Government* (Princeton: Princeton University Press, 1976), pp. 112–121.

[14] Mill, *Considerations on Representative Government,* p. 243.

Critics frequently raise two additional objections to the imperatives of the theory of mandates: (1) The representative, even if locally elected, should put the national interest first;[15] and (2) representatives bound by instructions cannot enter into the compromises that the enactment of legislation usually requires.[16] The first of these objections raises a serious issue for the theory of mandates as it applies to members of legislative bodies but is irrelevant to that theory as it applies to presidents and national parties. In both these latter cases the constituency *is* the nation as a whole. The second objection is compelling only against a certain kind of mandate; it has little, if any, bearing on mandates that indicate only general policy objectives.

By the late nineteenth century another body of thought critical of the theory of mandates had developed quite independently of that just noted. Here, the central criticism was not of the theory's imperatives but of its assumption that mandates are discoverable. Writing in 1913, A. Lawrence Lowell gave a lucid, though incomplete, statement of this view. First distinguishing "the main question which people must decide"—that is, which candidate is to occupy a given office—from "the grounds for their decision," he noted that an election usually settles the former quite clearly, while the latter "are often painfully obscure."[17] He then observed:

> Some momentous questions are usually debated between the parties, the arguments upon them helping to supply the motives that determine the popular verdict, and yet it is often hard to know how far any one of these

[15] In Burke's words, "Parliament is a *deliberative* assembly of *one* nation, with *one* interest—that of the whole—where not local purposes, not local prejudices, ought to guide, but the general good, resulting from the general reason of the whole. You choose a member, indeed; but when you have chosen him, he is not a member of Bristol, but he is a member of *Parliament*" (*Writings and Speeches,* vol. 2, p. 96).

[16] See Hanna Fenichel Pitkin, *The Concept of Representation* (Berkeley: University of California Press, 1967), pp. 146–147.

[17] A. Lawrence Lowell, *Public Opinion and Popular Government* (New York: Longmans, Green, and Co., 1913), p. 71.

motives was decisive, because there are commonly a
number of them operating with unequal force on different individuals. Unless some one problem of controlling
significance—like the free silver issue in the presidential
election of 1896—has dominated the situation, one cannot be sure that the public has passed a judgment on any
specific question.

Sir Henry Maine suggests that "the devotee of democracy is much in the same position as the Greeks with their
oracles. All agreed that the voice of an oracle was the
voice of a god, but everybody allowed that when he
spoke he was not as intelligible as might be desired."[18]

Note that Lowell's case against the theory of mandates, while
strong, is still too generous. He had no reliable information
about how many voters carried a concern about free silver
into the voting booth in 1896 or whose side they took, Bryan's
or McKinley's, if they did. The most that can be said *on the
authority of the election returns alone* is that McKinley's stand
on free silver did not count decisively *against* his election; that
claim, however, true by definition, tells us only what the electorate of 1896 was prepared to tolerate, not what it com-
manded.

That theorists have discussed with such passion whether a
representative *should* act in accordance with his constituents'
wishes at first blush seems odd, given Lowell's commonsense
observations about the difficulty of discovering what voters'
wishes *are*. It seems less odd, however, when one considers
what elections were like at the time of Burke's address to the
voters of Bristol or when John Stuart Mill wrote his *Considerations on Representative Government* one hundred years later.
In 1761 only 22 of 203 English boroughs had an electorate of
over 1,000 people,[19] and the situation was similar in 1861.[20]
Voting was public, and many voters voted simply as clients of

[18] Ibid., p. 73.
[19] Lewis Namier, *The Structure of Politics at the Accession of George
III,* 2d edition (New York: St. Martin's Press, 1968), p. 80.
[20] See Sir Ivor Jennings, *Party Politics,* vol. II (Cambridge: At the University Press, 1961), pp. 116–120.

leading citizens. In such circumstances the views that voters brought to voting about issues of policy, the qualifications of candidates, the merits of parties, and the proper activities of officials could be well known to voters and candidates alike, at least in many constituencies. It could also be known how much voters cared about the outcome of an election, how hard they found their choices, and how well informed they were. Only later, as electorates became much greater in size, the secret ballot came into general use, and populations became much more mobile, did this kind of contextual information, essential to assessing the meaning of an election, become increasingly scanty and unreliable. Elections outgrew knowable mandates.

When they take notice of the theory of mandates at all, modern students of party politics are apt to sound a skeptical note in the tradition of Lowell. Peter G. J. Pulzer, commenting on a charge by the Marquess of Salisbury that the government of the day had no mandate to abolish capital punishment, remarks that Lord Salisbury "gets no nearer than any other advocate of the mandate theory to explaining how the electorate's views on this topic could be singled out from their views on any other in the course of a General Election."[21] P. A. Bromstead observes:

> It is . . . said of a Government, which has been returned to power through the operation of the electoral system, that it has, by virtue of its electoral success, a mandate *to do certain things.* Unfortunately, we can never be quite clear what these things are. . . . Active politicians sometimes find it helpful to their arguments to claim that they have a mandate for a certain policy, or that their opponents are doing things without a mandate.[22]

Gerald Pomper, refusing to find in the election of 1920 any mandate against American participation in the League of Nations, argues that "the issue was clouded by other questions,

[21] Peter G. J. Pulzer, *Political Representation and Elections in Britain,* 3d edition (London: George Allen and Unwin Ltd., 1975), p. 145.
[22] "Mandate," p. 404, in Julius Gould and William L. Kolb, *A Dictionary of the Social Sciences* (New York: The Free Press, 1964).

by vagueness, and by the personalities of the candidates." If a mandate could not be clearly obtained on the issue of the League, he continues, "policy decisions in elections must be unlikely in general."[23] R. S. Milne and H. C. Mackenzie refer to the "doctrine of the mandate" as "largely discredited"; they then go on to ask how a voter can use his one vote "to express at the same time approval or disapproval of several issues."[24] The difficulty of obtaining mandates from elections, they add later, "is not mainly mechanical, arising from the circumstance that there is only a single election and several issues, but psychological, deriving from the complexity of the elector's own opinions and emotions, and the difficulty of distinguishing issues from images."[25]

It should be noted that several quite different sorts of assertions contribute to the overall tone of skepticism of commentary in this vein. Critics allege that

1. some particular claim of a mandate is unsupported by adequate evidence;
2. most claims of mandates are unsupported by adequate evidence;
3. most claims of mandates are politically self-serving; or
4. it is not possible in principle to make a valid claim of a mandate, since it is impossible to sort out voters' intentions.

Pomper's comments on the election of 1920 involve a proposition of the first sort, and he is surely right in his conclusion. The second and third propositions are probably true, also, though they can hardly be said to be definitely established.

The fourth proposition, however, is outdated. The sample survey has again given us the ability to discover the grounds for voters' choices. From surveys we can learn what voters regard as important in their estimates of parties and candidates,

[23] Gerald M. Pomper with Susan S. Lederman, *Elections in America,* 2d edition (New York: Dodd, Mead and Co., 1980), p. 214.
[24] R. S. Milne and H. C. Mackenzie, *Straight Fight* (London: The Hansard Society, 1954), p. 138.
[25] Ibid., p. 139.

how firm their choices are—indeed, virtually all of the contextual information about elections that was lost with the expansion of electorates in the nineteenth and twentieth centuries. Surveys do not enable us to distinguish with certainty a rationalization or a lie from a genuine, motivating conviction, but no one has ever been able to do that, even when very small numbers of voters were involved. It is thus of immense practical importance that the meaning of modern elections involving mass electorates can be as intelligible as elections in the days of Burke and Mill.

THE MANDATES OF '64 AND '72

If what I have just said is reasonable, one can reasonably pose as an empirical question whether voters issued mandates in voting for Lyndon Johnson and Richard Nixon. Table 7.2 presents some of the basic data required; it shows (as a percentage of all voters) the numbers of those in the two elections who cited various issues and sets of issues as reasons for liking or disliking the candidates and their parties. It is important to remember that the responses summarized in the table were volunteered, not prompted by questions about particular issues.

By any strict definition, opinion on New Deal issues in 1964 represents the closest approach to a mandate in either of the two elections. A near majority of all respondents cited one or more of these issues as a reason for preferring Johnson, twice the number favoring Goldwater on the same basis. While Goldwater's campaign was not so anti–New Deal as it has often been portrayed, his precampaign record gave voters ample reason to think him unfriendly to New Deal programs;[26] thus a claim that a strong plurality of the electorate had reaffirmed the nation's acceptance of the New Deal would be a reasonable summary of these data. Note, however, that the category *New Deal issues* subsumes a set of related issues.

[26] See Kelley, "The Presidential Campaign," pp. 76–77, in Cummings, *The National Election of 1964.* See also Page, *Choices and Echoes in Presidential Elections,* pp. 118–132.

TABLE 7.2

Selected Issues in Two Landslide Elections

Considerations	% Favoring Winner on Issue	% Favoring Loser on Issue
1964		
New Deal issues	49.1	24.8
Economic issues	14.8	12.6
Liberalism, conservatism	10.5	10.6
Relation to Big Business, common man	37.4	4.7
Medical care	8.9	2.3
Peace	16.1	4.2
Poverty program	5.9	2.2
Race-related issues	16.2	11.1
1972		
Vietnam War, peace	33.6	18.4
Foreign policy	20.7	6.1
Détente with U.S.S.R.	4.1	1.0
Policy toward Red China	7.4	1.6
New Deal issues	28.6	39.5
Monetary and fiscal policy	6.5	8.6
Welfare	17.3	5.2
Race-related issues	6.0	4.0
The Social Issue	15.2	8.1

For 1964, N = 1,113
For 1972, N = 830

Johnson's advantage on economic issues was not nearly so great as it was on the set as a whole, and the ideological trappings of the New Deal gave him no advantage at all. While the respondents concerned about the relationship of the candidates and their parties to Big Business favored Johnson overwhelmingly, such respondents did not constitute a majority and their attitudes suggest only the most general sort of guidance for policy.

In 1972 Nixon's handling of the Vietnam War won him more support than he derived from any other single policy and more than any single policy had earned for Lyndon Johnson. Nixon cannot be said to have received a strong mandate on the subject, however; as Table 7.2 shows, those citing the Vietnam War as a reason for favoring him fell far short of a majority. One can also question the likely stability of Nixon's support on the issue of the war, since his policy was interpreted by supporters in two different ways—either as the surest road to peace or as the best way to win the war.

Johnson's and Nixon's specific claims of meaningful mandates do not stand up well when confronted by evidence. (I say *meaningful* mandates because I do not regard as such Nixon's claim to have had a mandate for "change that will work. . . , change that will build a better life"[27] or Johnson's that he had a "mandate for unity, for a Government that serves no special interest . . . that is a servant of all the people.")[28] No majorities endorsed with their votes "the program that was begun by our beloved President John F. Kennedy"[29] or peaceful understanding with the Soviet Union. Nor did majorities endorse Nixon's positions on welfare or fiscal policy—the two issues on which he planned to say, "the people have spoken."

Both Johnson and Nixon did receive one-sided support on a number of issues—that is, their positions won favor with large majorities *of those for whom the issues in question were salient.* In 1964 Johnson was favored by about four to one by those citing the poverty program, medicare, and the peace issues as reasons for liking or disliking the parties and their candidates. Nixon received comparably one-sided support for his overtures toward Red China, his policy of détente with the Soviet Union, and his general conduct of foreign policy. He received

[27] *Public Papers of the Presidents of the United States: Richard Nixon,* vol. 1972 (Washington, D.C.: United States Government Printing Office, 1974), p. 1151.
[28] *New York Times,* November 4, 1964.
[29] Ibid.

less overwhelming but still substantial support on welfare and the Social Issue. A judgment of so far, so good, would have been a justifiable reaction by either man to these data. But a mandate? No. None of these policies was cited by more than 21 percent of respondents as a reason to like Johnson, Nixon, or their parties. The two presidents had a right to be encouraged by the public reception of these initiatives, but encouragement is not the same as command.

SOME SPECULATIONS

That neither the 1964 election nor that of 1972 produced a mandate is surely owing in part to the heterogeneity of voters' interests, perceptions, and beliefs. Consider the Vietnam War as an issue in the election of 1972. The war touched the lives of Americans in a multitude of ways, and the candidates and the press gave it almost ceaseless attention. Nonetheless, for some 45 percent of all voters the candidates' positions on the war were not an explicit consideration in evaluations of the candidates and parties, either because these voters saw the issue differently from others or because they cared about it less. That fact is dramatic evidence that American voters are of many minds, and this heterogeneity of opinion can be expected to reduce the likelihood of mandates in most elections and to make even rarer the highly specific mandates that theorists have regarded as particularly ill advised.

The normal tactics of candidates can also be counted upon to make mandates rare. Mandates are clearly not impossible; any presidential candidate willing to propose a sufficiently burdensome level of taxation could easily evoke one. But candidates hardly ever do anything grossly impolitic on purpose, not even candidates like George McGovern and Barry Goldwater. The positions they took were extreme only in comparison to those which candidates usually take; in fact, many millions of people shared most of their views.

This line of thought suggests that mandates are likely to be the unintended consequences of political mistakes, mistakes graver than any committed by either Goldwater or McGovern. There have been such. In the circumstances of 1932 the policies of the Hoover administration were politically disastrous. They easily invited the conclusion that President Hoover and his party were either unwilling or unable to take effective measures to relieve the suffering of the unemployed and the distress of many others that were attendant on an economy in collapse. In these circumstances Franklin D. Roosevelt's claim that voters had demanded "direct, vigorous action"[30] to put people back to work is eminently believable, though not demonstrable. It seems likely also that Alfred M. Landon's indiscriminate condemnation of the New Deal in 1936—a strategy that apparently offended his political instincts[31]—produced an endorsement of the spirit of the New Deal, if not a mandate for its substance.

For those who find Burke's criticism of the theory of mandates attractive, the case of 1932 is one to consider carefully. At the onset of the Great Depression, President Hoover found his own understanding of sound economic policy in conflict with a widespread demand for direct federal relief measures and for governmental intervention in key sectors of the economy. The Burke of the "Address to the Electors of Bristol" would have urged him to resist these pressures, as Hoover did, but it is hard to believe that Burke's counsel was good advice for this case. It is true that Hoover could have, and did, stick to his conceptions without prejudice to the right of the voters to replace him in 1932. Suppose, however, that the Democratic nomination of that year had gone to someone of similar convictions; after all, Roosevelt's nomination was in fact a close thing, and most of his rivals were economic conserva-

---

[30] See *The Public Papers and Addresses of Franklin D. Roosevelt*, vol. 2: *The Year of Crisis 1933* (New York: Random House, 1938), pp. 12–13.

[31] See Arthur M. Schlesinger, Jr., *The Politics of Upheaval* (Boston: Houghton Mifflin Co., 1960), pp. 601–625. Roosevelt's prescription for a vote-winning Republican strategy was, "First, I would repudiate Hearst. Then I would repudiate the duPonts and everything they stand for. Then I would say: 'I am for social security, work relief, etc. etc. But the Democrats cannot be entrusted with the administration of these fine ideals.' I would cite chapter and verse on WPA inefficiency—and there's plenty of it" (p. 603).

tives. The country would then have been saddled for the next four years with a president whose personal views of the national interest ran counter to the (highly probable) mandate for "direct, vigorous action." In such circumstances the Burkean prescription for the conduct of a representative could easily be a recipe for national disaster.

CHAPTER EIGHT

RULE BY THE WORST
OF THE MANY

The meaning that we assign to elections depends substantially on our assessments of the quality of the decisions by voters that go into them, and these assessments make a difference. In the words of V. O. Key,

> Obviously, the perceptions of the behavior of the electorate held by political leaders, agitators, and activists condition, if they do not fix, the types of appeals politicians employ as they seek popular support. . . . They may govern, too, the kinds of actions that governments take as they look forward to the next election. If politicians perceive the electorate as responsive to father images, they will give it father images. If they see voters as most certainly responsive to nonsense, they will give them nonsense. If they see an electorate as receptive to cold, hard realities, they will give it the cold, hard realities.[1]

The beliefs of ordinary citizens about the quality of voting are no less important in their consequences than those of politicians; as those beliefs vary, so will respect for elections and for democratic institutions generally.

The electorate's competence to choose the nation's leaders has been a subject of debate from the beginning of our history as a nation; indeed, the Constitution's provision for the choice of presidents by the Electoral College had its source in doubts of that competence. Critics of mass democracy, stressing the inherent difficulty of judging a candidate's capacity for leadership, have repeatedly argued that most voters lack the time,

---

[1] V. O. Key, Jr., with the assistance of Milton C. Cummings, Jr., *The Responsible Electorate* (Cambridge: Harvard University Press, 1966), p. 6.

means, and sense of responsibility required for the task. On these grounds, and on the basis of necessarily haphazard observation, many influential thinkers of the nineteenth and twentieth centuries have concluded that the American electorate is ill informed, "unable to imagine a future which must result from the unchecked operation of present forces,"[2] liable "to yield to extrarational or irrational prejudice and impulse,"[3] and apt to reach conclusions hastily "from a superficial inspection of the more prominent features of a question."[4]

By bringing a new and impressive kind of evidence to bear on the issues of this old debate, surveys of voters have powerfully influenced its terms and tone. *The American Voter,* the single most influential study of voting, portrayed an electorate "almost wholly without detailed information about decision making in government"[5] or "coherent patterns of belief"[6] and concluded that, "for a large part of the public, political affairs are probably too difficult to comprehend in detail."[7] Students of voting have added to these doubts about the electorate's competence by calling attention to an apparently perverse feature of free elections—that the least-informed voters "seem to hold the critical balance of power, in the sense that alternations in governing party depend disproportionately on shifts in their sentiments."[8] *The People's Choice* asserted that

> ... the party changers—relatively, the people whose votes still remained to be definitely determined during

[2] James Bryce, *The American Commonwealth,* vol. II (London: Macmillan, 1890), p. 348.

[3] Joseph A. Schumpeter, *Capitalism, Socialism, and Democracy,* 3d edition (New York: Harper and Bros., 1950), p. 262.

[4] Alexis de Tocqueville, *Democracy in America,* vol. I (New York: Vintage Books, 1954), p. 208.

[5] Angus Campbell, Philip E. Converse, Warren E. Miller, and Donald E. Stokes, *The American Voter* (New York: John Wiley and Sons, 1960), p. 543.

[6] Ibid.

[7] Ibid.

[8] Philip E. Converse, "Information Flow and the Stability of Partisan Attitudes," p. 136, in Angus Campbell, Philip E. Converse, Warren E. Miller, and Donald E. Stokes, *Elections and the Political Order* (New York: John Wiley and Sons, 1966).

the last stages of the campaign, the people who could swing an election during those last days—were, so to speak, available to the person who saw them last before Election Day. The notion that the people who switch parties during the campaign are mainly the reasoned, thoughtful, conscientious people who were convinced by the issues of the election is just plain wrong. Actually, they were mainly just the opposite.[9]

The American Voter reported that independents had a "somewhat poorer knowledge of the issues"[10] than partisans and that people who paid little attention to politics were—or, at any rate, seemed to be—"contributing very disproportionately to partisan change" in the early 1950's.[11] Elections, these statements suggest, involve not just rule by the uninformed many but rule by the worst of the many.

As Key noted, this view has disturbing implications both for the conduct of government and the conduct of campaigns. If the worst of the many decide the outcome of elections, then politicians should pay them particular heed. Stephen Shadegg, a professional campaign manager long associated with Senator Barry Goldwater, draws that implication quite bluntly. Voters, he argues, should be classified into three groups: "The Committed, the Undecided, and the Indifferent."

> The Indifferents are those who don't vote at all, or vote only in response to an emotional appeal, or as the result of some carefully planned campaign technique which makes it easy for them to reach a decision. The Indifferents decide elections.[12]

And, he adds, they can be persuaded to give their ballots "to a candidate whose philosophy is opposed to the cherished no-

---

[9] Paul F. Lazarsfeld, Bernard Berelson, and Hazel Gaudet, *The People's Choice,* 2d edition (New York: Columbia University Press, 1948), p. 69.

[10] Campbell, et al., *The American Voter,* p. 143.

[11] Ibid., p. 264.

[12] Stephen C. Shadegg, *How to Win an Election* (New York: Taplinger, 1964), p. 13.

tions of the voter."[13] To put it another way, Indifferents are easily misled.

Key, for one, disputed the notion that elections and the control of government are decided by the least-informed voters. He agreed that those independents who disavow partisan leanings are "not an impressive lot" and that their vote is highly volatile. But, he said,

> Some observers move bravely to the conclusion that the fate of the Republic rests in the hands of an ignorant and uninformed sector of the electorate highly susceptible to influence by factors irrelevant to the solemn performance of its civic duties. That conclusion is certainly not invariably, if ever, correct. In the election of 1952, an election with an unusually marked amount of party switching, this repulsive type of "independent" did not call the turn. Among the switchers from Truman to Eisenhower he was far outnumbered by people who regarded themselves as Democrats. . . .[14]

Key assigned primary responsibility for partisan change to two groups: *switchers,* those who changed their party preferences from one election to the next; and *new voters,* those who had not voted at the preceding election. He clearly hoped to show that these groups were not markedly less admirable than other voters, but in the end his efforts were not conclusive. He had no direct measures of how well-informed switchers and new voters were, relative to other voters, and thus had to rely on indirect measures of information, such as the amount of interest in politics that respondents declared. The data on interest in politics that he adduced, moreover, failed to support his argument in a striking way. New voters showed considerably less than average interest both in 1952 and 1960, the two elections for which he presented data. Although switchers were not markedly less interested in politics than Democratic standpatters in 1952, they were in 1960.

[13] Ibid., p. 10.
[14] Key, *The Responsible Electorate,* p. 92.

If true, the contention that the least-qualified voters decide elections is a damning indictment of elections as institutions. However strongly a democrat might reject the self-serving claims of the "best" to rule, he cannot favor the de facto rule of the worst. In any case, he would want to know whether the worst are in fact the rulers. The Voter's Decision Rule enables one to distinguish in a persuasive way between strongly and weakly committed voters and thus to bring new evidence to bear on this dispute about the role of swing voters. Just as important for an understanding of that role, however, is careful thought about who such voters are, the circumstances that increase or decrease their influence, and the standards that we should apply in evaluating their qualifications; for the issues in the dispute are tangled ones.

MARGINAL VOTERS IN THE JOHNSON AND NIXON LANDSLIDES

The swing voters that figure in the dispute that we are examining have in every case been electoral minorities.[15] Since no minority by itself can determine the outcome of a two-party election, it can be decisive only in a special sense, a sense which an example can help us to specify.

Suppose that two candidates, A and B, vie for the support of five voters—Mike, Wendy, Dan, Rick, and John—in a plurality election. In their propensity to vote for A, the five voters rank in the order given, with Mike the most favorable to A and John the least; in their propensity to vote for candidate B, the five rank in the reverse order. This ordering of propensities tells us that Mike will vote for A if Wendy does, that Wendy will vote for A if Dan does, and so on. In this situation

[15] Lazarsfeld, Berelson, and Gaudet classified 8 percent of their sample as "party changers" (*The People's Choice,* p. 66). Campbell and his co-authors were discussing about 25 percent of all voters in their comments on independents and 40 percent of the active electorate in those on "people who paid little attention to politics" (*The American Voter,* pp. 143–44 and p. 264). Key's "switchers" were from 10 to 19 percent of all voters in the period 1940–1960, and his "new voters" (in the same period) ranged from 13 to 30 percent of all voters. (*The Responsible Electorate,* p. 20).

Dan seems to play a uniquely pivotal role: Whomever he votes for will win, and whoever wins needs Dan's vote to do so.

Some such conception of ordered voting is implicit in the notion of a pivotal minority which decides the outcome of two-party elections. Marginal voters, defined as in Tables 5.4 and 6.1 above, necessarily include an electorate's "Dans"— that is, the least committed members of that half of the electorate most committed to the winning candidate.[16] Note, however, that swing voters defined in other ways need not be Dans and often are not. In our example Rick's vote (or that of any other voter except Dan) is not pivotal in the way that Dan's is, though in a landslide for A, Rick might have delayed making up his mind, have changed his preference from B to A, have voted for the first time, or have been independent, undecided, or indifferent. And, in two-candidate presidential elections since 1952, independents have never simultaneously cast a majority of their votes for the winner *and* cast votes that he needed to win, and party changers have done so in only two of those elections.[17] In four of the six elections for which Key gives data, his party shifters also failed either to support the winner or to supply him with votes that he needed.[18]

Thus, if one wants to compare the qualifications of that minority which can (in a special sense) swing an election with those of voters generally, one should examine the qualifications of marginal voters, as I have defined them. The standards to apply in assessing their qualifications are of course not self-evident, but for the moment let us take as given those invoked in arguments for and against the proposition that the worst voters decide elections. The good voter, most such arguments assume, takes an active interest in politics and elec-

[16] But not only the "Dans." For the procedure followed in defining marginal voters, see Chapter 4.

[17] The independents to which I am referring are those who declared no leaning toward either party. Party changers are those who declared their intention to vote for one candidate in preelection interviews but later reported a vote for another.

[18] See Key, *The Responsible Electorate*, p. 27.

tions, pays attention to campaigns, is well informed about campaign issues and public affairs generally, and, in deciding how to vote, is particularly concerned about the ideological positions of parties and candidates and about their stands on issues of public policy.

Given these standards, how good are marginal voters? What are they like? Since it is the ordering of commitments to the candidates of a particular election that makes some of its voters marginal, there is no reason to expect that the marginal voters of one election will resemble those of another. The marginal voters of 1964, however, were remarkably similar to those of 1972, as Table 8.1 shows. In every case but one, a group under- or overrepresented among marginal voters in one of these elections was under- or overrepresented among such voters in the other. Note, too, that the *extent* of a group's under- or overrepresentation was often nearly the same in both years.

Together, Tables 8.1. and 8.2 also show clearly that marginal voters in both elections were less well educated, less well informed, and more passive in their orientation to politics than were voters generally. Marginal voters showed to best advantage, though still below the average, in their participation in elections, in their attention to the campaign on television, and in their responses to some questions testing their knowledge of public affairs. Those with only an elementary-school education or less were substantially overrepresented among marginal voters in 1964, however, and slightly overrepresented in 1972. Substantially underrepresented among marginal voters in both elections were those who reported a strong interest in the campaign, attention to it, and political activity other than voting.[19]

Tables 8.3 and 8.4 show another striking contrast between

[19] Treating data on voters' interest and participation in politics as measures of their knowledge of public affairs, a frequent practice in studies of voting, may have led analysts to overly pessimistic conclusions. In 1964 and 1972, at least, marginal voters' responses to questions testing their knowledge compared more favorably with those of voters generally than their answers to questions about their interest and participation.

TABLE 8.1

**Representation of Selected Groups Among
Marginal Voters in 1964 and 1972**

Population Groups	All Voters (% of total)		Marginal Voters (over-/under-representation)	
	1964	1972	1964	1972
Males	45.6	44.3	.98	.85
Thirty-five or older	74.8	66.7	.95	.93
Whites	91.3	90.0	1.03	1.03
Blacks	8.4	8.8	.70	.71
Protestants	68.7	67.6	.99	.97
Catholics	24.4	24.8	1.04	1.08
Union member in household	26.1	26.4	1.02	.94
Voters with a family income of $10,000 or above	23.5	54.8	.97	.96
Voters with a grade-school education or less	21.1	15.3	1.21	1.04
Regular voters (voted in all or most presidential elections for which eligible)	85.2	85.8	.99	.94
Voters who voted for U.S. representative	87.3	87.2	.98	.93
Voters who thought politics not too complicated to understand	35.0	30.7	.58	.75
Voters who had written officials	20.0	31.3	.66	.65
Voters who attended a political meeting	10.6	11.0	.40	.72
Voters who tried to persuade others how to vote	35.8	34.5	.66	.65
Voters who were very interested in the campaign	43.8	35.7	.70	.73

TABLE 8.1 (Continued)

| | All Voters (% of total) | | Marginal Voters (over-/under- representation) | |
Population Groups	1964	1972	1964	1972
Voters who read about the campaign regularly in a newspaper	44.3	28.9	.82	.68
Voters who followed the campaign on television	91.4	90.0	.97	.96
Voters who knew which party had a preelection majority in Congress	68.6	73.0	.85	.94
Voters who knew which party had a postelection majority in Congress	85.2	63.3	.95	.92

NOTES: Each entry in the two left-hand columns is the percentage of the full sample of voters in the year indicated who were members of each group listed. For example, the first entry in the column farthest to the left indicates that 45.6 percent of the 1964 sample were males. Each entry in the two right-hand columns gives the extent to which each group was overrepresented or underrepresented among marginal voters, relative to the sample as a whole, and was arrived at by dividing the percentage of marginal voters who were members of a given group in a given year by the percentage of all voters who were members of that group in the same year. The first entry in the second column from the right, for example, indicates that the percentage of marginal voters who were males in 1964 was .98 of the percentage of the full sample who were males; thus, males were slightly underrepresented among marginal voters in that year. The third entry in the same column shows that whites were slightly overrepresented among marginal voters in 1964: The percentage of marginal voters who were white was 1.03 times as great as the percentage of all voters who were white. Marginal voters in 1964 and 1972 are defined as those with net scores from + 2 to + 4 inclusive and from + 1 to − 2 inclusive, respectively.

TABLE 8.2
Additional Comparisons of Marginal Voters to All Voters

Voters Who:	All Voters (% total)	Marginal Voters (over-/under- representation)
1964		
Had never voted in a primary	22.9	1.04
Always follow governmental activity	33.4	.66
Knew the name of the congressional incumbent	72.0	.92
Correctly named both congressional candidates	35.6	.80
Knew that Johnson favored the Civil Rights Act of 1964	78.4	.88
Knew that Goldwater opposed the Civil Rights Act of 1964	69.9	.87
Thought the Republicans more conservative than the Democrats	64.3	.80
Knew Goldwater was from Arizona	81.4	.91
1972		
Knew how many terms a president is eligible to serve	79.2	.93
Knew length of senatorial term	33.6	.78
Knew length of U.S. representative's term	36.4	.95
Thought McGovern more for busing than Nixon	41.4	.72
Thought McGovern more for withdrawal from Vietnam than Nixon	74.6	.87
Thought the Democrats more likely than the Republicans to declare an amnesty for draft evaders	47.4	.71

TABLE 8.2 (Continued)

Voters Who:	All Voters (% total)	Marginal Voters (over-/under-representation)
Thought the Democrats more likely than the Republicans to cut military spending	43.4	.74
Thought McGovern more liberal than Nixon	57.8	.83
Were rated as high or fairly high in political information by interviewers	39.5	.73

NOTES: Marginal voters in 1964 and 1972 are, respectively, those with net scores from + 2 to + 4 and from + 1 to − 2, inclusive. Numbers less than one in the right-hand column indicate that a group was underrepresented among marginal voters, while those greater than one indicate that a group was overrepresented.

marginal and other voters in 1964 and 1972. The two tables report, for each election, the over- or underrepresentation of forty concerns and sets of concerns among marginal voters relative to the frequency of these concerns among all voters. Of the eighty comparisons made, only eight show as high a salience for an issue among marginal voters as among voters generally, and only three show a higher salience. On the average, marginal voters simply had fewer likes and dislikes of parties and candidates.

In what they were concerned about, however, marginal voters were not very different from other voters. Though it may not be obvious from the two tables, in both elections the salience of any given concern among voters generally was highly correlated with its salience among marginal voters— that correlation was .97 for 1964 and .98 for 1972.[20] Those

[20] In 1964 the relationship between an issue's salience among all voters (x) and its salience among marginal voters (y) was well described by the formula $y = .87x − 1.65$. The comparable formula for the 1972 election was $y = .76x − .46$.

TABLE 8.3

Substantive Concerns of Marginal Voters in 1964 and 1972

	All Voters (% citing)		Marginal Voters (over-/under- representation)	
Considerations	1964	1972	1964	1972
New Deal Issues	78	75	.81	.76
Economic issues	29	40	.79	.80
Government spending	12	7	.75	.71
Monetary and fiscal policy	9	15	.67	.87
Election's economic impact	13	22	.85	.68
Ideological stance	38	31	.61	.65
Liberalism, conservatism	23	21	.61	.67
Farm policy	5	2	.60	1.05
Social Security, the aged, workers' welfare programs	21	9	.71	.78
Relationship to unions, labor	9	6	.78	1.00
Relationship to Big Business, common man	42	41	.76	.88
Competence of candidates	71	61	1.04	.87
Record, experience	30	31	1.13	.87
Strength of leadership	13	24	.85	.88
Realism	9	13	1.00	.85
Candidates' other traits	55	48	.82	.71
Integrity, sincerity	31	35	.65	.63
Appearance, family	12	6	.92	.67
Independence	5	3	.60	1.00
Foreign Policy	41	28	.83	.64
Military preparedness	6	8	.50	.63
Internationalism	6	5	.83	.67
Quality of stewardship	51	51	.75	.61
Governmental corruption	14	10	.64	.50
Race-related issues	28	10	.79	.70
Partisan unity	5	5	.40	.80
Partisanship	44	19	.80	.74
Conduct of campaign	31	15	.94	.80

NOTE: Marginal voters in 1964 and 1972 are, respectively, those with net scores from +2 to +4 and from +1 to −2, inclusive. Numbers less than one in the two right-hand columns indicate that a group was underrepresented among marginal voters, while those greater than one indicate that a group was overrepresented.

TABLE 8.4

**Some Additional Concerns of Marginal Voters
in 1964 and 1972**

Considerations	All Voters (% citing)	Marginal Voters (over-/under-representation)
1964		
Foreign Aid	4	.75
Peace	21	.76
Handling of trouble spots	7	.86
Medical care	11	.55
Poverty program	8	.37
Extremism	4	.50
Judgment, stability of candidates	20	1.00
Clarity of candidates' positions	19	.74
Scandals	8	.62
Goldwater Republicanism	23	.57
Relationship to J. F. Kennedy	19	1.00
1972		
Vietnam War, peace	55	.75
Relations with China	9	.78
Relations with U.S.S.R.	5	.80
The Social Issue	24	.71
Law and order	4	.00
"Amnesty, acid, abortion"	7	.43
Youth-related issues	12	.67
Welfare	23	.70
Watergate affair	5	.60
Conventions, Eagleton affair	11	.73
Eagleton affair	8	.88

NOTE: Marginal voters in 1964 and 1972 are, respectively, those with
net scores from +2 to +4 and from +1 to −2, inclusive. Numbers less
than one in the right-hand column indicate that a group was underrepresented among marginal voters, while those greater than one indicate
that a group was overrepresented.

matters which concerned many voters—New Deal issues, for
example, and the qualifications of candidates—also concerned many marginal voters, and those that concerned few
voters in the general population—for instance, the appear-
ances and families of the candidates—also concerned few
marginal voters. Nonetheless, there were a few notable variations in the degree to which particular concerns were underrepresented among marginal voters. In both 1964 and 1972
concerns about the competence of candidates, particularly
concerns about their records and experience, were less underrepresented (indeed, in 1964 they were overrepresented) than
most issues. In contrast, concerns about the ideological
stances of parties and candidates, about the integrity and sincerity of candidates, and about the quality of stewardship
were among the issues most underrepresented.

Any strong tendency for the *bias* of issues to run counter to
each other in the electorate as a whole and among marginal
voters—that is, for issues to have a Republican bias among
voters generally but a Democratic bias among marginal
voters, or vice-versa—would raise a tricky problem both for
campaign strategists and for democratic theorists. There were
few instances of such opposed biases, however, in the elections
of 1964 and 1972; they occurred on only six of forty issues in
the former election (ideological stance, monetary and fiscal
policy, the poverty program, quality of stewardship, race-related issues, and the independence of candidates) and on three
of forty issues in the latter (integrity and sincerity, the quality
of stewardship, and the vice-presidential candidates). Three of
these nine cases involved very small numbers of marginal respondents and thus a high probability of error in measurement. In both elections the bias of a given issue among all
voters showed a high correlation (.92 in 1964, .93 in 1972) with
its bias among marginal voters, though not so high a correlation as that for the salience of issues in the two groups. The
former correlation, in both years, was reduced by a tendency
for the bias of issues among marginal voters to have the same
direction as that among all voters but to be more pronounced:
Issues biased toward the Democrats among voters generally

were even more biased toward them among marginal voters, and similarly for issues biased toward the Republicans.

The picture of swing voters in 1964 and 1972 that emerges from the tables above is incomplete. From the data presented in them, for instance, we do not know how well-informed marginal voters were about the issues that were salient to them or about many other matters as important, or more important, than those about which we do have evidence. One should also remember that those tables deal in averages. All the data in them are perfectly consistent with the existence of a sizable body of exemplary citizens among marginal voters. Nonetheless, the findings clearly count on the side of those who have decried the competence of swing voters. In two elections very dissimilar in their results, marginal voters had very similar characteristics. In both, compared to voters generally, they were on average less well educated, less active politically, less interested in the campaign, less informed, and less attentive to politics. They were also concerned about fewer issues than other voters and less inclined to praise or fault candidates and parties for their ideological positions.

IMPLICATIONS

What do these findings imply about the quality of the collective decisions reached by voters in the presidential elections of 1964 and 1972? What would be implied if it should turn out that marginal voters in most elections are like those of 1964 and 1972?

It may be helpful to consider these questions, initially, in the context of an imaginary situation. Suppose an electorate consisting of three groups of voters—R, D, and M—must choose by majority vote between two candidates. Suppose further that

1. The members of group R are all better informed than the members of group D, who in turn are all better informed than the members of group M;
2. the members of each group always vote en bloc;

3. no one group casts a majority of the votes but any two groups do;
4. the members of R support one candidate, those of D support the other;
5. the members of M are undecided; and
6. we approach an election.

What can one say about the role of group M in this situation? Under what circumstances might one reasonably consider that role pernicious?

To evaluate the situation, we need to know, first of all, how the number of candidates came to be limited to two. Presumably, some system of nomination is responsible for that limitation. If the nominators chose the candidates only, or mainly, for their popularity with the members of M, M could rightly be said to have decided the election before it began. If the candidates were chosen only, or mainly, for their acceptability to R and D, however, M's balance-of-power role is of far less consequence for the qualifications of the eventually successful candidate. Group M will have the last say only because groups R and D have spoken first, and its choice will necessarily be the same as that of some better informed group.

Second, note that M's votes will *not* decide the election in a strict sense, a point I have made already about marginal voters. The votes of M and D, or of M and R, will do so, but not those of M alone. M's minority status constrains its influence in the election: Any appeals directed to its members must be reconcilable with those directed to at least one of the better informed groups.

Third, the acceptability of this situation depends on the costs and benefits of remedies for it. One remedy might be to limit the right to vote to members of R and D, or even to those of R only, since it is the best-informed group. That solution, however, is likely to mean that the interests of those excluded from the electorate will be disregarded. In the words of John Stuart Mill, "Rulers and ruling classes are under a necessity of considering the interests and wishes of those who have the suffrage; but of those who are excluded, it is their option whether they will do so or not; and however honestly disposed, they are in general too fully occupied with things which they *must* attend to, to have much room in their thoughts for anything which they can with impunity disregard."[21] Moreover, in modern states, it is a deadly insult to be denied suffrage, and its denial alienates from the regime some of those whom it needs to defend itself, enrich its treasury, and obey its laws. Other remedies, historically, for badly qualified voters—hereditary succession to leadership or the choice of leaders by lottery, appointment, or indirect election—all have serious shortcomings (to put the matter mildly) of their own.

Fourth, the kind of access to the members of group M that the candidates and their supporters enjoy is of great importance for one's evaluation of the situation. Suppose, for example, that group D's candidate has exclusive or markedly unequal access to group M by reason of a better organization or a better-financed campaign. In those circumstances he may find it relatively easy to exploit the ignorance of its members and so to mislead them. If so, group M's power is illusory, and its interests will suffer. So will the interests of group R, for it is deprived of any chance to bid for M's votes on the basis of some honest compromise of its interests with M's, and so it is likely to feel that the election has been rigged, as, in a sense, it has been.

Finally, the fact that M's members are less well informed than those of the other groups in itself tells us nothing about the qualifications of the former to choose wisely between the candidates. To make that judgment, we need to know how well informed the members of M are, *relative to what they should know.* The odds are overwhelming that any electorate—even the College of Cardinals—will have some members who are better informed than others, and the existence of such differences is perfectly consistent with every member of the group being well qualified to vote, or none being well qualified.

These observations on our imaginary situation suggest some conclusions about those that actually obtained in the elections of 1964 and 1972. To begin with, it is highly likely

---

[21] Mill, *Considerations on Representative Government,* p. 170.

that the marginal voters in those two elections who were least
interested in politics, and least knowledgeable about it, had
less—probably considerably less—influence on the parties'
choices of nominees than other voters. The *direct* influence of
such marginal voters was certainly less; those who know and
care little about politics do not become convention delegates,
attend party caucuses, or participate proportionately to their
numbers in presidential primaries.[22] Furthermore, there is little reason to believe that those involved directly in the choice
of the presidential candidates gave undue consideration to the
views of the uninformed when making those choices. On the
contrary, the temptation of the knowledgeable activist must
usually be to ignore the views of the ignorant, on the theory
that they will not feel hurt by what they don't know.[23]

Even if we ignore this background, the claims of marginal
voters to have cast the decisive votes in the elections of 1964
and 1972 are not so good as the claims of those voters whom I
have called the core supporters of the two winning candidates.
The former group gave the two victors their *margins* of victory, but the latter (defined in each case as that half of the

[22] On participation in presidential primaries, see Austin Ranney,
"Turnout and Representation in Presidential Primary Elections," *American Political Science Review* 66 (March 1972), pp. 21–37. See also the
survey data reported by the *New York Times*, March 2, 1980, comparing
voters in the New Hampshire primary with the potential electorate in
New Hampshire and with voters nationwide.

[23] Consider, for example, Stephen Shadegg's mailing of handwritten
postcards to some of Senator Barry Goldwater's Arizona constituents,
which said "Dear (first name) . . . Tuesday is Election Day. I sure hope
you'll vote and I hope you will vote for me. Barry." Shadegg explains:
  What a ridiculous, futile exercise! Anyone receiving such a card
  should know immediately that the candidate could not possibly
  have taken time to write the message personally. . . . I knew that
  most of the voters receiving that post card appeal couldn't be moved
  to cross the party line by a plea from their mother. But I also knew
  that if I were lucky, perhaps ten per cent of the cards would be received by the Indifferents. . . . I was convinced that a personal communication, a post card without any political slogan, just a request
  for a vote, made on a first-name basis, might be enough of a reason
  to secure their support (*How to Win an Election*, pp. 22–23).
One can imagine few better examples of an effort to win votes on the
cheap.

electorate most favorable to the winning candidate) gave them their victories. Tables 8.5 and 8.6 give us information about core supporters in the two elections comparable to that provided above for marginal voters. These voters, the tables show clearly, did not differ greatly in their characteristics from voters generally, either in 1964 or 1972. Nixon's core supporters were actually more inclined than the average voter to participate in politics and were better educated and better informed. While the comparable group of Johnson supporters were below average in these respects, they were not far below, nor is their below-average showing surprising, given the constituency of the Democratic Party.

Recall, furthermore, that we have been taking for granted the validity of the standards that critics have applied in evaluating the qualifications of marginal voters and of voters generally. The data, in this study and others, show that many voters (and, proportionally, even more marginal voters) are ignorant of some elementary facts about American politics and government and do not see the differences between candidates and parties in ideological terms. These facts, however, are far from compelling evidence that such voters are unqualified to vote. While at first blush it may be dismaying to learn that many voters in 1972 and 1964 did not know which party controlled Congress, the number of terms a president can serve, the names of congressional candidates, and the length of the terms of U.S. senators and representatives, none of these pieces of information is highly relevant to voting in presidential elections. Observers have also been appalled to learn that many voters are unaware of basic facts relating to important issues of policy, and it is true that a sizable minority of voters in 1964 did not know the stands of the two candidates on the Civil Rights Act of that year and that in 1972 many were ignorant of the candidates' stands on busing, withdrawal from Vietnam, amnesty for draft evaders, and military spending. But what issues should voters know about? No sensible model of democratic government would require all voters to care about the same set of issues or to be well informed about issues they do not care about. Ignorance or misinformation about matters which they do regard as important for their

TABLE 8.5

**Representation of Selected Groups among That Half
of the Electorate Most Strongly Committed
to the Winning Candidates, 1964 and 1972**

Population Groups	All Voters (% of total)		Half of Sample Most Strongly Committed to the Winner (over-/under-representation)	
	1964	1972	1964	1972
Males	45.6	44.3	.96	1.04
Thirty-five or older	74.8	66.7	1.00	1.07
Whites	91.3	90.0	.92	1.10
Blacks	8.4	8.8	1.88	.14
Protestants	68.7	67.6	.94	1.08
Catholics	24.4	24.8	1.13	.87
Union member in household	26.1	26.4	1.33	.82
Voters with a family income of $10,000 or above	23.5	54.8	.86	1.09
Voters with a grade-school education or less	21.1	15.3	1.13	.86
Regular voters (voted in all or most presidential elections for which eligible)	85.2	85.8	.98	1.04
Voters who voted for U.S. representative	87.3	87.2	.99	1.04
Voters who thought politics not too complicated to understand	35.0	30.7	.99	1.06
Voters who had written officials	20.0	31.3	.84	.99
Voters who attended a political meeting	10.6	11.0	.78	.97
Voters who tried to persuade others how to vote	35.8	34.5	.92	1.10
Voters who were very interested in the campaign	43.8	35.7	1.01	1.10

TABLE 8.5 (Continued)

Population Groups	All Voters (% of total) 1964	1972	Half of Sample Most Strongly Committed to the Winner (over-/under-representation) 1964	1972
Voters who read about the campaign regularly in a newspaper	44.3	30.4	.97	1.14
Voters who followed the campaign on television	91.4	90.0	.94	1.02
Voters who knew which party had a preelection majority in Congress	68.6	73.0	.93	1.07
Voters who knew which party had a postelection majority in Congress	85.2	63.3	.98	1.06

NOTE: The half sample most strongly committed to the winning candidate comprises, in 1964, those respondents with net scores from +4 to +20 and, in 1972, those with net scores from −2 to −20. Numbers less than one in the two right-hand columns indicate that a group was underrepresented among voters in that half of the sample most strongly committed to the winner, while those greater than one indicate that a group was overrepresented.

choices among candidates would surely count against the competence of voters, but the data just reviewed—and that relied upon by critics—do not show that kind of ignorance or misinformation. What little evidence exists—recall that reported in Chapter 4 above—suggests that voters do have knowledge about the issues that they themselves raise in canvassing their likes and dislikes of parties and candidates.

Table 8.3 shows that voters in 1964 and 1972 were more concerned with the competence of the candidates than with their ideological positions and that this emphasis was greater, relatively, among marginal voters. The voters in the two elections—to put the matter in the most pejorative way possi-

TABLE 8.6

**Additional Comparisons of All Voters to That Half
of the Electorate Most Strongly Committed
to the Winning Candidates, 1964 and 1972**

Voters Who:	All Voters (% total)	Half of Sample Most Strongly Committed to the Winner (over-/under-representation)
1964		
Had never voted in a primary	22.9	1.08
Always follow governmental activity	33.4	.91
Knew the name of the congressional incumbent	72.0	.95
Correctly named both congressional candidates	35.6	.87
Knew that Johnson favored the Civil Rights Act of 1964	78.4	1.01
Knew that Goldwater opposed the Civil Rights Act of 1964	69.9	1.04
Thought the Republicans more conservative than the Democrats	64.3	.91
Knew Goldwater was from Arizona	81.4	.97
1972		
Knew how many terms a president is eligible to serve	79.2	1.02
Knew length of senatorial term	33.6	1.12
Knew length of U.S. representative's term	36.4	1.08
Thought McGovern more for busing than Nixon	41.4	1.19
Thought McGovern more for withdrawal from Vietnam than Nixon	74.6	1.07
Thought the Democrats more likely than the Republicans to cut military spending	43.4	.99

TABLE 8.6 (Continued)

Voters Who:	All Voters (% total)	Half of Sample Most Strongly Committed to the Winner (over-/under-representation)
Thought the Democrats more likely than the Republicans to declare an amnesty for draft evaders	47.4	1.15
Thought McGovern more liberal than Nixon	57.8	1.06
Were rated as high or fairly high in political information by interviewers	39.5	1.08

NOTE: That half of the sample most strongly committed to the winning candidate comprises, in 1964, those respondents with net scores from +4 to +20 and, in 1972, those with net scores from −2 to −20. Numbers less than one in the right-hand column indicate that a group was underrepresented among voters in that half of the sample most strongly committed to the winner, while those greater than one indicate that a group was overrepresented.

ble—cared more about images than about ideology. But what does the term *images* mean in this context? The voters of 1964 and 1972 were in fact concerned for the most part with the record and experience of the candidates, their capacity for leadership, their judgment, their realism, and their integrity, not with their appearance. These concerns made voters the unconscious followers of Mill, who regarded just these things as among the most important criteria for making choices among candidates. And how important is ideological awareness for evaluating candidates? As descriptive terms the words *liberalism* and *conservatism* of ordinary political parlance serve a useful purpose; as criteria of evaluation they have little merit. When considering what the right solution to some public problem might be, it is unhelpful to ask whether a proposed solution is liberal or conservative, because the sets of positions commonly labeled as such are not united by, or derivable from, any clear set of principles. The logic, for instance, that makes opposition to abortion, gun control, minimum wages, school integration, and withdrawal from Vietnam conservative, and the contrary positions liberal, is surely obscure.

Finally, while unusual access to voters is a potential threat to the integrity of elections, it would be hard to argue persuasively that the outcomes of the 1964 and 1972 elections depended on the victorious candidates' unequal access to marginal voters. Although Johnson and Nixon were incumbent presidents and, as such, enjoyed a president's unequaled ability to attract news coverage, their challengers were both unusually well financed and the beneficiaries of massive canvassing campaigns. Moreover, marginal voters in the two elections—and party changers, party shifters, independents, and the undecided as well—split their votes, so that any advantage in access enjoyed by the two victors was either partial or only partially effective.

What are the implications of these findings for elections generally? That access to marginal voters was not one-sided in the 1964 and 1972 elections does not mean that it has not been, or could not be, in others. Nor, obviously, can one regard the knowledge that voters bring to voting as a matter of indifference to the health of democratic regimes. In the long run badly informed voters seem likely to get less of what they want from government, just as badly informed purchasers are likely to buy products unsatisfactory to them, and, thus, the badly informed may become a discontented element in the body politic. Before decrying the situation that actually obtains in elections, however, we ought to have better standards of evaluation than we now do, and we ought to recognize that the fear that presidential elections exemplify the rule by the worst of the many is to a large extent illusory. In 1964 and 1972 the impact on government of marginal voters was, and in most elections is highly likely to be, severely limited by our procedures for nominating presidents, the minority status of such voters, and the divisions among them.

CHAPTER NINE

1980: THE UNEXPECTED
LANDSLIDE

How the press assigns meaning to elections is important in itself and also because its approaches to that task are illustrative of those commonly employed. Journalists routinely interpret elections, as no other group in society does, and in recent years well-designed surveys of opinion sponsored by the press have become a major source of information about elections. No other interpretations of elections have the political significance that those of the news media do, at least in the short run: The press gets there first with the most publicity, and first impressions of elections tend to endure. Though reporters work under greater pressures and rarely employ advanced statistical techniques, their basic analytical moves are very similar to those of most academic students of politics, and the first-order questions that one can raise about the methods of both are much the same.

So far I have considered only briefly any approaches to interpreting elections but my own. In what follows I review critically what the press had to say about our most recent presidential election. The chief objective of that review is to evaluate the press's analytical methods and the evidence with which it buttressed its accounts of what the election meant. A secondary purpose is to advance some conclusions about the import of Ronald Reagan's victory.

In promising a review of what the press had to say about the 1980 election, I am of course taking a writer's liberty. In fact I have limited my attention mainly to what television news, the two major news magazines, and some prestigious newspapers and commentators said and did. These are not *the* press, but they do constitute the leadership of the press, a leadership which has the avid attention of most journalists and of politically active people generally.

"LANDSLIDE. YES, LANDSLIDE"

With virtual unanimity these voices of the press quickly proclaimed Ronald Reagan's victory a landslide. In the words of
Time,

> Landslide. Yes, landslide—stunning, startling, as-
> tounding, beyond the wildest dreams and nightmares of
> the contending camps, beyond the furtherest ken of the
> armies of pollsters, pundits and political profes-
> sionals. . . . Once the big count began all the shibboleths
> of the election—that Americans were confused, apathetic
> and wished a plague on all candidates and, above all, that
> they were closely divided—were swept away by a rising
> tide of votes. . . .[1]

Others characterized the election as "decisive"; a "shocker";
"a stunning," "stupefying," "roaring" landslide; "the most as-
tonishing landslide in election history"; the " '80 quake"; a
"tidal wave"; and a "Mt. St. Helens of disappointment and
anger."[2] The observation of a *New York Times* editorial that
"the President-elect's triumph was not a landslide of historic
proportions" was lonely in its moderation, even in the columns of the *Times*.[3]

Yet, by conventional criteria, that observation is surely
right. Reagan won a slightly larger share of the electoral vote

[1] *Time*, November 17, 1980.

[2] The quoted words and phrases come from (in order of quotation) the
New York Times, November 5, 1980; the *Washington Post*, November 6,
1980; the *Los Angeles Times*, November 5, 1980; the *Chicago Tribune*,
November 6, 1980; the *Wall Street Journal,* November 5, 1980; cover,
David Broder et al., *The Pursuit of the Presidency 1980* (New York:
Washington *Post*, Berkeley Books, 1980); the *New Orleans Times-Pica-
yune*, November 11, 1980; the *Washington Post*, November 6, 1980; and
the *Chicago Tribune*, November 6, 1980.

[3] *New York Times*, November 6, 1980. The *Washington Post*'s Haynes
Johnson was another who noted that Reagan's landslide was of smaller
proportions than a number of earlier ones (*Washington Post*, November
9, 1980).

than Johnson did in 1964 and almost as many states. But consider these additional facts:

   —Reagan won 55.4 percent of the major-party vote; in over half of the other presidential elections since the turn of the century, the winning candidate did as well or better.
   —Reagan's share of the total popular vote (50.9 percent) barely exceeded that of Jimmy Carter in 1976 (50.4 percent); in this century fourteen of twenty winning candidates have done as well.
   —Reagan's share of the total *potential* vote (26.6 percent) was the third lowest of any winning candidate since 1932.

To an unusual degree in 1980, the count of electoral votes and states exaggerated the winner's popular margin. For each percent of the major-party vote that Reagan won nationally, he won 1.64 percent of the electoral vote and 1.56 percent of the states. These ratios are the highest for any winning candidate in this century and show that Reagan benefited greatly from the geographical distribution of his vote.[4] The 1980 presidential election was a big landslide only in the division of electoral votes and states; in the division of *voters* it was at best a small landslide.

Other indicators of electoral decisiveness support this judgment. The victor's popular vote in 1980 could have been matched by the effective mobilization of his major opponent's adherents more easily than in any other recent landslide. Compare the loser's mobilization ratio for these five elections:

---

[4] To win in the electoral college, Carter would have had to win all those states that Reagan carried by less than 56 percent of the major-party vote. Although this figure is four percentage points below the comparable one for McGovern and six percentage points below that for Goldwater, the distribution of Reagan's vote made his victory as secure against countermobilization as Eisenhower's in 1952. It was an appreciation of how well distributed Reagan's support was that led David Broder to predict a Reagan victory at a time when two national polls by his paper yielded conflicting and statistically inconclusive results and when many other analysts rated the outcome as too close to call.

1964	111.9%
1972	88.7
1956	84.5
1952	73.9
1980	65.6

The ratio for 1980—that is, the percentage of Carter's adherents (voting and nonvoting) who would have had to cast ballots for his vote to have equaled Reagan's—is the lowest by some 8 percentage points,[5] and it is the only one of the five to represent a degree of mobilization actually achieved by candidates in recent elections.

Moreover, the commitment of voters to candidates in 1980 was unusually weak, at least as weak as it had been in 1976: While the press used no measure of commitment so finely calibrated as net scores,[6] its data support that conclusion. Twenty-seven percent of the respondents in the Gallup postelection survey reported changing their choice of candidates during the campaign. That figure is 6 percentage points higher than the comparable one for 1976 and more than double that for 1972.[7] In three surveys the number of voters who said that

[5] In calculating the ratio for 1980, I based the estimate of the candidates' support among nonvoters on data gathered by the *New York Times* and CBS News in their postelection survey. See the *New York Times*, November 16, 1980.

[6] Calculation of net scores from the data produced by the University of Michigan's 1980 National Election Study support this conclusion fully. If one defines weakly committed voters as those with net scores between ±2, for instance, then the data show that more than one-third of all voters were weakly committed to both Reagan and Carter, that 38 percent of Reagan's vote came from weakly committed voters, and that Reagan, to win, needed 71 percent of the vote that he received from such voters. Thus, the proportion of weakly committed voters in 1980 and the percentage of the winners' vote received from them were about the same as they had been in 1976 and 1972 and were considerably greater than they had been in any of the other five elections since 1952 (see Tables 3.4 and 3.6 above). Changing the definition of weakly committed voters to all those with net scores between ±1 or ±3 does not change this result.

[7] Gallup Poll release for December 7, 1980. The *Washington Post*, reinterviewing in the week before the election a sample of voters originally surveyed in September, found that 30 percent had either switched their preferences from one candidate to another or had become unde-

they had decided how to vote in the week before election day ranged from 23 percent to 35 percent.[8] In 1964 and 1972 half that many or less, and in 1976 no more than that, waited until the last *two weeks* to decide.[9] Three surveys found that about 10 to 12 percent of their respondents did not decide how to vote until election day itself.[10] About the same proportion waited that long in 1976,[11] but only about half that many did so in either 1964 or 1972.[12] Attitudinally, the 1980 election was another close landslide.[13]

It was also one in which many voters found their choice not only hard but unattractive. *Time*'s survey of mid-October found that 43 percent of Reagan's adherents among registered voters were "more interested in voting against Carter than for

---

cided (November 2, 1980). The *New York Times*–CBS News postelection survey, in which voters surveyed shortly before election day were reinterviewed shortly after it, found 12 percent of the respondents to have changed their choice of candidates in the last four days of the campaign (*New York Times*, November 16, 1980).

[8] The *Times*–CBS election-day survey found 23 percent; the ABC News election-day survey, 27 percent; and the Gallup Poll postelection survey, 35 percent. Some 18 percent told Gallup interviewers that they had decided how to vote after watching the Carter-Reagan debate, a response which the other two surveys did not permit.

[9] These data are from the relevant national election studies of the University of Michigan's Center for Political Studies.

[10] The Gallup Poll postelection survey, the ABC News election-day poll, and the NBC–Associated Press election-day poll.

[11] Gallup Poll release for December 7, 1980.

[12] Data from the 1964 and 1972 national election studies of the University of Michigan's Center for Political Studies.

[13] Other survey findings attest to the general weakness of voters' commitments in 1980. A *Time* story, based on a poll in mid-October, reported that "sixty-one per cent of the voters admit being unmoved by anyone in the race" (November 3, 1980). *Newsweek*, reporting the result of the *Newsweek* poll of October 17–20, noted that "lightly committed voters represent a quarter of Carter's total, a fifth of Reagan's. Combined with the truly undecided, this group amounts to about one-third of the electorate" (November 3, 1980). Lightly committed voters were those who indicated only a moderate preference for their candidate and only moderate opposition to the others. The *Newsweek* findings were similar to those of the Gallup Poll in mid-September. In the *Times*–CBS election-day survey, one-third of the respondents said that they supported the candidates of their choice "with reservations."

Reagan," while 37 percent of Carter's adherents said that they were "really just anti-Reagan."[14] Earlier in the month the Gallup Poll had compared the percentages of voters giving Carter and Reagan "highly favorable" ratings with those given candidates in earlier races.[15] Arranged in order from high to low, the ratings can be seen in Table 9.1. Reagan's rating had been higher earlier in the campaign and probably improved later. In particular, Reagan's performance in the Carter-Reagan debate made many voters more comfortable at the prospect of a Reagan presidency.[16] Nonetheless, on election day, the *Times*-CBS survey still found 18 percent of Reagan voters who said that their votes were more anti-Carter than pro-Reagan, in addition to the 36 percent who supported Reagan with reservations.[17] The story of Reagan's presidency should note that on election day he was a relatively unpopular victor.[18]

For some reporters the rising tide of votes on election night did sweep away the evidence that many voters were weakly committed and dissatisfied with their choice, but it should not have. As the data for the 1972 election show, a large margin of victory does not necessarily mean resolute voters: It is quite

[14] *Time*, November 3, 1980.

[15] Gallup Poll release for October 19, 1980.

[16] In the *New York Times*-CBS News postelection survey (November 7–12, 1980) 45 percent of the respondents said that "the way Ronald Reagan handled himself in the debate with Jimmy Carter" made them feel "more comfortable about what kind of a President he might be."

[17] Figures are computed from data appearing in the *New York Times*, November 9, 1980. The findings of the NBC News–Associated Press election-day survey were similar: 37 percent of those who voted for Reagan did so with reservations, while 14 percent said they liked none of the candidates.

[18] Calculating credit ratings from the data of the University of Michigan's 1980 National Election Study makes this point dramatically. In 1980 fully one-quarter of all voters made "lesser of evils" choices, only 6 percent "better of goods" choices. The ratio of the former to the latter was thus the highest for any election since 1952. (See Table 3.8 above). Reagan received net positive credit ratings from 41.8 per cent of all those respondents who voted. His mean credit rating was −.11 and his median credit rating zero. This showing is the poorest for any victorious candidate for whom credit ratings can be calculated. (See Table 3.9.)

TABLE 9.1

Percentages of "Highly Favorable" Ratings Given Presidential Candidates, 1952–1980

Candidate	Date of Survey	Rating
Eisenhower	Mid-October 1956	59%
Johnson	Mid-October 1964	49
Eisenhower	August 1952	47
Kennedy	Mid-September 1960	42
Carter	Late September 1976	41
Nixon	October 1972	41
Nixon	Mid-September 1960	40
Nixon	Early September 1968	38
Stevenson	August 1952	37
Stevenson	Mid-October 1956	33
Carter	*October 10–12, 1980*	*30*
Ford	Late September 1976	28
Humphrey	Early September 1968	25
Reagan	*October 10–12, 1980*	*23*
McGovern	October 1972	21
Goldwater	Mid-October 1964	16

SOURCE: Gallup Poll release for October 19, 1980.

possible to fashion a one-sided electoral outcome from individual decisions that carry little conviction. Nor was the failure of the polls to predict a sizable victory for Reagan a sufficient reason to disregard the evidence of weak commitment and negativism when interpreting that victory later. During the campaign the press had often noted the volatility of voters' preferences. Given such volatility, a last-minute swing toward one candidate or the other is quite possible; it takes only a small push to raise one end of a teeter-totter.[19] For accuracy in predicting as well as in interpreting the election, the press

[19] As David M. Alpern and his associates noted in their postelection report for *Newsweek* (November 17, 1980). For an extended discussion of the performance of the polls in predicting the 1980 election, see Everett C. Ladd and G. Donald Ferree, "Were the Pollsters Really Wrong?" *Public Opinion* (December, January, 1981), pp. 14–17.

should have paid greater heed to its own evidence; most survey organizations for the press stopped polling too soon.

The press exaggerated the one-sidedness of Reagan's victory; reportorial language as well as the economy suffered from inflation in 1980. Such exaggeration may have owed something to a desire both to give the winner his due and to avoid rehashing old stories about perplexed and unhappy voters. The techniques of television coverage probably also contributed. On election night the three networks devoted themselves almost entirely to calling wins and losses state by state, recording their calls on huge, two-color maps and in running tallies of the electoral vote, and thus conveying the impression of a runaway election. Finally, the press (following virtually unanimous expert opinion) had advertised a very close race. Given that fact, a big victory must have seemed a better story than a modest one, and surprise became midwife to a landslide. Whatever the reasons for the exaggeration, however, it did not advance understanding of what had happened.

"THE COLLAPSE OF A COALITION"

In a number of accounts of the 1980 election, the traditional Democratic coalition appeared high on the casualty list. Stories in *Time, Newsweek,* the *New York Times,* and the *Wall Street Journal* all proclaimed its downfall,[20] supporting their claims with analyses of the voting of particular social and demographic groups.

Such analyses are a standard feature of election stories, and their popularity is easy to understand. The data required are readily available, and the style of thought is seductive. We commonly speak of the black vote, union vote, or Catholic vote and think of these entities as the building blocks of coali-

[20] *Time,* November 17, 1980; *Newsweek,* November 17, 1980; *New York Times,* November 5, 1980; and the *Wall Street Journal,* November 5, 1980. The *New York Times* said that the Democratic coalition had "collapsed"; *Time,* that it had been "dismembered"; the *Wall Street Journal,* that it had been "wrecked"; and *Newsweek,* that it had been "shredded."

tions that constitute the support for parties and candidates. Within limits it makes sense to do so. Many groups have distinctive interests and outlooks and are accessible through more-or-less distinctive channels of communication. Parties and candidates must consider how to reconcile the diverse interests of such groups and how to unite them into winning combinations.

A *New York Times* story by Adam Clymer was a workmanlike example of the genre. Appearing under the headline "The Collapse of a Coalition," the story reported that

> the old Democratic coalition deserted President Carter yesterday with defections reminiscent of the defeat of George McGovern in 1972.
>
> Roman Catholics went against the President, he gained little better than an even split among voters from union households, and his margins among Jews, liberals and low-income voters fell well below the percentages that Democrats usually get. . . .
>
> And Mr. Carter neither repeated the unusual strength he showed in 1976 among such predominantly Republican groups as white Protestants, nor made the compensating gains he had counted on among blacks or the teachers. . . . In fact, the teachers went for Ronald Reagan. . . .
>
> Mr. Reagan did not lose any significant element of the Republican base. Eighty-four per cent of Republicans backed him. He got the votes, as nearly as this poll [the *Times*-CBS election-day poll] could identify them, of "big business and the country club set."[21]

The huge sample of the *Times*-CBS survey (over 12,000 voters) enabled Clymer to make reliable statements about the voting of such relatively small groups as Jews, liberal Democrats, and those eighteen to twenty-one years old. He compared the voting of groups in 1980 with their voting in 1976 and 1972 and with what they had "usually" done. To good effect, he drew more often on cross-tabulations of data than is

[21] *New York Times*, November 5, 1980.

common in this kind of reporting, noting, for instance, the presidential preferences of women for and against the Equal Rights Amendment. And yet some of the story's uses of data were quite misleading, and so was its headline, though Clymer was doubtless not responsible for the latter.

Almost all of Clymer's citations of data (like those of most reporters who write stories of this sort) were of the actual vote of various groups, as when, for instance, he observed that "the President carried black voters overwhelmingly, but Mr. Reagan's 14 percent showing was almost as good a vote as Mr. Ford's 16 percent."[22] This deployment of data takes all too literally the coalition metaphor, for it implies that opinion in particular groups is wholly independent of opinion in the general electorate. Clearly, no such independence exists for most groups; much of the variation from election to election in a group's vote for a given party's candidates reflects variations in the general popularity of the candidates, not differences in the party's appeal to the group as such. To put the matter another way, what party coalitions amount to in electoral terms is a certain *distinctiveness* in the voting of some groups, an *inclination* toward one or the other party's candidates which modifies the impact on voting of movements of opinion that are more general.[23] That a group's vote is the same in two elections may therefore mask a substantial change in its partisan inclination, while a difference may falsely suggest a change. For example, Richard Nixon's share of the votes of college graduates was 61 percent in 1960, 63 percent in 1972. Relative to his vote in the electorate at large, the earlier showing was by far the better one: In 1960 the college-educated voted 11 percentage points more Republican than all voters, in 1972 only one percentage point more Republican. Or again, consider the votes of independents for Eisenhower in 1952— 65 percent—and Gerald Ford in 1976—57 percent. Eisenhower's 8-percentage-point advantage over Ford among independents was no more than that which he enjoyed among all voters; thus, the pro-Republican inclination of the indepen-

[22] Ibid.
[23] Cf. Campbell et al., *The American Voter*, p. 301.

dent vote in the two cases was just about the same. Analyses
of variations in the appeal of the parties to particular groups
should focus not on the group's vote but on the *bias* of its vote.

Clymer's use of the actual vote of groups is misleading for a
second reason: The 1980 election featured three candidates
who drew significant support, while the two elections with
which he most frequently compared it did not. Consider, for
instance, the statement that "Mr. Carter drew the votes of 57
percent of the liberals, as against the 70 percent he got in
1976."[24] True, but another equally true statement puts the
matter in a different light: Reagan's share of the liberal vote in
winning (27 percent) barely improved upon Ford's share in
losing (26 percent). There may be no ideal way of comparing
the results of an election involving only two candidates with
those of a contest among three, but computing a group's
major-party vote in both races is a start toward a reasonable
basis for comparison.[25] In 1980 Carter drew 68 percent of the
major-party vote of liberals, only 2 percentage points less than
he drew in 1976. That figure is surely a better indication of his
appeal to liberals in 1980 as *against that of his Republican
challenger* than the one Clymer cites. Recall, moreover, that
Carter's general popularity was lower in 1980: The Democratic share of the major-party vote of liberals in 1976 exceeded that of all voters by about 19 percentage points, in
1980 by about 27. Thus, contrary to what the raw figures suggest, among liberals the advantage of the Democratic candidate over the Republican candidate *increased* in 1980. For liberals, Ford was a more attractive Republican candidate than
Reagan, a conclusion foursquare with common sense.

Table 9.2 is based on data from the Gallup Poll in the period 1952–1980. In constructing it, I have taken into account

[24] *New York Times*, November 5, 1980.
[25] The results of the ABC News election-day poll suggest that Carter's
share of the major-party vote was about the same as the vote that he
would have received if Anderson voters had been forced to choose between Carter and Reagan. In a two-way race the ABC sample would
have given Reagan 56 percent of its votes and Carter 44 percent. Reagan's share of the major-party vote in the election itself was 55 percent
and Carter's 45 per cent.

TABLE 9.2

The Partisan Inclinations of Selected Social and Demographic Groups, 1952–1980

Group	Mean Partisan Inclination 1952–1980	Deviation from Mean Partisan Inclination							
		Eisenhower 1952	Eisenhower 1956	Nixon 1960	Goldwater 1964	Nixon 1968	Nixon 1972	Ford 1976	Reagan 1980
Nonwhite	−34	−1	+15	+16	+1	−4	−15	+1	−11
Democrats	−32	0	−11	−2	+7	−4	+3	+2	+4
Union families	−13	−4	−2	−2	+1	−3	+5	+1	+4
Catholics	−12	+1	+4	−16	−2	−2	+2	+6	+7
Manual labor	−8	−2	0	−2	−2	−1	+3	+1	+2
Grade-school educated	−8	+1	0	+3	+4	−3	−3	+1	−3
Under 30 years	−5	−1	+4	+1	+3	0	−5	+2	−4
East	−3	+2	+5	0	−4	−2	−2	+2	−1
High-school educated	−1	+1	−1	−1	+1	+2	+5	−1	0
Men	−1	−2	−2	−1	+2	+2	+2	−2	+4
30–49 years	−1	−2	−2	−3	−1	−1	+6	+2	+3
South	0	−7	−7	−1	+9	+3	+9	−3	−2
Women	+1	+2	+3	+1	0	−2	−1	+2	−3
Midwest	+1	+2	0	+1	−1	+1	−3	+1	−1
West	+1	+1	−2	0	0	+1	−4	+2	+3
50 years and older	+3	+3	+1	+1	0	+1	−1	−3	−1

White collar	+ 3	+2	+ 3	− 1	+2	+1	− 1	−3	− 2
Whites	+ 3	−2	− 2	− 2	−1	+2	+ 3	+1	+ 2
Protestants	+ 7	+1	− 2	+ 5	−1	+1	+ 1	−9	− 4
College educated	+ 8	+3	+ 3	+ 3	+1	+1	− 7	−1	− 3
Prof. and business	+ 9	0	+ 2	0	−1	+4	− 2	−1	− 1
Independents	+ 9	+1	+ 4	− 2	−3	0	− 2	0	+ 2
Republicans	+39	−3	− 1	+ 6	+2	+1	− 6	+4	− 3

NOTE: The *partisan inclination* of a group in any particular election is the difference between the Republican candidate's share of the group's major-party vote and his share of the national major-party vote, subtracting the latter from the former. A group's *mean partisan inclination* is simply the mean of its partisan inclinations in each of the eight elections from 1952 to 1980. The figures in columns two to nine are the differences derived by subtracting a group's mean partisan inclination from its partisan inclination in the indicated election; thus, negative signs in those columns mean that the group was less inclined toward the candidacy indicated than it was toward Republican candidates on the average, while positive signs have the opposite meaning. All the data that figured in the calculations came from the Gallup Poll except that for regions in 1980, which came from the *New York Times*–CBS News election-day survey.

the two objections just made to Clymer's use of data. The first column shows how distinctive a group's vote was on average during the period, with negative numbers indicating an inclination toward the Democrats and positive numbers an inclination toward the Republicans. The first entry in the column, for instance, shows that Republican candidates' average share of the major-party vote of blacks (or, more precisely, non-whites) was 34 percentage points less than their average share of the major-party vote nationally. Entries in the remaining eight columns show how much more or less distinctive a group's major-party vote was for particular candidates than it was for Republican candidates on the average. Thus, to explain awkwardly but precisely, the first entry in the second column shows that Eisenhower in 1952, relative to his share of the major-party vote among all voters, received one percentage point less of the major-party vote of blacks than Republican candidates did on the average, relative to their share of the national major-party vote. The first entry in the third column shows that Eisenhower's share of the major-party vote of blacks in 1956, relative to his share of the major-party vote nationally, was 15 percentage points greater than Republican candidates' average share of that vote, relative to their share of the national major-party vote. And so on.

The central message of the table is stability in the inclination of groups over the entire period. The pro- and anti-Republican inclination of particular groups for particular candidates is, in most cases, close to the average shown in the first column: Seventy-nine percent of the entries in the eight right-hand columns show a deviation from the average of 3 percentage points or less, and 88 per cent show a deviation of 4 percentage points or less. The largest deviations are mainly localized in five groups: Southerners, blacks, Democrats, Catholics, and Protestants. The candidacies of John F. Kennedy and Jimmy Carter, respectively, probably account for a major amount of the deviation in these last two groups. Groups significantly biased toward one party or the other preserved that bias during the whole period. In only one case (Protestants in 1976) did a group with an average bias of more than 3 percentage points reverse its bias in a particular election. For the whole period also, there are few pronounced trends in the data. Southerners, manual workers, union families, and Catholics show a tendency toward increasing support for the Republicans, while blacks, white-collar workers, the college educated, and those with a grade-school education or less show some increase in support for the Democrats. The election of 1980 does not stand out as exceptional in Table 9.2; certainly, the data reveal nothing like the collapse of the Democratic coalition. The bias of particular groups was close to the average for Republican candidates. In sixteen of the twenty-three groups that bias deviated 3 percentage points or less from the average, and in twenty-one, 4 percentage points or less. There is some depolarization shown in the data; that is, Reagan tended to do better than the average Republican candidate in groups whose average bias since 1952 has been Democratic, and he tended to do worse among groups with an average Republican bias. The largest changes in inclination in 1980 came among Democrats, union families, men and Catholics, changes which benefited Reagan, and among blacks, Protestants, and the young, which worked to his disadvantage. What the "collapse" of the Democratic coalition mainly amounted to, however, was that fewer of its members cast their ballots for a Democratic loser than they have typically cast for Democratic winners. In other words, the Democratic coalition did not really collapse; the biases in voting of those groups which constitute the coalition changed only marginally.[26]

Table 9.2 also suggests the limitations of demographic analysis as an aid to understanding elections. Note that the biases

[26] Table 9.1 does cast an interesting sidelight on Reagan's appeal, however. The signs of the entries in the columns for 1972 and 1980 are the same in all but four cases, indicating that Reagan's performance was above average in the same groups in which Nixon's was above average, and below average in those in which Nixon's was below average. In this specific sense, the appeal of the Republican candidate in 1980 did resemble that of Nixon in his victory over George McGovern, and (note also) was *unlike* that of Eisenhower in 1956 or Nixon in 1960.

of the two explicitly political groups—Democrats and Republicans—dwarf those of all other groups except blacks. Of the
other twenty groups only two (Catholics and union families)
have shown an average bias of 10 or more percentage points,
and ten groups listed have had an average bias of less than 3
percentage points. Blacks and the parties aside, membership
in social and demographic groups is quite weakly related to
voting. The biases of such groups are not trivial in their effect
in particular times and places, but they exert a relatively modest influence on the outcome of most elections.

Thus, the explanatory value of demographic analyses of
voting is not very great. Reports of election results by groups
explain an election's outcome in much the same sense that reports of results state by state do: Given all the particular outcomes in particular groups (or states) in an election, the outcome in the electorate as a whole must be whatever it is. Like
the election results themselves, demographic analyses can
raise interesting questions: Why, for instance, did Catholics
show a greater inclination toward Ford and Reagan than toward any other Republican candidate since 1952? To answer
such a question, however, one must go beyond demography to
examine the beliefs and attitudes that are the immediate de-
terminants of voters' choices.

"A Profound and General Turn to Conservatism"

Except for Barry Goldwater, no presidential candidate for a
long time has been so clearly identified with conservatism as
Ronald Reagan, and, not long before the event, many
doubted that so conservative a candidate could be elected.
The survey evidence available to the press, however, inhibited
the natural inclination to attribute Reagan's victory to a national shift toward conservatism. Those voices of the press
who proclaimed such a shift did so largely without reference
to polling data. Those who paid attention to polls, however,
did not stress ideology or ideological change as a major factor
in Reagan's victory.

A column entitled "Tidal Wave" by Anthony Lewis, the

New York Times's able analyst of public affairs, and a piece entitled "The Anti-Liberal Revolution" in the *National Review*[27] are examples of interpretations of the former sort. In Lewis's view ideological change was the source of Reagan's victory and of the outcome of other races as well:

> What happened in the 1980 election reflected a profound and general turn to conservatism in the country.
>
> Particular issues this year worked to arouse conservative feelings. Abroad, there was the sense of American impotence, symbolized by the hostages in Iran. At home there was economic frustration, especially over the inflation.
>
> But movement to the right began long before 1980. The Republicans would clearly have written [*sic*] the trend to victory four years ago if it had not been interrupted by public revulsion at the crimes of Richard Nixon.[28]

On behalf of its similar thesis, the *National Review* offered no evidence of any kind. In support of his, Lewis cited (1) the results in races for the Senate; (2) Reagan's electoral-vote landslide; (3) a statement of Congressman Richard Cheney that the 1980 returns showed those of 1976 to have been an aberration; (4) the "fact" that Jimmy Carter "won in 1976 only because he was a Southerner, a professed fiscal conservative"[29] and (5) his (Lewis's) personal conviction that "the majority wanted to vote Republican all along this year but had personal doubts about Reagan that he dispelled in the debate."[30]

Lewis's argument is unimpressive just as it stands. In his interpretation of the presidential and senatorial elections he seems to assume, as no experienced analyst should, that voters elected conservative candidates in 1980 primarily for their conservatism and rejected liberal candidates primarily for their liberalism. As John Sears remarked soon after the elec-

[27] November 28, 1980.
[28] *New York Times*, November 6, 1980.
[29] Ibid.
[30] Ibid.

tion, "Obviously, quite a number of the people elected to Congress on Tuesday are more conservative. The question is whether that is what the voters intended."[31] And while the "sweep of the liberal disaster" does indeed suggest "a broader trend,"[32] it does not necessarily follow that the source of the trend was a popular conversion to conservatism; George Will's view, that voters were rebuking the Democratic Party, is an obvious alternative hypothesis.[33] Lewis's other points are even shakier. Congressman Cheney's views are hardly so laden with authority that, absent the grounds for them, they should command our assent. The 1976 election was so close that a great number of things could have given Carter his margin, but no good evidence suggests that his fiscal conservatism and southern origins were indispensable to his victory or that of a Democratic candidate. As argument, personal convictions are unpersuasive.

In postelection news stories ideological interpretations of the election as unqualified as Lewis's were rare.[34] Adam Clymer, for instance, reported that those who voted for Reagan "appear to have been motivated more by dissatisfaction with President Carter than by any serious ideological commitment to the Republican's (Reagan's) views."[35] *Time* reached the same conclusion.[36] In their postelection reports Clymer's colleague Hedrick Smith and F. Richard Ciccone of the *Chicago Tribune* made no mention of ideology as a factor in the election's outcome.[37] The *Washington Post*'s Haynes

[31] *New York Times*, November 9, 1980.

[32] *New York Times*, November 6, 1980.

[33] See the *Washington Post,* November 6 and 13, 1980.

[34] A *Wall Street Journal* editorial attributed Carter's defeat to his gross misjudgment of "the nation's swing to the right" (November 5, 1980), however, and James J. Kilpatrick saw the Senate returns as a repudiation of the "pervasive liberalism" of Carter's party (*New Orleans Times-Picayune*, November 7, 1980). *Newsweek* said, rather ambiguously, that Reagan had "harnessed a tide of time-for-a-change conservatism" (November 17, 1980).

[35] *New York Times*, November 9, 1980.

[36] November 17, 1980.

[37] *New York Times*, November 5, 1980, and *Chicago Tribune*, November 5 and 6, 1980.

Johnson said that it would be premature to read Reagan's triumph "as some sort of ideological mandate,"[38] while David Broder very cautiously observed that there was "perhaps some ideology in Tuesday's voting."[39]

The evidence from press surveys justifies such caution and skepticism, for it contradicts the claims that voters shifted toward conservatism and that this ideological shift elected Reagan. The Gallup Poll found no more voters describing themselves as "right of center" in 1980 than it had in 1976,[40] and Louis Harris noted a decline since 1968 in the proportion of the electorate describing itself as conservative.[41] On some issues a shift toward the conservative side occurred, but none did on other issues that are usually regarded as dividing liberals from conservatives.[42] Many of those who voted for Reagan considered themselves conservatives—estimates ranged from

[38] *Washington Post*, November 9, 1980.

[39] *Washington Post*, November 6, 1980.

[40] Gallup Poll release for November 13, 1980.

[41] ABC News–Harris Survey release for November 11, 1980. In addition, Warren E. Miller, reporting respondents' placement of themselves on the seven-point liberal-conservative scale in the University of Michigan's 1980 National Election Study, observes that "despite the swirl of controversy over the magnitude of the nation's swing to the right, our data give little support to the view that there has been any dramatic change, at least since 1972. The proportions of self-declared liberals and conservatives have remained virtually constant, with at most a gentle drift favoring the conservative position" ("Policy Directions and Presidential Leadership: Alternative Interpretations of the 1980 Presidential Election," paper prepared for delivery at the 1981 Annual Meeting of the American Political Science Association, New York, September 3–6, 1981, p. 7). Data from the 1980 National Election Study also enable one to compare the ideological affiliations of the electorate in 1980 with those in earlier years by means of a liberal-to-conservative index, constructed from responses to thermometer questions in national election study surveys. See Warren E. Miller, Arthur H. Miller, and Edward J. Schneider, *American National Election Studies Sourcebook*, 1952–1978 (Cambridge: Harvard University Press, 1980), p. 95. By this measure, the proportion of voters who were conservative increased substantially between 1964 and 1980, though not between 1970 and 1980. This comparison is suspect, however, because the wording of thermometer questions in 1968 and before differed from that after 1968.

[42] Gallup Poll release for November 13, 1980.

40 to 55 percent—but many did not.[43] Some 29 percent of
self-designated conservatives did not vote for Reagan, while
over one-quarter of all liberals did.[44] And even his conservative supporters did not necessarily vote for Reagan's conservatism. Given ten statements describing reasons for their
choice and asked to check the two most important, only 11
percent of Reagan's supporters in the *Times*-CBS election-day
poll checked, "He's a real conservative."[45]

Survey evidence does support the editorial observation of
the *Los Angeles Times* that conservatives gave Reagan a base
of support, though not his victory,[46] but the nature of the evidence produced by the press's polls makes assessment of the
size of that base difficult. Voters' ideological affiliations interest observers of politics mainly because they are thought to
summarize voters' positions on a range of policy issues, to indicate a general orientation which governs attitudes toward
many specific matters of controversy. So conceived, the ideological positions of voters become an economical way to describe their motivations, and a movement across ideological
lines of any sizable group of voters is an event with wide rami-
fications for political action. There is a difference, however,
between what is posited by this conception of ideology and
what is measured by asking people whether they are liberals
or conservatives (the most common way of ascertaining their
ideological affiliations), for in fact the relationship is quite
weak between the positions that voters take on specific issues
and the ideological labels that they apply to themselves. In the
words of one recent study,

 . . . there was a modest relationship, both in 1972 and
 1976, between ideological location and several statements

[43] The higher estimate comes from the ABC News election-day survey,
the lowest ones from the *New York Times*-CBS News election-day survey
and the ABC News–Harris Survey of October 22 to November 3, 1980.
[44] *New York Times*–CBS News election-day poll. The comparable figures
from the ABC News election-day survey were 29 percent and 23 percent and
from the NBC News-Associated Press election-day survey, 24 percent and 27
percent.
[45] *New York Times*, November 9, 1980.
[46] November 5, 1980.

of policy preferences. The correlations with issue positions are also reasonably stable across the same period. At the same time, the correlations are of a relatively modest magnitude; they are certainly too small to warrant the conclusion that ideological location is simply a summary of policy preferences.[47]

Partisanship seems to be one reason for the weak correlation between self-designated ideological affiliation and preferences on policy issues: ". . . Republican liberals are more likely to see conservatives as closer to their own issue positions than are Democratic liberals, and Republican conservatives are more likely than Democratic conservatives to see conservatives as closer to their own issue positions."[48] Another reason for the relative weakness of the correlation is that different people give different meanings to ideological labels. Some of those who call themselves liberals or conservatives, for instance, construe those terms very narrowly, or give them meanings opposite the usual ones, or even give them no meaning at all. Others may use them in a way that is sensible linguistically but not politically, like the respondent to a *New York Times*–CBS News survey who counted herself a conservative—"I don't butt into people's business. I don't go out and bar-hop. I dress conservatively"—but favored governmental payments for abortions, safety regulations for factories, and efforts to provide jobs and low-cost housing.[49] The self-declared conservatism of a very substantial portion of the Reagan voters as revealed by surveys cannot, therefore, be equated with issue-based conservatism, nor does the relatively high correlation between ideological position and voting[50]

[47] Warren E. Miller and Teresa E. Levitin, "Ideological Interpretations of Presidential Elections," *American Political Science Review* 73 (September 1979), p. 766.

[48] Ibid., p. 767.

[49] *New York Times*, January 22, 1978.

[50] This high correlation does not, however, enable one to account well statistically for the way the electorate votes. In 1972, for instance, University of Michigan interviewers asked each respondent to locate himself and the candidates on a seven-point scale ranging from extremely liberal to extremely conservative. If one takes a vote for the candidate that a re-

imply an equally high correlation between voting and the positions on issues that journalists, scholars, and political activists commonly associate with liberalism and conservatism.

These limitations of self-labeling as a measure of ideological orientation make attractive another way of proceeding, which is to examine the consistency of voters' opinions on issues that observers of politics associate with liberal-conservative differences. Philip Converse has used such a procedure[51] and so, more recently, have Norman Nie and his associates.[52] The approach is attractive in concept because it focuses directly on what most analysts of elections want to summarize by invoking ideology—voters' views on issues of policy.

Thus far, the approach has failed to show ideological thinking to be widespread in the electorate or strongly related to voting. While Nie and his associates found a high average correlation (gamma coefficient) between voters' opinions on selected pairs of issues in the elections of 1964, 1968, and 1972,[53] that finding does not count heavily for the thesis that

---

spondent placed nearest his own position as an indication of ideological voting, the votes of 51 percent of those respondents who voted could be counted as ideological. In the same year 67 percent of all votes were "partisan" in the same sense, that is, were cast by voters voting consistently with their partisan identification. The accuracy of predictions from ideological affiliation in 1972 was quite high—85 percent—but only 60 percent of the responses permitted any prediction, either because respondents saw no ideological difference between the candidates or because they confessed to not having thought much about where to place themselves on the scale. This kind of test also exaggerates the apparent amount of ideological voting because it takes no account of projection, that is, of the tendency of some voters to attribute their own ideological position to the candidate they favor for other reasons.

[51] In "The Nature of Belief Systems in Mass Publics."

[52] See Norman H. Nie and Kristi Andersen, "Mass Belief Systems Revisited: Political Change and Attitude Structure," *Journal of Politics* 36 (1974), pp. 540–587; Norman H. Nie, Sidney Verba, and John R. Petrocik, *The Changing American Voter,* enlarged edition (Cambridge: Harvard University Press, 1979); and Norman H. Nie and James N. Rabjohn, "Revisiting Mass Belief Systems Revisited: Or, Doing Research Is Like Watching a Tennis Match," *American Journal of Political Science* 23 (February 1979), pp. 139–175.

[53] Nie, Verba, and Petrocik, *The Changing American Voter,* pp. 124–137.

ideological thought is common. Comparison of opinions on issues, two at a time, is an extremely weak test of consistency on a range of issues; indeed, as Nie and Rabjohn acknowledge, the existence of a "unidimensional liberal-conservative attitude continuum" cannot be confirmed by such a test.[54] More to the point is the "index of attitude consistency" featured in *The Changing American Voter*, which summarizes the consistency of voters' opinions on a number of issues simultaneously,[55] but the use made of the index there casts no light on actual levels of consistency. For Nie and his associates, voters with "coherent issue positions" in any given year are those whose consistency—however great it was—put them in the most liberal or most conservative third of all voters in the period 1952–1972.[56] Moreover, the index is a relatively poor predictor of voting. In the elections from 1956 to 1972, the correspondence between voting and ideological position as measured by the index was greatest in 1964, when 73 percent of those respondents with "coherent issue positions" voted in accordance with them.[57] In the same year 83 percent of those who identified with one of the major parties (or said that they leaned toward one) voted consistently with that identification. Party in fact outpredicted ideology in every year for which *The Changing American Voter* reported results and did so, of course, for a greater proportion of the total electorate.[58]

Clearly, ideology informs the political views of some voters and so enters into voting, but ideology, like demography, explains poorly what has been happening in recent elections,

[54] Nie and Rabjohn, "Revisiting Mass Belief Systems Revisited," p. 159.

[55] For an account of the index's construction, see Nie, Verba, and Petrocik, *The Changing American Voter*, appendix 2B, pp. 400–402.

[56] Ibid., pp. 294, 296.

[57] Ibid., p. 297.

[58] The proportion of respondents with coherent issue positions ranged from 61 percent in 1956 to 73 percent in 1968 (see ibid., p. 294); the proportion of those with a partisan identification in the same period (1956–1972) averaged 92 percent. I am including in the count of partisans those independents who said that they "leaned" toward one of the major parties.

though for a different reason. No clear set of facts exists about the extent and nature of voters' ideological affiliations in recent elections or about the relationship of such affiliations to voting. What the press and many others have been measuring is not issue-relevant ideology, and issue-relevant ideology has yet to find its appropriate measures.

A Referendum on the Economy

Particular issues figured prominently in many election stories, among them the adequacy of Carter's leadership, the economy, the hostages in Iran, "cultural anxieties,"[59] national defense, Carter's attacks on Reagan, and the alleged decline of American prestige abroad. To evaluate this aspect of press coverage issue by issue would be extremely tedious. It is also unnecessary; not many *kinds* of evidence were involved. I shall look in detail only at the press's treatment of economic issues. These were seen by many as important to Reagan's victory and by some as the key to it. The *Christian Science Monitor,* for example, said that the "1980 results appear uniquely tied to economic performance."[60] Joseph Kraft called inflation "the big issue in the campaign,"[61] and the *Chicago Tribune* declared that "in simple terms, Carter's economic failures caused his defeat."[62]

What were the grounds for such judgments? Did economic issues enter into most voters' choices? Did other issues figure less? Was opinion more lopsided on economic issues than on others? Did economic issues add greatly to Reagan's margin of victory? Would there have been a Reagan victory without them? As we shall see, unequivocal answers to some of these questions are hard to extract from any information that the press either presented or had at hand.

Most political reporters were probably persuaded quite early and for good reason that economic problems would have

[59] The phrase is George Will's *(Washington Post,* November 6, 1980).
[60] November 10, 1980.
[61] *Washington Post,* November 9, 1980.
[62] November 6, 1980.

a powerful impact on the outcome of the 1980 election. The "misery index"—a term Carter had used in 1976 to refer to the sum of the rates of inflation and unemployment—had climbed sharply since his inauguration. That fact could hardly help him, particularly when Carter's opponents were continually reminding voters of it. Reagan made inflation and joblessness the keynote of his challenge, as Senator Edward Kennedy had in his bid for the Democratic nomination.

A considerable body of research also testifies to the normal potency of economic issues in elections. Several careful studies have shown a strong relationship between the division of the vote in congressional and presidential elections and changes in real income from election to election.[63] A similarly strong relationship has held between voting and responses to some kinds of questions about the personal finances of voters; in general, the more politically pointed the question, the stronger is the relationship, as Table 9.3 shows. In that table the responses to questions one, two, and four show a relatively weak association between economic situation and voting. That result should not be surprising, because one can easily be better or worse off financially without seeing government as at fault. Questions three and five produced strikingly different results: The right-hand column shows that, on the average, 88 percent of those who associated a better or worse economic future with the outcome of the election voted in line with that conviction.[64] Of course the electoral impact of such perceptions will vary with the number who share them. Thus, evidence of the potency of pocketbook issues in past elections tells us nothing specific about their potency in 1980.

[63] See particularly Gerald Kramer, "Short-Term Fluctuations in U.S. Voting Behavior, 1896–1964," *American Political Science Review* (March 1971), pp. 131–143; and Edward R. Tufte, *Political Control of the Economy* (Princeton: Princeton University Press, 1978).

[64] Note, however, that this result may exaggerate the correspondence between responses and voting, since some respondents without a strong conviction on the issue raised by these questions may simply name the party for which they intend to vote.

TABLE 9.3

**Voting and Responses to Questions about
the Voter's Financial Situation
(data from the elections of 1960, 1964, and 1972)**

Question	% of Cases Predicted 1960 1964	% of Cases Predicted Correctly 1960 1964	% of Predictions That Are Correct 1960 1964
1. So far as you and your family are concerned, would you say that you are pretty well satisfied with your present financial situation, more-or-less satisfied, or not satisfied at all?	58.7 59.7	34.7 35.3	59.2 59.1
2. During the last few years, has your financial situation been getting better, getting worse, or has it stayed the same?	53.0 61.0	31.4 36.7	59.1 60.2
3. Do you think it will make any difference in how you and your family get along financially whether the Republicans or Democrats win the election?	34.8 32.5	30.9 30.3	88.8 93.1
	1972	*1972*	*1972*
4. Would you say that you (and your family) are better or worse off financially than you were a year ago?	48.2	29.5	61.3

TABLE 9.3 (Continued)

Question	% of Cases Predicted 1972	% of Cases Predicted Correctly 1972	% of Predictions That Are Correct 1972
5. Looking ahead again, do you think that your family would get along better financially in the next four years if the Democrats or the Republicans win the election, or wouldn't it make much difference?	42.3	34.9	82.6

RULES FOR PREDICTION:
Question 1: If "pretty well satisfied," predict a vote for the party of the incumbent president; if "not satisfied at all," predict a vote for the opposition party.

Question 2: If "getting better," predict a vote for the party of the incumbent president; if "getting worse," predict a vote for the opposition party.

Questions 3, 5: Predict a Republican or Democratic vote as indicated by the respondent.

Question 4: If "better off," predict a vote for the party of the incumbent president; if "worse off," predict a vote for the opposition party.

The Salience of Economic Issues

For how many voters in 1980 were economic issues a consideration? In the press one sort of evidence of their salience came from responses to a free-answer question that asked voters to name "the most important problem facing this country today." In early October a Gallup column featured data produced by this question, and after the election a *New York Times* story which stressed the importance of economic issues in Reagan's victory noted that "seventy-three per cent of the

TABLE 9.4

**National Problems and Voting in the Elections
of 1960, 1964, and 1968**

Question: What would you personally feel are the most important problems the government should try to take care of when the new President and Congress take office in January? Who do you think would be the most likely to do what you want on this, the Democrats, the Republicans, or wouldn't there be any difference?"

Responses:	*1960*	*1964*	*1968*
Percent of cases which permit a prediction	75.2	66.7	72.7
Percent of cases correctly predicted	67.2	60.3	59.8
Percent of predictions that are correct	89.4	90.4	82.2

PREDICTIVE RULE: Predict that the voter will vote for the party he sees as most likely to take care of the problem he mentions first, unless he sees no difference between the parties in that regard; in which case predict a vote for the party he sees most likely to take care of the problem he mentions next, unless he sees no difference between the parties; and so on.

NOTE: The question quoted above is from the 1960 survey; similar but not identical questions were asked in the other two. In all three surveys respondents were encouraged to name up to three problems. The sizes of the samples varied from 1,207 to 1,406.

public now calls the economy the nation's greatest problem."[65]

Many students of voting regard responses to the "most important problem" question as one of the best measures of the salience of issues in the repertory of survey research; certainly, it is reasonable to suppose that voting reflects voters' assessments of how well the candidates and parties will deal with the nation's greatest problem. The Gallup Poll has used the question for a long time, and the University of Michigan's Center for Political Studies has used variants of it in several of

[65] *New York Times,* November 16, 1980. Some 40 percent of the public had cited inflation as the most important problem, about 10 percent unemployment, and the rest some other economic problem.

its national election studies. Table 9.4 shows the results produced by applying a predictive rule to responses to the question in the Michigan studies of 1960, 1964, and 1968. The rule
yields quite accurate predictions for those voters whose answers permit one: For the three elections, an average of 87
percent of all predictions are correct.

But remember that the *New York Times*'s story told us how
many voters called some economic problem "most important," *not* how many saw a candidate as likely (or more likely
than his opponents) to handle that problem to their satisfac-
tion.[66] The distinction is important, for, as Table 9.5 demonstrates, more voters in 1980 saw economic problems as worrisome than saw the election as a way out of them.[67] When
asked the first question quoted there, 10 to 12 percent of the
respondents failed to name one of the candidates as better
able to handle the economy. That question's prefatory "if you
had to choose," moreover, nudges respondents toward a
choice. When explicitly asked either to name a candidate or to
say that they saw little difference among them, as in the table's
second question, 30 percent or more failed to name a candidate. Questions three and four reveal an even larger proportion who may have seen the problem but not the solution.
Thus, the datum cited in the *Times*'s story cannot be taken to
indicate the number of voters who took account of economic
issues in making their choices among the candidates, and
Table 9.5 suggests that the proportion who did so could have
been considerably below 73 percent.

The evidence of the table is inconclusive, however, because,
in another way, the *Times*'s use of the "most important problem" question might have led to an underestimation of the salience of economic issues. Interpreting that question literally,

[66] In the survey on which the story relied, this question was not asked,
though it had been in earlier *Times*-CBS surveys.

[67] That they should have done so was of course to be expected. In the
Michigan national election studies that were the source of the data for
Table 9.3, from 39 to 54 percent of all respondents named a problem as
most important but failed to name one of the parties as "most likely to do
what you want" about the problem.

TABLE 9.5

**Perceptions of Differences in the Ability of Candidates
to Handle Economic Problems**

Question: "Now, if you had to choose between Ronald Reagan,
Jimmy Carter and John Anderson, which one do you feel would
do a better job of handling the economy?"

Responses:	11/2	10/29-30	10/22-24	10/14-16	9/22
None	2%	2%	3%	2%	3%
Not sure	8	6	9	8	9

Source: ABC News–Harris Survey releases of October 2, October 23, November 2, and November 4, 1980.

Question: "Which candidate—Reagan, Carter or Anderson—do you
think would do the best job of solving the nation's economic
problems, or don't you see much difference between the candidates on this?"

Responses:	10/22-24	10/8-10	9/22-24
Not sure	5%	6%	6%
No difference	25	26	26

Source: NBC News–Associated Press Poll releases of September 30, October 13, and October 28, 1980.

Question: "Do you think that if (Ronald Reagan, Jimmy Carter) is
elected President in 1980, the economy will get better, get worse,
or stay about the same?"

Responses:	10/30-11/1	10/16-20	9/23-25	9/10-14
Don't know to either question	14%	12%	10%	12%
Expectations the same for both candidates	26	27	24	25

Source: CBS News–*New York Times* Surveys for the dates noted. The data derive from a cross-tabulation of responses to two questions, one about Carter,
the other about Reagan.

TABLE 9.5 (Continued)

Question: "Do you think the President has the power to solve the nation's economic problems, or are the economic problems too complicated for any President to solve?"

Responses:	*10/8-10*
Not sure	5%
Problems too complicated	66

Source: NBC News–Associated Press Poll release of October 13, 1980.

---

interviewers for the *Times*-CBS survey recorded only one problem for each respondent. The Gallup Poll, which allowed respondents to name more than one, found a greater number of voters concerned with economic issues,[68] and it is easy to see a possible reason for that finding. A voter most concerned about inflation may be almost equally concerned about unemployment (or taxes) and as ready to take account of it in voting; given a chance he will name both problems. Moreover, the problem that emerges from the *Times*-CBS procedure as most important to a plurality of voters need not be most important in any other sense. Specifically, it need not be the problem with the widest impact on voting: Just as a candidate

[68] In September the *Times*-CBS poll asked the "problems" question in two separate surveys. In the first, 63 percent of the respondents called some economic problem most important; in the second, 62 percent did so. Sandwiched between these two surveys was one by Gallup in which 77 percent of those interviewed called either "unemployment" or "inflation/the high cost of living" the most important problem. Differences in what the two polling organizations regarded as economic problems cannot explain this substantial difference; Gallup's definition was less expansive than the *Times*'s. While sampling error may account for part of the discrepancy, Gallup's allowing of multiple responses seems the likely source of much of it, especially since a similar procedure in the University of Michigan's 1980 National Election Study produced similar results. In that study, interviewers recorded up to three "most important problems" per respondent and found (in November) that 30 percent of all respondents named unemployment, 54 percent inflation, 11 percent taxes and government spending, and 21 percent other economic problems. (See Miller, "Policy Directions and Presidential Leadership," table 12.)

TABLE 9.6

Reasons Offered for Choices of Candidates

Question: "What would you say was the single most important reason you had for voting for [your choice of candidate]?"

Responses:

Reason	% Mentioning Reason
Time for a change	11
The economy	9
He was the best candidate	8
Dissatisfaction with Carter	8
Dissatisfaction with Reagan	8

Source: CBS News–*New York Times* survey of November 7–12, 1980. Sample
was 1,857 respondents who were registered and voted for president.

Question: "What was the MAIN REASON why you voted for Reagan—
that is, why do you think he was the best man?"

Responses:

Reason	% Mentioning Reason
Dissatisfied with Carter	22
Need a change	21
Like Reagan's economic policies	17
Like Reagan's policies	14

Source: Gallup Poll survey of November 7–10, 1980, as reported in the Gallup
Poll release of December 7, 1980. Sample was of 1,556 adults.

could be everyone's second choice but the first choice of no
one, so more voters might share a secondary concern than
would agree on the primacy of any particular problem.

Table 9.6 reports the most frequent responses to a second
free-answer question designed to elicit voters' motivations.
This one asked respondents to state their "main" or "most
important" reason for voting as they did. Anyone who might
want to minimize the role of economic issues in 1980 would
surely call attention to these data. Less than 10 percent of
those respondents who voted gave the economy as the reason

for their choice of candidates and less than 20 percent of those who voted for Reagan did so.

This question is even more likely to lead to an underestimate of an issue's salience, however, than the one just discussed. As a response to the "most important problem" question, economic problems competed only with other problems—the danger of war, for instance, or the Iranian crisis—to achieve the status of "most important." To be named the "main reason," economic issues had to compete with the full range of other possible motivations. Moreover, the "main reason" question encourages vague, uninterpretable responses. Depending on how we are asked, we may give either a relatively specific set of reasons for an action or one or more very general ones. This kind of question pushes the respondent in the latter direction: "I didn't like Carter's economic policies, his religiosity, and his inability to get the hostages home" may thus become an ambiguous "I didn't like Carter" or "it's time for a change." We do not know, and cannot, how many of those who voted for a change or out of dissatisfaction with one of the candidates—among the most frequent responses to the "reason" question—may have been motivated in part by economic issues. Just as the best may be the enemy of the good, in this case the search for the most important hampers the search for the important.

The questions quoted in Table 9.7 (I shall call them *list* questions) were a third approach that the press took to assessing the salience of issues. The data that appear in the table were widely quoted. The *Washington Post*'s David Broder, for example, reported that "The ABC News poll . . . showed that 31 per cent of the voters thought government spending an important problem,"[69] while an Associated Press dispatch noted that "more voters mentioned inflation as the reason for their vote than any other topic . . . the second most important reason, the voters said, is strengthening America's position in the world."[70] The *New York Times, Newsweek,* the *Los Angeles Times,* the *Wall Street Journal,* and *Time* all drew upon data

[69] *Washington Post*, November 6, 1980.
[70] *New Orleans Times-Picayune*, November 5, 1980.

TABLE 9.7

Economic Issues in Exit Poll Lists

Question: Please put a checkmark next to the 1 or 2 issues where you MOST LIKED the stand of the presidential candidate you voted for: (CHECK A MAXIMUM OF 2 BOXES)

Government spending	( )	Equal Rights Amendment	
Foreign affairs	( )	(ERA)	( )
Inflation	( )	Problems of the poor	
U.S. military strength	( )	and elderly	( )
Tax cuts	( )	Energy	( )
		Abortion	( )

Responses:

Government spending	31%	Foreign affairs	25%
Inflation	22		
Tax cuts	19		

Source: ABC News General Election Exit Poll, November 4, 1980. The sample consisted of 11,250 voters.

Question: Which Issues Were Most Important in Deciding How You Voted Today? (CHECK UP TO 2 BOXES)

Balancing the federal		E.R.A./abortion	( )
budget	( )	Inflation and the economy	( )
Crisis in Iran	( )	Needs of the big cities	( )
Jobs and unemployment	( )	U.S. prestige around the	
Reducing federal income		world	( )
taxes	( )		

Responses:

Balancing the federal		U.S. prestige around the	
budget	21%	world	16%
Jobs and unemployment	24		
Reducing federal income			
taxes	10		
Inflation and the			
economy	33		

Source: CBS News–*New York Times* Exit Poll of November 4, 1980. The sample consisted of 12,782 voters.

TABLE 9.7 (Continued)

Question: Which one or two of the following issues were MOST important when you decided for whom you would vote for President? (MULTIPLE RESPONSES ACCEPTED)

Reducing unemployment	( )	Handling relations with Iran and the Arab countries	( )
Strengthening America's position in the world	( )		
Cutting federal taxes	( )	Controlling inflation	( )
Standing up for basic American values	( )	Insuring peace	( )

Responses:

Reducing unemployment	16%	Strengthening America's position in the world	33%
Cutting federal taxes	12		
Controlling inflation	38		

Source: NBC News–Associated Press Exit Poll of November 4, 1980. The sample consisted of 11,629 voters.

---

produced by one or more of the lists in Table 9.7 or by others with a similar format.

These data have some common features. *Some* economic issue was the item most frequently checked in each list—inflation in two cases, government spending in one. (For purposes of comparison, the percentage of respondents picking the leading noneconomic item appears in each panel of the table.) Among economic issues, tax cuts were the least frequently checked in all three lists, and, in the two in which unemployment and inflation both appeared, the latter was checked with considerably greater frequency than the former.

To doubt the accuracy of the data in Table 9.7, however, it is sufficient to look at them and to consider how they were produced. At least, that should suffice. The proportion who checked a given topic varies greatly from list to list: That for taxes, from 10 to 19 percent; for inflation, from 22 to 38 percent; for unemployment, from 16 to 24 percent. Sampling error should not be the source of variations of this magnitude, since all three samples were huge and well drawn. It seems clear, rather, that the number of respondents who picked any particular item depended to some unknown degree on what else they could pick. In the ABC survey, for example, the counterparts of those who checked unemployment on the other lists had no place to go but to some other issue or to no response. It is probably true also that all three lists presented fewer items to Carter voters descriptive of their motives than was the case for Reagan voters. If so, the answers of Carter voters may easily have inflated the apparent salience of some issues. For instance, did the difference between the NBC–Associated Press and *Times*-CBS figures for unemployment arise in part because the former list offered "insuring peace" as an option while the latter did not? Like responses to the "most important problem" question, those to list questions may overstate and understate salience simultaneously. The lists both *prompt* the respondent *and* limit the number of issues that he can name; the lists also ignore the possibility that issues may figure negatively in a decision, inclining a voter against the candidate for whom he votes or for a candidate for whom he does not.[71]

What can one conclude from the evidence just reviewed about the extent to which economic issues entered into voters' choices in 1980? About 10 percent of all respondents gave "the economy" as the main reason for their choice of candidates. At least 44 percent checked one or more economic issues as "most important" in deciding their vote in the *New York Times*-CBS News exit poll, and over 70 percent saw some economic issue as the "nation's most important problem." These data, none of which was produced by a procedure well calculated to measure salience, leave the analyst great freedom to emphasize or deemphasize the role of economic issues in 1980 as his hunches—or preconceptions—dictate.

[71] This latter objection applies with less force to the ABC News list than to the others that appear in Table 9.6, since ABC also invited respondents to indicate their dislikes of each of the candidates by checking items from its list. This procedure did not wholly meet my objection, however, since respondents could express likes only about the candidate for whom they voted.

The Bias of Economic Issues

Uncertainty about the salience of economic issues in 1980 necessarily casts doubt on press estimates of how greatly economic issues favored Reagan. Press surveys tell us how voters divided, but not the balance of opinion among those who actually took economic issues into account in their voting. Let us set this point aside for a moment, however, and review briefly the bias of economic issues among survey respondents generally. One can summarize as follows:

(1) *The economy as an issue had a large pro-Reagan bias, though far from a total one.* Two surveys taken near election day, one by ABC News and Louis Harris, the other by the *New York Times* and CBS News, supply the best evidence for this view. Calling the "economic issue" one of the two "key elements" working for a Reagan victory, Harris reported that "by a substantial 50–27 percent, Reagan is viewed as doing 'a better job [than Carter] of handling the economy,' the first Republican in modern times to win the economic issue decisively."[72] The *Times* story carried a similar message: "The economy, as it had been all fall, remained Mr. Carter's greatest problem. Thirty-one per cent of those polled said they feared it would get worse if the President was re-elected."[73] Table 9.8 shows the data on which these statements were based.

If we ask *how much* Reagan was preferred to Carter as a manager of the economy, the figures in the first panel of that table give an apparently straightforward answer: Of those who chose either Reagan or Carter, 65 percent chose Reagan. As presented, the data in the second panel fail to tell us Reagan's advantage. They report answers to two questions in which a respondent might either have associated a better economic future with a candidate *or* have predicted the same future with both, and one cannot tell from the table how many

[72] ABC News–Harris Survey release of November 4, 1980.
[73] *New York Times*, November 3, 1980.

TABLE 9.8

The Economy as an Issue:
Responses from Two Late Preelection Surveys

Question: "Now, if you had to choose between Ronald Reagan, Jimmy Carter, and John Anderson, which one do you feel would do a better job of handling the economy?"

Responses:	*Reagan*	*Carter*	*Anderson*
	50%	27%	13%

Source: ABC News–Harris Survey of November 2, released November 4, 1980.

Question: "Do you think that if (Ronald Reagan, Jimmy Carter) is elected President in 1980, the economy will get better, get worse, or stay about the same?"

Responses:	*Reagan*	*Carter*
Economy will:		
Get better	38%	19%
Get worse	20	31
Stay the same	31	42

Source: CBS News–*New York Times* Survey of October 30–November 1, 1980.

---

did which. Cross-tabulation of responses yields that information,[74] however, and shows that 60 percent of the respondents clearly preferred one candidate to the other and that 66 percent of these preferred Reagan. Thus, the two surveys give about the same result.[75]

[74] I am grateful to Michael Kagay for providing the cross-tabulation.
[75] In several surveys, Reagan was consistently preferred as a manager of the economy over the course of the general election campaign. The questions in Table 9.7 were asked several times, and, though the candidates had their ups and downs, the advantage for Reagan was clear each time. It was clear also in answer to questions about the economy in NBC News–Associated Press and *Newsweek* surveys. In mid-October a poll for *Time*, however, found more confidence in Carter than in Reagan "when it comes to dealing with the economy," and by an appreciable margin. (See *Time*, November 3, 1980.)

(2) *Inflation as an issue had a larger pro-Reagan bias than economic issues generally or than unemployment, taxes, and spending, specifically.* In its election-day survey ABC News gave voters a chance to check up to two issues from a list,[76] indicating on which of them they most disliked the stands of each of the candidates. Thirty-seven percent of the sample checked inflation for Carter, only 5 percent for Reagan, yielding an apparent Carter disadvantage of more than seven to one. For government spending the count was Carter, 27 percent, and Reagan, 9 percent, a disadvantage for Carter of three to one; and on tax cuts Carter had a slight advantage—10 percent of the sample disliked his position, while 11 percent disliked Reagan's. Data collected earlier permit a direct comparison of the bias of inflation and unemployment as issues (see Table 9.9) and show Reagan to have had a greater advantage on the former than on the latter. The Gallup data show an edge for Reagan on inflation of three to two, and on unemployment an edge of six to five. In the NBC News–Associated Press data, the comparable ratios are two to one and three to two.

How seriously can one take these indications of Reagan's advantage on economic issues? Unfortunately, all are suspect, those from ABC News because of the shortcomings of list questions, the rest because closed-ended questions draw answers from respondents who do not care about the issue posed or do not care about it *as voters.* For those estimates which were based on evidence derived from the latter sort of question, however, one can make a reasonable guess about the probable direction of error: The estimates of Reagan's advantage were too low.

Consider those questions which asked respondents to say which candidate they preferred as manager of the economy. The large number of voters who considered the economy the nation's foremost problem argues that few of those who saw a difference between the candidates regarded that difference as irrelevant to voting, though some may have. Those who saw no such difference but still named a candidate, probably a

---

[76] The same list that appears in Table 9.6.

TABLE 9.9

Differences in Opinion on Inflation and Unemployment

Question: "This card lists various problems with which the man elected president this November will have to deal. Regardless of which man you happen to prefer—Carter, Reagan or Anderson—please tell me which one you, yourself, feel would do a better job of handling each of the following problems."

| Responses: | Man Who Would Do the Better Job of Handling: | |
	Inflation	*Unemployment*
Reagan	44%	41%
Carter	28	32
Anderson	14	14

Source: Gallup Poll Release of October 26, 1980. The sample consisted of 1,768 likely voters, and interviews were conducted in person September 1–15 and October 10–12, 1980.

Questions: "Which candidate—Ronald Reagan, Jimmy Carter or John Anderson—do you think would do the best job solving the nation's inflation problems, or don't you see much difference between the candidates on this?"

"Which candidate—Ronald Reagan, Jimmy Carter or John Anderson—do you think would do the best job solving the nation's unemployment problems, or don't you see much difference between the candidates on this?"

Responses:	Best Job on Inflation	Best Job on Unemployment
Reagan	39%	33%
Carter	16	20
Anderson	10	9

Source: NBC News–Associated Press Poll release of September 30, 1980. The sample consisted of 1,512 likely voters, and interviews were conducted by telephone on September 22-24, 1980.

larger group, are likely either to have named a candidate randomly or to have named the one they preferred on other grounds, more probably the latter. Responses of the first sort would have depressed estimates of the issue's bias toward Reagan. So would those of the second sort, since Reagan enjoyed a larger apparent advantage on economic issues than he did as a choice for president.

This reasoning can be tested. The two questions in Table 9.10 raise the same issue but differ in one important respect: The second is better designed to encourage respondents who see no difference between candidates to identify themselves. The two questions were included in surveys taken at about the same time on three different occasions. If the reasoning just set forth is correct, responses to the second question should show a greater advantage for Reagan than those to the first. And uniformly they do, in two cases markedly. The unprompted responses to the likes-dislikes questions in the University of Michigan's 1980 National Election Study show a still greater advantage for Reagan. In that study 53 percent of all respondents who voted mentioned one or more economic issues as something they liked or disliked about the candidates or parties.[77] Of those respondents, 79 percent saw those issues as favoring Reagan. Almost 90 percent of those who raised the issue of inflation counted it for Reagan. Reagan's advantage on economic issues was not only great but very great.

Weakly Committed Voters

None of the evidence examined so far tells us how much economic issues helped to bring weakly committed voters into the Reagan fold, adding to his vote at the margin. Many reports paid little attention to this question, but some did address it. The methods used to identify marginal voters were reasonable in the circumstances: The *New York Times*'s Adam Clymer examined the salience and bias of issues among voters who, in

---

[77] I have counted as references to economic issues all references to inflation, unemployment, taxes, monetary policy, government spending, the federal budget, and the election's impact on wages, salaries, and income.

TABLE 9.10
How "No Difference" Can Make a Difference

Question: "Now, if you had to choose between Ronald Reagan, Jimmy Carter and John Anderson, which one do you feel would do a better job of handling the economy?"

Responses:

Date of Survey	Reagan	Carter	Anderson	None, not sure	Reagan Advantage Economy	Vote Pref.
10/22–24	47%	28%	13%	12%	62.7%	51.7%
10/14–16	48	30	12	10	61.5	51.9
9/22	45	27	16	12	62.5	52.2

Source: ABC News–Harris Survey releases of October 2, October 23, and November 2, 1980.

Question: "Which candidate—Reagan, Carter or Anderson—do you think would do the best job of solving the nation's economic problems, or don't you see much difference between the candidates on this?"

Responses:

Date of Survey	Reagan	Carter	Anderson	None, not sure	Reagan Advantage Economy	Vote Pref.
10/22–24	39%	21%	10%	30%	65.0%	53.8%
10/8–10	43	17	8	32	71.7	55.1
9/22–24	44	18	10	32	69.0	56.0

Source: NBC News–Associated Press Poll releases of September 30, October 13, and October 28, 1980.

NOTE: The *Reagan advantage* is the percentage of the respondents who favor Reagan, of those who favor either Reagan or Carter.

the four days before November 4, had changed their minds either about the candidate they preferred or about voting at all. For those who made their decisions late, ABC News and the Gallup Poll did the same, the latter more extensively than the former. The Gallup organization, both for the Gallup Poll and for *Newsweek*, also examined the preferences and views of uncommitted and "soft" voters, the latter being defined as "those who qualify their presidential choice by indicating that they only moderately support their candidate and at the same time are only moderately opposed to his opponents."[78] These ways of identifying weakly committed voters do not identify precisely the same people, but probably come close to doing so. In the *New York Times*–CBS News election-day survey, for example, only 12 percent of those who had made their decisions in the last week of the campaign said that they strongly favored the candidate of their choice.

The evidence from these sources suggests that the salience and bias of economic issues were about as great among marginal voters as among voters generally. Clymer reported that

> about one registered voter in five changed his or her mind about whom to vote for, or whether to vote at all, in the last four days of the Presidential campaign, and about three-fifths of that group made a change that hurt President Carter. . . . Economic arguments were cited most frequently by those who switched in a way that helped Mr. Reagan. About a third of them said either that the economy was the reason for their change or that it was the greatest failure of Mr. Carter's term.[79]

Newsweek found that "lightly committed" voters—a quarter of Carter's adherents and a fifth of Reagan's—did "not differ much from voters generally in their views on the candidates' capabilities or their stands on issues."[80] The proportion of soft and undecided voters in the *Newsweek* poll who named either Carter or Reagan as the candidate best able to deal with inflation was somewhat smaller than that among registered voters as a whole, but the issue's pro-Reagan bias among such voters was somewhat greater. The lightly committed also had about the same amount of confidence in the ability of each of the major-party candidates to handle the economy as did all

[78] Gallup Poll release of October 5, 1980.
[79] *New York Times*, November 16, 1980.
[80] *Newsweek*, November 3, 1980.

registered voters. The *New York Times*–CBS News election-day poll found that voters who had made their choice in the week before election day cited inflation as an issue important to their votes more frequently than those who had decided earlier, and cited "a balanced federal budget," "reduced federal income taxes," and "jobs and unemployment" no less frequently. There is one discordant piece of evidence: Data reported by the Gallup Poll show that Reagan voters who made their choice on election day gave his economic policies as their main reason for choosing him much less frequently than Reagan voters generally.[81] In the main, however, the evidence indicates that economic issues helped Reagan very considerably in expanding his support beyond his committed conservative and Republican base.

Was the performance of the economy the central issue in 1980? The evidence produced by the press permits no firm conclusion. Certainly, that evidence suggests strongly that the economy was an issue that counted with many voters, including many whose allegiance to their preferred candidate was weak. The evidence suggests also that inflation was particularly worrisome to voters and that it attracted more of them to the Reagan standard than unemployment or government spending, though these were also concerns of many. These findings are not trivial, but they are vague—too vague to justify claims that inflation was the election's big issue or that Carter lost because the economy was in trouble.

OTHER ISSUES

The quality of the press's evidence about the salience of the noneconomic considerations that entered into voting in 1980 was no better than that for economic issues, and the information collected and published about most such considerations was much more fragmentary. The information that does exist justifies two conclusions: (1) If any set of considerations surpassed economic issues in salience, it was those bearing on the

[81] Gallup Poll release of December 7, 1980.

qualifications of candidates. Asked to give the main reason for voting as they did, voters said something about the candidates at least as often as they cited policy issues or problems. According to the Gallup Poll, 40 percent of those who voted for Reagan gave his leadership, Carter's lack of accomplishment, and general dissatisfaction with Carter as their main reason for supporting the Republican candidate.[82] Many of these responses may have had their origin in the performance of the economy, as I have already noted, but many may not have. (2) Foreign policy and international affairs were clearly less salient than domestic policy issues. At no point during the general election campaign were issues of foreign policy cited as the nation's most important problem, or as the main reason for supporting a candidate, with anything like the frequency of economic issues.[83] In none of the exit poll lists did a foreign policy issue rank first as a reason for liking a candidate, though from one-quarter to one-half of the ABC News sample checked "foreign affairs" or "U.S. military strength."[84] To a direct question about whether they were more concerned about the "economy and domestic problems" or about "the U.S. position abroad and foreign policy in general," respondents chose the former, two to one.[85]

Hardly any basis exists for estimating the salience of any other issues. Responses to the "main reason" and "most im-

[82] Ibid.

[83] In a Gallup survey of September 12–15, some international or foreign policy problem was called the nation's most important by 15 percent of the sample; an October survey by the *New York Times* and CBS News found 19 percent citing Iran, the danger of war, relations with the Soviet Union, or other problems of foreign affairs. Neither Gallup nor the *New York Times* reported any respondents who said such problems were the main reason for their votes.

[84] In one of ABC's lists. Percentages of respondents citing various foreign policy issues in the lists were as follows: foreign affairs, 25; U.S. military strength, 22; Carter's handling of the Iran hostages, 26 (ABC News); strengthening America's position in the world, 33; relations with Iran and the Arab countries, 7 (NBC News and the Associated Press); Iran, 14; U.S. prestige around the world, 16 (CBS News and the *New York Times*).

[85] NBC News release of October 28, 1980, reporting the results of an NBC News–Associated Press survey of October 22–24, 1980.

portant problem" questions were dominated overwhelmingly by references to the candidates, the "need for a change," and economic and foreign policy problems. Nothing else was mentioned by more than 4 percent of those responding,[86] a result not believable as an indication of the actual salience of other concerns. Closed-ended questions might have been, but were not, used to identify roughly those who took particular issues into account in voting.[87] The exit poll lists together included nine items that did not concern the economy, foreign policy, or the qualifications of candidates.[88] Of these, the item most frequently checked was the vague "standing up for American values" (24 percent); that checked least often was "the needs of big cities" (2 percent). For reasons already noted, such responses are not reliable indicators of salience, and that point is underscored by widely divergent results for abortion and the Equal Rights Amendment. Six percent of the respondents to the ABC News exit poll checked the former and 18 percent the latter, while "E.R.A./abortion" was checked by only 7 percent of those responding to the *Times-* CBS election-day survey.

Reporters sometimes cited a strong relationship between voting and opinion on an issue to indicate the latter's importance, as, for example, when David Broder, having remarked that "the interviews with voters Tuesday contain clear evidence that there were important issues . . . in Tuesday's voting," noted that voters concerned about the problems of the

[86] Energy problems were called most important by 4 percent of all respondents in the Gallup survey of September 12–15 and in the *New York Times*–CBS News survey of September 19–25.

[87] To be used for that purpose, such questions should be accompanied by one filter designed to discourage positive responses from those who see no difference between the candidates on the issue posed and another to identify respondents who regard the issue as irrelevant to their vote. On occasion, press surveys used one or the other of these types of filters but rarely, if ever, used them together.

[88] These were "the Equal Rights Amendment," "abortion," "E.R.A./abortion," "problems of the poor and elderly," "energy," "Carter's decision not to debate Reagan and Anderson together," "the Billy Carter–Libya investigation," "the needs of the big cities," and "standing up for basic American values."

poor and elderly "went for Carter, 78 percent to 16 percent."[89]
As I have already argued, the implications of such evidence
are far less clear than Broder's statement suggests. Consider
the data arrayed in Table 9.11 which show how responses to
twenty-five questions on noneconomic issues were related to
preferences for candidates: In the table this relationship varies
by issue, but it also varies—and more strongly—with the type
of question asked. On the average 90 percent of those responding to closed-ended questions that asked for direct comparisons of candidates had preferences consistent with their
opinions. The comparable figures for other closed-ended
questions and for list questions were 63 percent and 67 percent, respectively. Note another feature of the data: In eighteen of twenty-five cases, those respondents who took
minority positions were more likely to have preferences
consistent with their opinions than those who took majority
positions. For list questions the difference was small, but
for closed-ended questions it was 8 percentage points on
average.

What is one to make of these facts? The weaker relationship
between opinions and preferences among holders of majority
views could mean—but probably does not—that minorities
are more passionate in their opinions. More likely, it reflects
the presence among majorities of swing voters, whose votes
are likely to be weakly correlated with their opinions on any
given issue. The very strong relationship between preference
and responses to closed-ended, candidate-comparison questions may derive in part from their tendency to discourage
positive responses from those without genuine opinions (in
Table 9.11 such questions drew fewer positive responses than
other closed-ended questions, though far more than list questions), but that strength may also be partly spurious, deriving
from a tendency of such respondents simply to name the candidate they prefer. At the very least, the anomalies of Table
9.11 argue for a skeptical attitude toward measures of the consistency of voting and opinion as evidence of the latter's electoral significance.

[89] *Washington Post*, November 6, 1980.

TABLE 9.11

Consistency of Opinions on Issues and Preferences for Candidates in Responses to Selected Questions on Noneconomic Subjects

Subject and Question	% Giving Positive Response*	% Favorable to Reagan	% Whose Opinion and Preference for a Candidate Were Consistent, of Respondents:			Question Type
			Giving Positive Responses	With Pro-Carter Opinions	With Pro-Reagan Opinions	
Threat of War:						
1. Candidate best for keeping U.S. out of war	51	31	88	84	98	Closed-ended
2. Candidate best able to keep us out of war	66	32	86	80	99	Closed-ended
3. Candidate disliked because might get us into war	33	12	70	70	74	List
Foreign and defense policy:						
4. Candidate disliked for stand on foreign affairs	44	61	72	68	75	List
5. Candidate best able to protect U.S. interests overseas	68	46	94	92	96	Closed-ended
6. Candidate best for strengthening U.S. position abroad	55	60	95	96	94	Closed-ended
7. Candidate disliked for stand on						

Question						Type
8. U.S. should, should not be more forceful toward U.S.S.R. even at risk of war	77	65	68	64	70	Closed-ended
9. Should spending next year on defense and the military be increased or decreased?	83	73	66	66	66	Closed-ended
Competence of candidates:						
10. Most forceful and decisive candidate	60	63	80	90	74	Closed-ended
11. Candidate disliked as weak leader	45	89	78	83	77	List
12. Candidate best able to get job done	60	60	97	98	97	Closed-ended
13. Candidate who won't get things done	31	90	77	78	77	List
14. Most intelligent candidate	50	42	90	86	96	Closed-ended
15. Candidate not intelligent enough	20	43	85	81	90	List
Integrity of candidate:						
16. Candidate with highest ethical standards	61	38	87	83	94	Closed-ended
17. Candidate who seems hypocritical	32	44	84	83	85	List
Social issues:						
18. Favor or oppose Equal Rights Amendment	74	46	63	56	72	Closed-ended
19. Favor or oppose Equal Rights Amendment	74	47	69	62	77	Closed-ended

TABLE 9.11 (Continued)

Subject and Question	% Giving Positive Response*	% Favorable to Reagan	% Whose Opinion and Preference for a Candidate Were Consistent, of Respondents:			Question Type
			Giving Positive Responses	With Pro-Carter Opinions	With Pro-Reagan Opinions	
20. Candidate disliked for stand on E.R.A.	33	25	54	45	57	List
21. Favor or oppose leaving abortion to woman and her physician	85	26	52	47	63	Closed-ended
22. Candidate disliked for stand on abortion	17	33	35	28	49	List
Other issues:						
23. Candidate disliked for stand on problems of poor and elderly	20	18	44	47	28	List
24. Candidate with greatest concern for average citizen	65	40	92	88	98	Closed-ended
25. Candidate who made especially unfair charges	63	55	90	89	91	Closed-ended

SOURCES: Questions 1, 6, NBC News–Associated Press Survey, October 22–24, 1980; questions 2, 5, 10, 12, 14, 16, 24, News-week Poll, October 1980; questions 3, 4, 7, 11, 13, 15, 17, 20, 22, 23, 25, ABC News General Election Exit Poll; questions 8, 18, New York Times–CBS News election-day survey; questions 9, 19, 21, NBC News–Associated Press election-day survey.

MANDATES AND NEW BEGINNINGS

Among the first to announce the mandate of the 1980 election was the vice-president-elect, George Bush. Before an audience of Republicans on election night, he declared that Reagan's victory was

> ... not simply a mandate for a change but a mandate for peace and freedom; a mandate for prosperity; a mandate for opportunity for all Americans regardless of race, sex, or creed; a mandate for leadership that is both strong and compassionate ... a mandate to make government the servant of the people in the way our founding fathers intended; a mandate for hope; a mandate for hope for the fulfillment of the great dream that President-elect Reagan has worked for all his life.[90]

This set of mandates, surely, is an odd mixture of the specific, the sweeping, the vacuous, and the far fetched.

As if to prove that a mandate, like beauty, is in the eye of the beholder, others—though rarely those who reported the results of surveys—followed with a wide variety of claims. Some saw the electorate as having declared *for* conservative policies, more effective administration, "the goals to which Reagan is committed,"[91] and "new solutions that will strike practical people as responses to the real issues,"[92] and as having stood *against* liberal excesses, the political and governmental status quo, and a "perfect-world-or-nothing philosophy."[93] Others thought that voters had called for economic growth, an end to inflation, an increase in the nation's military strength, firmness and forcefulness in relations with the Soviet Union and other nations generally, reduced spending on domestic programs, an eventual balanced budget, less governmental regulation of business, less governmental interference

---

[90] Transcript, ABC News election-night telecast.

[91] Roscoe Drummond in the *Christian Science Monitor*, November 7, 1980.

[92] *New Orleans Times-Picayune*, November 9, 1980.

[93] *Washington Post*, November 9, 1980.

in the private lives of citizens, opposition to the dictatorships of both right and left, and an end to busing for the purpose of desegregating schools. In pressing their views, few gave more than the barest hint of what they meant by the term *mandate,* or of the source of their knowledge that one did or did not exist.

From our review of the issues in 1980, it should be clear that press surveys yield no conclusive evidence of a mandate in the election of Ronald Reagan. This is not to say that all the claims were preposterous. In response to closed-ended questions, majorities—often substantial majorities—did say that they favored reductions in federal spending, taxes, governmental regulation, unemployment, and the rate of inflation. They also said that they wanted a more militant foreign policy, increased defense spending, the Equal Rights Amendment, registration of firearms, a liberal policy on abortion, and continuance of informal relations with Taiwan. We do not know, however, how many voters took these issues into account *in voting,* or how many of those who did endorsed either Reagan's position or Carter's. Whether the electorate of 1980 issued a mandate should therefore be an open question to readers of the press, and the absence of mandates in the landslides of 1972 and 1964 argues for skepticism.

Many reports on the election suggested that Reagan's victory might signal a new era in party politics, though usually they did so in a speculative vein. Not a journalist but an historian of American politics, Robert Kelley, made the most unequivocal claim that the 1980 election had been midwife to a new party system:

> A new "critical election" has occurred, stimulated by the cultural crisis of the 1960's, the economic crisis of the 1970's, and a revived Soviet threat. . . . A new balance of forces exists, the sixth "party system." It may be an equal balance, as was true of the second and third party systems, or we may see one party dominant as in the fourth and fifth. How long will it last? Past history suggests a long time.[94]

[94] *New York Times,* November 9, 1980.

As evidence for this view, Kelley noted that "a majority of
Catholics and the white South . . . as well as a large component of the Jewish voters, have shifted into the reviving Republican Party."[95] He also invoked the "discovery" of scholars that U.S. political history has "gone through a series of
roughly 40-year oscillations, or party systems."[96]

Evidence of this quality will not support so grand a thesis. A
majority of Catholics have *not* shifted into the Republican
Party. About 30 percent of Catholics now identify with the
Republicans, many fewer than consider themselves Democrats.[97] White southerners have moved away from identification with the Democratic Party but mainly toward independence, not Republicanism.[98] Catholics and white southerners
each gave Reagan a majority of their *votes* in 1980 (the former
a bare majority), but the *inclination* of Catholics remained
Democratic, as Table 9.2 shows. Relative to the Republican
share of the national major-party vote, Reagan improved
upon Ford's showing in each of the groups that Kelley mentioned, but not strikingly.

Consider now the "40-year oscillations." Like Kelley, many
students of party politics see five party-systems in our history:
the Federalists and the Jeffersonian Republicans; the system
which pitted Democrats against National Republicans and,
later, the Whigs; a Civil War system which endured until the
1890's; a Republican-dominated alignment from 1893 until
1932; and, after 1932, the New Deal party-system. Forty years
is a reasonable estimate for the duration of the third and

[95] Ibid.

[96] Ibid.

[97] As shown by the University of Michigan's 1980 National Election
Study. This estimate counts as Republicans those independents who said
they leaned toward the Republican Party. Twenty percent of all respondents called themselves "strong" or "not so strong" Republicans. Comparable figures for Catholic identification with the Democratic Party are
56 percent and 43 percent, respectively.

[98] The University of Michigan's 1980 National Election Study found
32 percent of southern whites identifying with, or leaning toward, the
Republican Party. The comparable figure for identification with the
Democratic Party was 53 percent.

fourth party-systems. It fits the facts for the first two, however, only if one does some rather fancy defining. We cannot count the forty-odd years duration of the fifth party-system for this theory of oscillation, since Kelley is seeking to prove that the fifth party-system has just ended. This accounting leaves us with two, possibly three, cases in support of the theory and with at least one clear exception. Chance quite often presents us with regularities of this order.

Evidence that the 1980 election was not a critical election, that preexisting divisions in the electorate did not alter sharply, is far more persuasive than any evidence Kelley advances. In fact, the ideological composition of the electorate did not change. Nor, in the aggregate, did the partisan identifications of voters change. Moreover, the partisan inclinations of social and demographic groups were close to their norms for the period since 1952. Participation in the 1980 election was the lowest since 1948, and the issues of policy which seemed to have worked most strongly for Reagan—inflation, defense expenditures, and firmness in dealing with the Soviet Union—are not ones on which the two parties are locked into positions. For instance, the New Deal party-system survived a bout with inflation in 1946, and in the early sixties John F. Kennedy made firmness abroad and increased defense expenditures Democratic issues. The hostage issue, which may have been important among marginal voters, was wholly transient.[99]

I do not mean to argue that party ties have not weakened in recent years—they have—or that a successful Reagan administration could not alter the relative popularity of the parties. What happened in the election of 1980 did not change the party balance greatly, but what President Reagan *does* might do so, particularly if he can satisfy voters on economic issues, the issues central to the New Deal party-system. These views are close to those expressed by some prominent Republicans.

[99] For an excellent discussion of what recent history may portend for the party system, see Jonathan M. Rich, *Changes in the American Party System: Realignment or Disintegration?* (Princeton University senior thesis, 1981).

William Brock, the former party chairman, saw the 1980 election as a *possible* "breakpoint" in party history: "In this election we have brought together the elements of a new coalition. The cementing of that coalition depends on our performance in office."[100] Congressman Jack Kemp, warning that the election was not a mandate to repeal the New Deal, also stressed performance as the key to the Republicans' future: "If the Republican Party fails to bring prosperity to the American people, the American people will turn away from it, and 1980 will look like an Eisenhower victory."[101] For this nonmillenarian interpretation of the election, Kemp had an explanation that may hold for other Republicans as well: "I want to be part of a majority party. My future is inextricably linked to the ideas I have advocated."[102]

INTERPRETING ELECTIONS

The press made an extraordinary effort to find out what voters were thinking and doing in 1980. That effort featured extensive and repeated polling of national samples over the entire course of the campaign, surveys in a considerable number of individual states, the reinterviewing of respondents, and post-election polls. The enormous election-day samples, uncontaminated by the responses of nonvoters, enabled reporters to do analyses that would have been meaningless with samples of the usual size. The surveying of popular opinion on this scale is an important commitment to an interpretation of elections well grounded in fact, and its benefits have already been substantial. In 1980 some editorials and columns of opinion still indulged in what might be called oracular journalism, making ill-supported claims of mandates, ideological revolution, and party realignment. Political reporters mindful of survey results, however, rarely joined in such claims.

The promise of press surveys is far from being fully realized, however. I shall not repeat here all the criticisms that I

---

[100] *New York Times*, November 6, 1980.
[101] *New York Times*, November 27, 1980.
[102] Ibid.

have already made, but some points deserve special emphasis and others should be added.

The press's interpretation of the 1980 election was at its weakest in sorting out the effects of particular issues on the outcome. Some accounts gave little or no attention to the impact of issues on marginal voters, which is rather like ignoring the last lap in covering a race. Press surveys also failed to ask the right kinds of questions. In tracing the influence of particular issues, the first and basic step is to find out which issues actually figure in voters' choices. The closed-ended questions, list questions, and one-response, free-answer questions on which the press largely relied are not well suited to that purpose, even when care is taken to test the association of responses with voting. Likes-dislikes questions that permit each respondent several responses are a far better approach to sorting out which issues count in decisions and how they count. Such questions do not prompt responses; they give the respondent an opportunity to answer in concrete terms; and they reduce the likelihood that issues important to voting will be overlooked. The press could also improve its current methods by filtering closed-ended questions better.[103]

Many interpretations of the 1980 election lacked historical perspective. The exaggeration of the one-sidedness of Reagan's victory overlooked obvious features even of the recent historical record. Some accounts of the voting of particular social and demographic groups were little more than bare reports of how each group's vote divided in 1980; these reports were informative, certainly, but contributed less than they could have to an understanding of what was, and was not, different about the election of 1980. Responses to survey questions were frequently reported without reference to similar data from earlier elections or even from earlier in the campaign. Most such information, so presented, informs no one but the specialist. Moreover, both continuities *and* discontinuities are an important part of any election, just as positions maintained may be as significant in a battle as those won and

---

[103] As indicated in footnote 87 above.

lost. As the press's archives of survey data grow, so, probably, will the use of them in reporting elections, but even now a wealth of data exists that would have enabled the press to show trends and to put facts in context.

Postelection interpretation of the 1980 election gave too much attention (relatively) to why the winner won and too little to why the vote divided as it did. In any election some issues and attitudes propel voters toward the victor, others toward his opponent (or opponents). To ignore the latter in interpreting an election gives a distorted view of it, for such factors limit the victor's victory and qualify its meaning. It is a significant fact, for instance, that Nixon, while winning reelection in 1972 by an immense landslide, nonetheless lost on bread-and-butter issues. Summing up in 1980, the press dwelt largely on pro-Reagan, anti-Carter influences, gave some (but not great) attention to the views of weakly committed voters, and had little to say about the influences that worked against Reagan's election. A foreign reader of some reports might have found it mysterious that anyone had voted against the new president, but almost half the electorate did.

Once the election was over the press folded its tents too quickly. In the few days surrounding an election, it is probably impossible to collect, process, and interpret adequately the data now collected by news agencies.[104] But why should interpretation of a presidential election be limited almost entirely to that period? Coverage of an election can reasonably be thought of as a branch of investigative journalism, the products of which can appear at any stage of the investigation. To the objection that presidential elections interest no one a few

[104] The use of multiple-response "likes-dislikes" questions would increase the time required for the analysis of data, since responses must be coded. As administered in the Michigan national election studies such questions also require a considerable amount of interviewing time (about ten minutes, on the average). Both problems could be mitigated to some extent, and probably with little loss, by asking respondents for fewer responses than Michigan interviewers do. Many of the analyses that I did for my account of the 1972 election used one set of data in which five responses for each "likes-dislikes" question were coded and another in which only three responses were coded. Differences in results were small.

months after they are over, one can cite the sales of T. H. White's books, which surely show that new material on an election, or old facts in a new light, interests readers.

These criticisms have point, because a good deal is at stake in the interpretation of elections—for politicians, the press, and everyone else. Political advantage hangs on it, and so in part does the intelligibility of elections as institutions. Because interpretation is intrinsically difficult, and because many speak from partisan motives, disagreement about what messages voters have actually sent to their leaders will doubtless always be with us. Still, there is a true state of affairs to be got at, there are methods more or less well designed to get at it, and voters want their messages heard. If the press (and scholars) give widely varying accounts of the same election, or accounts consisting chiefly of oracular assertions, reasonable people are apt to conclude that everyone is either guessing, pleading a cause, or making it up. That conclusion is a deadly one both for confidence in elections and confidence in the press.

APPENDIX I

As noted above, the theory of voting on which I rely was proposed by Richard A. Brody and Benjamin I. Page in their article, "Indifference, Alienation and Rational Decisions: The Effects of Candidate Evaluations on Turnout and the Vote," and by Thad W. Mirer and myself in "The Simple Act of Voting." The first of these sources reports tests of the theory against voters' evaluations of candidates in the 1968 presidential election, the latter against voters' likes and dislikes of candidates and parties in presidential elections from 1952 to 1968, inclusive. "The Simple Act of Voting" also examines in great detail the sources of errors in the Rule's predictions. More recently, Thomas E. Mann has tested the theory against data from ten races for the U.S. House of Representatives in 1976. (See his *Unsafe at Any Margin: Interpreting Congressional Elections,* pp. 63–71.) This appendix reports some additional tests.

Tables A.I.1 and A.I.2 bring up to date similar tables in "The Simple Act of Voting" (see pp. 576, 586). The new information is fully consistent with the conclusions stated there: The Rule is a considerably better basis than party identification for predicting both the division of the vote in presidential elections and the votes of individual voters. The Rule's predictions of the latter are less accurate than those based on voters' stated intentions, but it permits a greater number of correct predictions than intentions do. It is also a slightly better basis for predicting the division of the vote.

Table A.I.3 reports the results of a regression analysis of the Rule's predictions of individual respondents' votes in 1964 and 1972.[1] The table shows errors of prediction to be signifi-

---

[1] In this analysis I used that version of data for the 1972 election in which up to three responses to the "likes-dislikes" questions only were coded for each respondent.

A Comparison of Results in Predicting the Votes of Individual Voters in Accordance with the Voter's Decision Rule, from Partisan Identifications and from Stated Intentions

Election	Sample Size[a]	% of Cases in Which Data Permit a Prediction from:			% of Cases in Which Votes Were Correctly Predicted from:			Accuracy[c]		
		The Rule	Party Ident.[b]	Intended Vote	The Rule	Party Ident.[b]	Intended Vote	The Rule	Party Ident.[b]	Intended Vote
1952	1184	98.5	94.3	87.9	87.1	76.1	82.8	88.4	80.9	94.1
1956	1270	98.5	90.5	89.2	85.2	75.3	83.1	86.5	83.2	93.1
1960	1413[d]	98.9	91.3	87.0	88.2	78.5	81.9	89.1	86.0	94.1
1964	1113	99.6	94.1	88.7	90.3	78.4	84.1	90.7	83.4	94.8
1968	1027	99.1	91.6	86.6	80.9	68.9	77.0	81.6	75.2	89.0
1972	834	99.2	91.2	86.3	83.7	66.3	80.6	84.4	72.7	93.3
1976	1662.5[d]	98.6	89.1	82.9	84.1	72.6	76.3	85.3	81.5	92.0
1980	972	97.6	90.8	86.1	75.1	67.8	74.7	76.9	74.3	86.7
MEAN		98.8	91.6	86.8	84.3	73.0	80.1	85.4	79.7	92.1

[a] Samples are samples of persons who voted, excluding those who refused to say how they voted or who said that they didn't remember how they voted.
[b] Includes all those who identify with a party and independents who say they lean toward a party.
[c] Correct predictions as a percentage of all predictions.
[d] Weighted samples.

TABLE A.I.2

Results in Predicting the Division of the Major-Party Vote in Accordance with the Voter's Decision Rule, from Partisan Identifications and from Stated Intentions

Election[a]	% of Actual Vote for Major Parties That Was Democratic		% of Major Party Vote Predicted to Be Democratic		
	Sample	Population	The Rule	Intended Vote	Party Ident.[b]
1952	41.7	44.6	45.0	42.7	59.2
1956	40.2	42.2	44.8	42.6	58.0
1960	49.0	50.1	49.4	45.1	58.5
1964	67.4	61.3	69.5	72.3	65.5
1968	40.9	42.7	41.9	38.6	59.3
1972	35.5	37.5	38.7	31.1	55.7
1976	51.1	51.1	53.0	48.7	57.1
1980	49.1	44.7	49.0	48.6	57.3
Abs. value pred. minus actual vote in:	Sample[c]		2.1	2.6	11.8
	Population[c]		2.7	4.1	11.2

[a] Sample sizes as in Table A.I.1.

[b] Includes all those who identify with a party and independents who say they lean toward a party.

[c] Figures in this row are the means of the absolute values of deviations of the predicted vote from the actual vote.

cantly related to low net scores, indecision in voting intentions, changes of intention, predictions of votes inconsistent with respondents' party identifications, Republican identifications in 1964 and Democratic identifications in 1972, predictions of votes for the losing candidates, and the total number of respondents' responses to the likes-dislikes questions. All of these factors were identified as sources of error in "The Simple Act of Voting," and it is worth noting again that errors from these sources could be expected to occur even if voters were applying the Rule exactly.

For most people, the most problematic element of the

TABLE A.I.3

Regression Analysis of the Accuracy of Predictions in Accordance with the Voter's Decision Rule (1964 and 1972 samples pooled)

Variables	Regression 1.1		Regression 1.2	
	b	t	b	t
Democratic identification	.04	1.64		
Republican identification	.02	.97		
Indecision	−.26	−13.68***	−.27	−14.30***
Change of intention	−.73	−28.01***	−.75	−28.09***
Log_2 absolute value of net score	−.05	−7.65***	−.04	−6.16***
Response dissonance	.03	1.94		
Total number of responses	.01	5.05***		
Counteridentification prediction	−.11	−6.53***	−.08	−5.56***
Countertrend identification '64	.05	2.04*		
Countertrend identification '72	.05	2.10*		
Countertrend prediction '64	−.04	−1.84		
Countertrend prediction '72	−.10	−4.21***		
Log_2 no. days before election of preelection interview	−.009	−1.60		
Log_2 no. days after election of postelection interview	−.002	−.34		

Dependent variable: accuracy of prediction				
F-ratio	94.92		307.48	
No. of observations	1,823		1,823	
R^2	.42		.40	

b = net (partial) regression coefficient
t = t-value of regression coefficient
*** <.001
  * <.05

DEFINITIONS OF VARIABLES

Dependent variable

Accuracy of prediction	1 if the prediction was correct, 2 if it was not

Independent variables

Democratic identification	1 if respondent identifies with the Democratic Party, 0 if he does not
Republican identification	1 if respondent identifies with the Republican Party, 0 if he does not

TABLE A.I.3 (Continued)

Counteridentification prediction	1 if respondent is predicted to vote for the party with which he identifies or if he is an independent, 0 if the respondent identifies with one party but is predicted to vote for another
Countertrend identification '64	1 if respondent is *not* a Republican in 1964, 0 if he is
Countertrend identification '72	1 if respondent is *not* a Democrat in 1972, 0 if he is
Indecision	1 if the respondent stated a preference for a candidate in his preelection interview, 0 if he did not
Change of intention	1 if respondent reported voting for the candidate he preferred in his preelection interview or if he stated no such preference, 0 if he reported not voting for the candidate he preferred in his preelection interview
Countertrend prediction '64	1 if predicted to vote Democratic in 1964, 0 if predicted to vote Republican
Countertrend prediction '72	1 if predicted to vote Republican in 1972, 0 if predicted to vote Democratic
Response dissonance	1 if all the respondent's likes and dislikes favor the same candidate, 0 if they do not

Voter's Decision Rule is its assumption that the voter weighs equally his likes and dislikes of parties and candidates in arriving at a decision. Michael Kagay has investigated the reasonableness of that assumption in research comparing the predictive efficiency of the Rule and of the Stokes Six Component Model of voting decisions. (See Stokes et al., "Components of Electoral Decision.") Expressing both in linear equations, Kagay notes that the Rule (except in the role it assigns to party identification) is equivalent to the Stokes model with two assumptions built in: (1) that the coefficients of the six components are equal in any given year, and (2) that the constant term remains the same from year to year. He tested these assumptions by regression analysis.

TABLE A.I.4

A Comparison of Results in Postdicting the Votes of Individual Voters in Accordance with the Voter's Decision Rule and the Stokes Six Component Model

Election	Sample Size	$\bar{R}^2$ [a]	Six Component Model Correct Postdictions	No. of Errors	$\bar{R}^2$	The Rule (attitudinal component) Correct Postdictions	No. of Errors	Difference in No. of Errors
1952	1,181	.531	87.8%	144	.530	88.0%	142	−2
1956	1,266	.508	85.2	187	.507	85.9	179	−8
1960	1,406[b]	.571	88.6	160	.568	87.7	173	+13
1964	1,111	.543	89.5	117	.537	90.0	111	−6
1968	911[c]	.547	88.3	106	.543	87.8	111	+5
1972	830	.481	84.9	125	.458	84.2	131	+6

Source: Michael R. Kagay, "Two Models of Voter Decision-Making: Stokes' 'Six Components' and the Kelley-Mirer 'Rule.'"

[a] $\bar{R}^2$ computed as $1-(1-R^2)(N-1)/(N-K)$, where K is the number of parameters.

[b] Weighted sample. Raw N = 885.

[c] Wallace voters are excluded from the sample.

Kagay found neither assumption to hold statistically; that is, he found statistically significant differences in the constant term of the Six Component Model from year to year and statistically significant differences in the coefficients of the six components in several elections. As Table A.I.4 shows, however, these differences are practically inconsequential. The Rule and the Six Component Model make virtually the same postdictions.

Kagay's research of course does not exclude the possibility that unequal weighting by respondents of *some* kinds of considerations may be an important source of error in the Rule's predictions. Differences in the weights (coefficients) of "domestic issues" and "foreign policy issues," two of Stokes's six components, may be practically trivial; that does not necessarily mean that differences in the weights of, say, "economic issues" and "race-related issues" are trivial too. Taking my lead from Kagay, I ran a series of regressions to compare the predictive efficiency of the Rule with that of a large family of two-component models. The regression representing the Rule included as independent variables Republican and Democratic identification (as defined in Table A.I.3) and respondents' net scores. Each of the other regressions included both identification variables and *two* net scores—the first for one of the issues listed in Tables A.I.5 and A.I.6, the second for all other considerations.[2] For example, in one two-component model one of these net scores was based solely on responses relating to the integrity and sincerity of candidates, the other on all the other responses. If the assumption of equal weighting of considerations is a substantively serious distortion of reality, equations for the two-component models should have had a statistically better fit to the data than the equation for the Rule, *and* they should yield substantially better postdictions.

The results are summarized in Tables A.I.5 and A.I.6. Of the seventy-seven regression equations for the two-component models, twenty-one showed a better fit in a statistical sense than did the regression for the Rule. In no case, however, did any two-component model add as much as nine-tenths of one percent to the proportion of the votes correctly postdicted; in the one case in which there was a substantively significant difference in that regard (that for 1972 involving the Social Issue), the advantage was with the Rule. On the average, and excluding the Social-Issue case, the two-component models increased the proportion of votes correctly post-dicted by only seventy-three thousandths of one percent.

The University of Michigan's surveys in 1960 and 1964 yielded other data useful for assessing the consequences of the

---

[2] Because I made this test early in my research, the issues listed in Tables A.I.5 and A.I.6 differ in detail in their definitions from the similarly labeled issues of Appendix II.

TABLE A.I.5

A Comparison of Results in Postdicting the Votes of Individual Voters in Accordance with the Voter's Decision Rule and with a Series of Models in which Voters' Attitudes Are Partitioned into Two Components, 1964

Issue	Statistically Significant Difference in Coefficients?	Difference in % of Votes Correctly Postdicted
Foreign policy	Yes	−0.3
Peace	Yes	−0.3
Military spending	No	0.0
Handling of trouble spots	No	0.0
Internationalism	No	0.0
Foreign aid	No	+0.1
New Deal issues	Yes	−0.3
Economic issues	No	−0.5
Government spending	No	0.0
Fiscal policy	No	0.0
Election's economic impact	Yes	−0.2
Ideological stance	Yes	+0.2
Liberalism, conservatism	No	+0.2
Extremism	No	0.0
Relationship to Big Business, common man	Yes	+0.4
Welfare	No	0.0
Poverty program	Yes	0.0
Welfare statism	No	+0.2
Social Security, worker's welfare programs	Yes	0.0
Medical care	Yes	0.0
Relationship to unions	Yes	+0.2
Competence of candidates	No	0.0
Experience	No	0.0
Strength of leadership	No	−0.1
Realism	No	0.0
Judgment, stability	No	+0.1

TABLE A.I.5 (Continued)

Issue	Statistically Significant Difference in Coefficients?	Difference in % of Votes Correctly Postdicted
Candidate's other traits	No	+0.1
Integrity, sincerity	Yes	+0.2
Appearance, family	No	0.0
Clarity of positions	No	0.0
Independence	No	+0.1
Quality of stewardship	No	0.0
Corrupt government	No	+0.2
Scandals	No	+0.2
Partisanship	Yes	0.0
Goldwater Republicanism	Yes	+0.2
Party unity	No	0.0
Conduct of campaign	No	0.0
Race-related issues	No	+0.3
Relationship to John F. Kennedy	No	+0.1
Vice-presidential candidates	No	0.0

assumption of equal weighting. In 1960 respondents were asked, "What would you personally feel are the most important problems the government should try to take care of when the new President and Congress take office in January?" And "Who do you think would be the most likely to do what you want on this, the Democrats, the Republicans, or wouldn't there be any difference?" Interviewers recorded up to three problems in the order in which they were mentioned. In 1964 the questionnaire distinguished problems the government "should do something about" from those it "should stay out of." Again up to three problems were recorded in the order mentioned for each category.

For each election I examined the relationship of these responses to voting, in two regressions. In the first regression of the 1960 data I treated the first, second, and third mentioned

A Comparison of Results in Postdicting the Votes of Individual Voters in Accordance with the Voter's Decision Rule and with a Series of Models in Which Voters' Attitudes Are Partitioned into Two Components, 1972

Issue	Statistically Significant Difference in Coefficients?	Difference in % of Votes Correctly Postdicted
Vietnam War, peace	No	+0.6
Foreign policy	No	+0.2
Relations with Red China	No	−0.4
Relations with U.S.S.R.	No	0.0
Military spending	Yes	+0.3
Internationalism	No	+0.1
New Deal issues	Yes	+0.2
Economic issues	Yes	+0.3
Government spending	No	0.0
Election's economic impact	Yes	−0.3
Fiscal policy	Yes	+0.2
Ideological stance	No	+0.3
Liberalism, conservatism	No	+0.2
Welfare	No	+0.1
Social Security, the aged	Yes	0.0
Relationship to unions	No	0.0
Relationship to Big Business, common man	No	0.0
The Social Issue	No	−10.0
Law and order	No	0.0
"Amnesty, acid, abortion"	No	0.0
Race-related issues	No	−0.2
Youth-related issues	No	+0.1
Competence of candidates	No	+0.2
Experience	No	+0.2
Strength of leadership	No	−0.2
Realism	No	+0.1

TABLE A.I.6 (Continued)

Issue	Statistically Significant Difference in Coefficients?	Difference in % of Votes Correctly Postdicted
Candidates' other traits	Yes	+0.3
Integrity, sincerity	Yes	+0.7
Appearance, family	No	0.0
Independence	No	0.0
Corruption	No	+0.1
Watergate affair	No	+0.2
Partisanship	No	+0.2
Party unity	No	0.0
Conduct of campaign	No	+0.1
Eagleton affair	No	+0.8

problems each as independent variables, assigning values to each as follows:

Respondent believes the Democrats are more
likely to handle the problem well   +1
Respondent believes the Republicans are more
likely to handle the problem well   −1
Respondent sees no difference in the way the
parties would handle the problem, *or* the re-
spondent does not respond to the question   0

The first regression for the 1964 election included six problem-variables, reflecting the difference in questions in the two
years, but each was assigned values in the manner just described. In the second regression for each election I included
only one problem-variable, the value of which for any given
respondent was the sum of the three (1960) or six (1964)
problem-variables of the first regression. This procedure is the
equivalent for these data of calculating the Rule's net score,
since each problem (or issue) mentioned is treated as equal in
weight to all others. All regressions included respondents'

TABLE A.I.7

Issues and Voting: Two Models Contrasted

1960 Election

Regression 1			
Independent variables	b	(s)	t
First problem	.18	(.015)	11.7
Second problem	.09	(.017)	5.5
Third problem	.08	(.021)	4.0
Democratic ident.	.22	(.032)	6.7
Republican ident.	−.24	(.034)	−7.0
Constant	.47		
Dependent variable			
Vote in 1960			
F-ratio	391.2		
Standard error	.32		
No. of observations	1413		
R^2	.58		
% correctly postdicted	85.9		

Regression 2			
Independent variables	b	(s)	t
Problems summed	.12	(.007)	17.5
Democratic ident.	.22	(.034)	7.0
Republican ident.	−.24	(.032)	−7.1
Constant	.46		
Dependent variable			
Vote in 1960			
F-ratio	640.3		
Standard error	.33		
No. of observations	1413		
R^2	.58		
% correctly postdicted	85.8		

1964 Election

	Regression 1				Regression 2		
Independent variables	b	(s)	t	Independent variables	b	(s)	t
Problems for action:				Problems summed	.11		19.6
First problem	.19	(.017)	11.0	Democratic ident.	.04		1.0
Second problem	.07	(.019)	3.5	Republican ident.	−.35		8.2
Third problem	.03	(.024)	1.2	Constant	.76		
Problems to avoid:							
First problem	.10	(.023)	4.6				
Second problem	.10	(.033)	2.9				
Third problem	.07	(.046)	1.6				
Democratic ident.	.04	(.041)	.92				
Republican ident.	−.33	(.043)	7.9				
Constant	.75						
Dependent variable				*Dependent variable*			
Vote in 1964				Vote in 1964			
F-ratio	173.9			F-ratio	442.2		
Standard error	.31			Standard error	.32		
No. of observations	1113			No. of observations	1113		
R^2	.56			R^2	.54		
% correctly postdicted	87.7			% correctly postdicted	87.5		

partisan identifications (defined as in Table A.I.3) as independent variables.

The results are summarized in Table A.I.7. The first-mentioned problem in 1960 has a regression coefficient double that of the problem mentioned next, and a similar result obtains for 1964 with problems "to do something about." It seems clear that people assign a greater weight to the problem they mention first than to those they mention later. But compare the results of the two regressions for each election: The values of the identification variables, the constant terms, the standard errors, and the R^2's are virtually the same. So are the proportions of the vote correctly postdicted. The constraining assumption of the equal weighting of issues makes no difference in one's ability to account for votes even when, with data of this sort, one would seem fully justified in expecting otherwise.

APPENDIX II

DEFINITIONS OF ISSUES

Below are the definitions of the issues discussed in Chapters 4 and 5 (and elsewhere in the text). In each case the phrases indicate the kind of responses that pertain to the issue or set of issues; the numbers listed are the codes for these responses. Both the phrases and their codes are taken from the codebooks for the 1964 and 1972 National Election Studies conducted by the University of Michigan's Center for Political Studies. In the definitions the letter *R* is used as an abbreviation for respondent.

1964

1. Military preparedness
   1504, 2504, 3504, 4504, 5640, 6640, 7640, 8640, 5694, 6694, 7694, 8694

Democrats (Republicans) have strong and effective (weak, ineffective) foreign policy, provide strong (poor) military position, will (can't) keep up defenses, have a good scientific program, will undertake enough (not enough) technological development, can handle communists, are soft on communism. Johnson (Goldwater) offers good defense, preparedness (weakness, unpreparedness), will raise (reduce) defense spending, will pursue a firm (weak) foreign policy, has good (poor) stand on draft.

2. Handling of trouble spots
   1560, 2560, 3560, 4560, 5660, 6660, 7660, 8660

Democrats (Republicans) would handle trouble spots better (badly), e.g., Cuba, Vietnam. Johnson (Goldwater) can (can't) handle specific trouble spots, e.g., the Middle East, Cuba, Congo, Berlin, Vietnam, Cyprus.

3. Peace
   1580, 2580, 3580, 4580, 5680, 6680, 7680, 8680
R thinks there is better chance for peace with Democrats and
Johnson (Republicans and Goldwater). Democrats (Republicans will work for disarmament, will limit nuclear testing and
use of weapons. Democrats (Republicans) are war party, oppose disarmament, favor nuclear testing and use of nuclear
weapons. Johnson (Goldwater) will keep peace, is working for
disarmament, will keep us out of war, worked for test ban, will
control nuclear weapons. Johnson (Goldwater) is warlike, too
militaristic, against disarmament. There will be too much of a
threat of force in foreign policy, poor control of nuclear weapons under Johnson (Goldwater).

4. Foreign aid
   1540, 2540, 3540, 4540, 1550, 2550, 3550, 4550
Democrats (Republicans) favor (oppose) foreign aid—military, economic, or unspecified; would spend too much on foreign aid—military, economic, or unspecified.

5. Internationalism
   1510, 2516, 3510, 4516, 1520, 2524, 3520, 4524, 5613, 6611,
   7617, 8611, 5621, 6622, 7621, 8622
Democrats (Republicans) are internationalist (too interna-
tionalistic), will work and cooperate with UN and allies, meddle too much in other countries' affairs, favor (oppose) trade,
favor low (high) tariffs, have poor stand on trade and tariff,
are isolationist, are too isolationistic, mind their own business,
haven't enough interest in rest of world, have America as their
first concern, are too selfish. Johnson (Goldwater) is internationalist (too internationalist); favors aid to, cooperation with,
other countries, UN; is too sympathetic to UN, our allies; is
too much for foreign spending; is isolationist, too isolationistic; will reduce spending abroad, foreign aid; is not interested
enough in helping other countries, UN; will put UN, allies in
their place.

6. Foreign policy
   MILITARY PREPAREDNESS + HANDLING OF TROUBLE SPOTS
   + PEACE + FOREIGN AID + INTERNATIONALISM + 1502,

2502, 3502, 4502, 1570, 2570, 3570, 4570, 5601, 6601, 7601, 8601, 5603, 6603, 7603, 8603, 5635, 6635, 7635, 8635, 5670, 6670, 7670, 8670, 1590, 2590, 3590, 4590, 5690, 6690, 7690, 8690

As for subjects noted above and: Democrats (Republicans) offer a good (bad) foreign policy, would raise or maintain (lose, have lost) U.S. prestige in the world, would make other countries like us better (dislike us more). Johnson (Goldwater) handles foreign policy well, does not know how to handle world (military) situation, is familiar with world (military) situation, has experience (not enough experience) abroad and travel, foreign countries respect (don't respect) him. R likes (doesn't like), agrees (disagrees) with Johnson's (Goldwater's) foreign policy. Johnson (Goldwater) will (wouldn't) stop communism abroad, can (can't) handle Russia, is soft on communism, will win (lose) prestige race with Russia, will raise (lower) America's prestige in the world. Also other (unspecified) foreign policy issues.

7. Government spending
   1120, 2121, 3120, 4121, 1130, 2130, 3130, 4130, 5080, 6081, 7080, 8081

Democrats (Republicans) would spend less (more) money than the other party, will balance budget, are economy-minded (too economy-minded), will decrease (increase) national debt, don't spend enough, would spend more and spending is good for the economy, are for deficit spending. Johnson (Goldwater) will cut spending, run government economically, will not economize, will spend too much.

8. Monetary and fiscal policy
   1340, 2340, 3340, 4340, 5440, 6440, 7440, 8440

Democrats, Johnson (Republicans, Goldwater) have good (bad) fiscal policy; e.g., interest rates, taxes, money policy, budgets.

9. Election's economic impact
   1350, 2350, 3352, 4350, 1370, 2370, 3370, 4370, 5450, 6451, 7450, 8451, 1360, 2360, 3360, 4360

Times are (would be) better (are bad, would be bad) under Democrats (Republicans). Democrats (Republicans) are party

of prosperity, would take care of recession, would be good for
employment (higher wages, more jobs, better working conditions) would bring depression and recession, are bad for employment (lower wages, fewer jobs, worse working conditions). Johnson (Goldwater) will bring better (worse) times, a
lower (higher) cost of living, less (more) employment, an increase in the minimum wage. Democrats (Republicans) would
do (did) something about (wouldn't help) inflation, high cost
of living, high prices.

10. Economic issues
    GOVERNMENT SPENDING + MONETARY AND FISCAL POL-
    ICY + ELECTION'S ECONOMIC IMPACT

11. Social security, the aged, workers' welfare programs
    1300, 2300, 3300, 4300, 5591, 6591, 7591, 8591, 1792,
    2792, 3792, 4792, 5792, 6792, 7792, 8792
R likes (dislikes) Democrats' (Republicans') stand on worker
welfare programs, e.g., unemployment compensation, minimum wage, social security. R likes (dislikes) Johnson's (Goldwater's) stand on social security, unemployment compensation. R likes (dislikes) Democratic (Republican) Party
because it's good for (bad for), better for, has helped. will
help, has kept (will keep) in check, is made up of old people,
the aged. R likes (dislikes) Johnson (Goldwater) because good
for, will help (will keep in check) old people, the aged.

12. Poverty program
    1390, 2390, 3390, 4390, 5490, 6490, 7490, 8490
R likes (dislikes) Democrats', Johnson's (Republicans', Goldwater's) stand on antipoverty program, manpower retraining.

13. Medical care
    1330, 2330, 3330, 4330, 5594, 6594, 7594, 8594
R likes (dislikes) Democrats' (Republicans') stand on medical
care, e.g. medicare, socialized medicine, health insurance program. R likes (dislikes) Johnson's (Goldwater's) stand on
medical care, e.g., medicare, care for the aged.

14. Relationship to Big Business, common man
    1615, 2615, 3615, 4615, 1702, 2702, 3702, 4702, 1713,

2713, 3713, 4713, 1731, 2731, 3733, 4731, 1633, 2633, 3633, 4633, 5702, 6702, 7702, 8702, 5714, 6714, 7714, 8714, 5731, 6731, 7731, 8731

The Democratic (Republican) Party is good (bad, too good, better) for, has kept (will keep) in check, has helped (will help, will help at the expense of others), is made up of, is controlled by workers, common people, the poor, all the people, every-one, "the people," lower-income people, working-class people, the average man, special interests, Big Business, businessmen, industry, the upper classes, big (rich, powerful) people, Wall Street. Johnson (Goldwater) is good for, will help, will keep in check all the people, everyone, "the people," common people, poor people, working-class people, the laboring man, privileged people, business, Big Business, industry. Johnson (Goldwater) is for equitable policies.

15. Relationship to labor, unions
    1451, 2451, 3451, 4451, 1620, 2620, 3620, 4620, 1721, 2721, 3721, 4721, 5550, 6550, 7550, 8550, 5720, 6720, 7720, 8720

R likes (dislikes) Democrats' (Republicans') labor policy, e.g., stand on right-to-work issues, Taft-Hartley. Democrats (Republicans) are good (bad, better, too good) for, have kept (will keep) in check, have helped (will help), will help at expense of others, are made up of, are controlled by labor unions, labor union bosses, union members, labor. R likes (dislikes) Johnson's (Goldwater's) stand on labor, union corruption, right-to-work laws, Taft-Hartley, Hoffa. Johnson (Goldwater) is good for, will help, will keep in check labor, labor unions.

16. Farm policy
    1440, 2440, 3440, 4440, 5541, 6541, 7541, 8541, 1760, 2760, 3760, 4760, 5760, 6760, 7760, 8760

R likes (doesn't like) Democratic (Republican) farm policy, e.g., likes stand on price supports, (other) aid to farmers. R likes (dislikes) Democratic (Republican) Party because it's good for (bad for), better for, has helped, will help, has kept (will keep) in check, is made up of farmers. R likes (dislikes) Johnson (Goldwater) because good for, will help (will keep in check) farmers.

17. Liberalism, conservatism

    1270, 2270, 3270, 4270, 1280, 2280, 3280, 4280, 5470, 6470, 7470, 8470, 5480, 6480, 7480, 8480. Also included in GOLDWATER REPUBLICANISM: 3280, 4280, 7480, 8480

R likes (dislikes) Democrats' (Republicans') liberal philosophy, liberal (northern) wing, conservative philosophy, conservative wing, states' rights position. R likes (dislikes) the Dixiecrats. Johnson (Goldwater) is liberal, too liberal, conservative, reactionary, middle of the road, too (not too) radical, more liberal than most in his party; will listen to and bring in liberals; is more for social welfare and/or government economic activity; favors social welfare; represents conservative wing of party; will bring in and listen to conservatives; is opposed to social change. Johnson will continue New Deal, Fair Deal.

18. Extremism

    1970, 2970, 3970, 4970, 5970, 6970, 7970, 8970

R likes Democrats' (Republicans') stand on extremism. R doesn't like extremists in party, party's connection with extremism (e.g., A.D.A., John Birch Society). R likes (dislikes) Johnson's (Goldwater's) stand on extremism, connection with extremists.

19. Ideological stance

    LIBERALISM, CONSERVATISM + EXTREMISM + 1210, 2210, 3211, 4211, 1220, 2220, 3221, 4221, 1230, 2230, 3231, 4231, 1250, 2250, 3250, 4250, 1264, 2263, 3264, 4263, 1291, 2291, 3291, 4291, 5409, 6409, 7409, 8409, 6430, 5431, 8430, 7431, 5460, 6460, 8461, 7461

As for subjects noted above, and: Democrats (Republicans) favor (less, too many, too few) government economic controls; we need (don't need) some planned economy; need some (less) control of private enterprise or business; there is too much (too little) interference with private enterprise or business. Democrats (Republicans) favor (less, too much, too little) government economic and/or social welfare activity; favor (less, too much, too little) government activity; government should take care of things too big for states or private enterprise. Democrats (Republicans) favor (oppose) individualism, individual initiative, private enterprise, state-local rights; are for (against) social reform, social change and progress; will change things for the better, improve conditions; have socialistic philosophy (which R likes, doesn't like); are too radical. Democrats, Johnson (Republicans, Goldwater) have good (bad) stand on communism. Johnson (Goldwater) would cut down government activity, stop socialism, is socialistic, is for the welfare state. Johnson (Goldwater) is for (against) big government; will use power of federal government; will handle problems states and private enterprise can't; won't (would) give states, private enterprise their rights; is against (for) individual initiative.

20. New Deal issues
ECONOMIC ISSUES + SOCIAL SECURITY, THE AGED, WORKERS' WELFARE PROGRAMS + POVERTY PROGRAM + MEDICAL CARE + RELATIONSHIP TO BIG BUSINESS, COMMON MAN + RELATIONSHIP TO LABOR, UNIONS + IDEOLOGICAL STANCE + FARM POLICY

21. Record, experience
5020, 7020, 5030, 6030, 7030, 8030, 5040, 6040, 7040, 8040, 1160, 2160, 3160, 4160, 5411, 6411, 7411, 8411
Johnson (Goldwater) has war, military experience; was a war hero; has successful (unsuccessful) record; was (is) a good (poor) senator; has (does not have) enough government or political experience; has experience in civil government. Johnson is a good (bad) president, was a good (bad) vice-president. Democrats (Republicans) do (have done) a good (poor) job (without other specifications). Johnson (Goldwater) would handle domestic affairs well (poorly). Has (lacks) the experience to handle domestic affairs.

22. Strength of leadership
5110, 6110, 7110, 8110, 5120, 6120, 7120, 8120, 5130, 6132, 7130, 8132
Johnson (Goldwater) is (is not) a leader, a great natural-born leader (no other specification). Johnson (Goldwater) is a

strong (weak) man, is decisive (indecisive), is (is not) self-confident and aggressive. Johnson was able to take over after death of Kennedy. Johnson (Goldwater) will save America; America needs a man like him; a man you can follow; people have confidence in him. Johnson (Goldwater) is inspiring (colorless, uninspiring).

23. Realism
    5230, 6230, 7230, 8230
Johnson (Goldwater) understands (does not understand) the problems, people; is well (poorly) informed; is (is not) realistic; is (is not) down-to-earth.

24. Judgment, stability
    5291, 6291, 7291, 8291, 6210, 8210
Johnson (Goldwater) is stable, balanced; is fanatic, unstable, dangerous; is impulsive; doesn't think before he talks; stirs up trouble.

25. Competence of candidates
    RECORD, EXPERIENCE + JUDGMENT, STABILITY + STRENGTH OF LEADERSHIP + REALISM + 5010, 6010, 7010, 8010, 5141, 7141, 5240, 6240, 7240, 8240, 5360, 6360, 7360, 8360, 5601, 6601, 7601, 8601, 5170, 6170, 7170, 8170, 5160, 6160, 7160, 8160, 5050, 6050, 7050, 8050, 5280, 6281, 7280, 8281, 1100, 2100, 3100, 4100
As for subjects noted above, and: Johnson (Goldwater) is (is not) a good man; is well (not well) experienced. Johnson (Goldwater) is a politician (positive reference); is (is not) well educated, scholarly, intelligent, smart; is stupid, not intelligent enough; is in good (poor) health; is (is not) too old; knows (does not know) how to handle foreign policy well; has (has not) enough experience abroad; is (is not) familiar with world, military situation; is man of humility (not humble enough); knows his own limitations (too cocky); doesn't pretend to know all the answers (too self-confident). Johnson (Goldwater) is a good (poor) protector, would (would not) take care of things, knows (doesn't know) what to do, is a good (poor) administrator, has good (lacks) executive ability, is a good

(poor) organizer, is (is not) hardworking, would be a full-time (part-time) president, would stay on the job, is ambitious. Democrats (Republicans) would provide good, efficient (inefficient), businesslike (unbusinesslike), wasteful, bureaucratic administration.

26. Integrity, sincerity
   5201, 6200, 7201, 8200, 5330, 6330, 7330, 8330, 6141, 8141
Johnson (Goldwater) is (is not) a man of integrity, principles, high ideals, high morals; is (is not) honest; is (is not) sincere; promises everything; won't make deals; is too ambitious; is a "politician" (negative reference).

27. Appearance, family
   5270, 6270, 7270, 8270, 5300, 6303, 7300, 8303
R likes (dislikes) Johnson's (Goldwater's) family, wife, daughters, relatives. Johnson (Goldwater) has good family life; has nice (bad) personality; is (is not) pleasant; has a nice face, good sense of humor. R likes Johnson (Goldwater) as a person.

28. Clarity of positions
   5404, 6404, 7404, 8404
Johnson's (Goldwater's) position on issues is clear (unclear). Johnson (Goldwater) lets you know (not know) where he stands, talks straight to the point; is inconsistent.

29. Independence
   5150, 6150, 7150, 8150, 5810, 6810, 7810, 8810. Also included in PARTISANSHIP: 6810, 8810
Johnson (Goldwater) is (is not) independent; is (is not) his own boss; is run by others (no one runs him); is (is not) controlled by his party; is (is not) controlled by party bosses; is not a machine man.

30. Candidates' other traits
   INTEGRITY, SINCERITY + APPEARANCE, FAMILY + CLARITY OF POSITIONS + INDEPENDENCE + 5100, 6100, 7100, 8100, 1140, 2140, 3140, 4140, 5210, 7210, 5220, 7220, 5250, 6250, 7250, 8250, 5262, 6260, 7262, 8260, 5313,

6313, 7310, 8313, 6295, 8295, 5340, 6340, 7340, 8340, 5380, 6380, 7380, 8380, 5820, 6820, 7820, 8820, 5391, 6391, 7391, 8391. Also included in QUALITY OF STEWARD-SHIP: 5210, 7210, 5220, 7220

As for subjects noted above, and: Johnson (Goldwater) has (lacks) dignity. Democrats (Republicans) did (did not) dignify government; go at things without (with) fuss; act quietly, con-fidently (unconfidently). Johnson (Goldwater) is a public ser-vant, man of duty, patriotic; will be good for the country; is religious (irreligious), R likes (does not like) his religion; is wealthy, made his own money, worked his way up, won't be tempted or influenced by money; is too rich, has too much money; kind, warm likable; does (doesn't) get along with peo-ple; does (doesn't) have people's interests at heart; is dictato-rial, craves power; is (is not) democratic (in a nonpartisan sense). Johnson (Goldwater) is (is not) well known. R likes Johnson (Goldwater) because he's not a real Democrat (Re-publican), not like most Democrats (Republicans). R likes (doesn't like) Johnson (Goldwater) because he's from the South, Texas (West, Arizona).

31. Scandals
    5292, 6292, 7292, 8292

R likes (doesn't like) Johnson's (Goldwater's) stand on cor-ruption in government. R refers to Baker and Jenkins scan-dals, corruption, immorality in government.

32. Quality of stewardship
    INTEGRITY, SINCERITY + SCANDALS + CLARITY OF POSI-TIONS + 1110, 2110, 3110, 4110, 1820, 2820, 3820, 4820, 1950, 2950, 3950, 4950, 5210, 7210, 5220, 7220. Also in-cluded in CANDIDATE'S OTHER TRAITS: 5210, 7210, 5220, 7220; in GOVERNMENTAL CORRUPTION: 1110, 2110, 3110, 4110

As for subjects noted above, and: Democrats (Republicans) would (would not) provide honest government, would be more honest than opposition, would (would not) create a "mess in Washington," would not play politics in running government, would (would not) use patronage, would bring

graft and corruption, would buy votes. R thinks one can
(can't) trust Democrats (Republicans), know (don't know)
where they stand. Democrats (Republicans) keep (don't keep)
their promises, are more stable. Democrats (Republicans) are
(are not) interested in the good of the country, are (are not)
just interested in staying in power. Johnson (Goldwater) is a
public servant, man of duty, conscientious; is patriotic, for
Americans; will be good for the country.

33. Governmental corruption
    SCANDALS + 1110, 2110, 3110, 4110. Also included in
    QUALITY OF STEWARDSHIP: 1110, 2110, 3110, 4110
As for subjects noted above, and: Democrats (Republicans)
would (would not) provide honest government, ͻ would be
more honest than opposition, would (would not) create a
"mess in Washington," would (would not) use patronage,
would bring graft and corruption, would buy votes.

34. Partisanship
    1800, 2800, 3800, 4800, 1810, 2810, 3810, 4810, 2880,
    4880, 1860, 2860, 3860, 4860, 1870, 2870, 3870, 4870,
    1900, 2900, 3900, 4900, 5405, 6406, 7405, 8406, 5800,
    6800, 7800, 8800, 6810, 8810. Also included in INDEPEN-
    DENCE: 6810, 8810; in GOLDWATER REPUBLICANISM: 3870,
    7405, 7800
R has always (never) been a Democrat (Republican); R is
"just" a Democrat (Republican); R just couldn't vote Democratic (Republican); Democratic (Republican) is the traditional (family) vote for R. R speaks of Democrats (Republicans) in positive, personal, affective terms, e.g., as good people
or nice people, or in negative, personal, affective terms, e.g., as
bad or lazy people; indicates that he dislikes Democratic (Republican) Party bosses, cheap politicians—that they are too
political, partisan (in negative sense); indicates that he likes
(dislikes) local party. R likes (dislikes) faction that has influence or is controlling party (e.g., liberals, southerners) (e.g.,
conservatives, easterners). R just likes (doesn't like) Democratic (Republican) Party; it is a good (bad) party. R likes
Johnson (Goldwater) because he will support and continue

(won't support) Democratic (Republican) policies. R likes
(dislikes) Johnson (Goldwater) because he is a Democrat
(Republican), the Democratic (Republican) nominee, a good
Democrat (Republican). R thinks Johnson (Goldwater) is
controlled by Democratic (Republican) Party; controlled by
party bosses.

35. Goldwater Republicanism
    3280, 4280, 3870, 4970, 7405, 7480, 8480, 7830, 8830,
    7820, 7800. Also included in PARTISANSHIP: 3870, 7405,
    7800; in LIBERALISM, CONSERVATISM: 3280, 4280, 7480,
    8480
R likes (dislikes) Republicans' conservative philosophy, likes
(dislikes) the conservative wing of the Republican Party, likes
(dislikes) Republican states' rights position, thinks Republicans too radical, likes faction controlling the Republican
Party, doesn't like the party's connection with extremism, e.g.
John Birch Society. R likes (dislikes) Goldwater because he
will support and continue Republican policies; is conservative, reactionary, middle of the road, too (not too) radical; represents the conservative wing of the Republican Party; will
bring in conservatives; is opposed to social change; would listen to conservatives. R likes (dislikes) men around Goldwater.
R likes Goldwater because he's a Republican, the Republican
nominee, a good Republican.

36. Party unity
    1830, 2830, 3830, 4830
Democratic (Republican) Party is well organized, sticks together, is united, has bad organization, is split and its leaders
fight among themselves too much.

37. Conduct of campaign
    1841, 2841, 3841, 4841, 5841, 6841, 7841, 8841, 1850,
    2850, 3850, 4850, 5350, 6350, 7350, 8350
Positive (negative) references to conventions, the campaigns
the parties have waged. R likes (dislikes) Johnson's (Goldwater's) speeches and campaign tactics, Democrats' (Republicans') promises, platform. R thinks Johnson (Goldwater) a
good (poor) speaker who makes a good (poor) appearance.

38. Raced-related issues
    1400, 2400, 3400, 4400, 1410, 2410, 3410, 4410, 1420,
    2420, 3420, 4420, 1670, 2670, 3670, 4670, 1770, 2770,
    3770, 4770, 5770, 6770, 7770, 8770, 5500, 6500, 7500,
    8500, 5510, 6510, 7510, 8510, 5520, 6520, 7520, 8520
Democratic (Republican) Party has good (poor) stand on civil
rights; is more for (less for, too much for, not enough for) civil
rights, e.g., it favors integration, desegregation, FEPC, civil
rights law, and opposes the poll tax, segregation. Democrats
(Republicans) are bad (good, better, too good) for Negroes,
have kept (will keep) them in check, have helped (will help)
them, have helped them at the expense of others, are made up
of and controlled by Negroes. Johnson (Goldwater) is good
for and will help Negroes; will keep them in check; has good
(bad) stand on civil rights; is for (against) civil rights, e.g.,
favors desegregation, school integration, civil rights law; is
willing to go easy on desegregation and school integration.

39. Relationship to J. F. Kennedy
    1020, 2020, 1911, 5911, 5852, 6852, 6913
R likes (dislikes) John F. Kennedy, likes Democrats because
they will carry on in the Kennedy tradition, thinks country
should not change horses in midstream, thinks Democrats
should be given more time, likes Johnson because he will
continue policies of the Kennedy administration; thinks
Johnson should be given a chance. R likes (dislikes) Johnson's
connection with Kennedy, Truman, FDR. R thinks Johnson
won't change policies of Kennedy administration.

40. Vice-presidential candidates
    1060, 2060, 3062, 4062, 5860, 6860, 7860, 8860
R likes (dislikes) Democratic (Republican) vice-presidential
candidate, thinks him a good (bad) choice for a nominee, likes
(dislikes) Johnson's (Goldwater's) connection to his party's
vice-presidential nominee.

1972

1. Vietnam War, peace
   1155–1161, 1163, 1175–1177

R refers to situation in Vietnam, Indochina, Southeast Asia. Democrats and/or McGovern (Republicans and/or Nixon) offer a better (poorer) chance for peace, offer a better chance for peace in Vietnam, failed to end war in Vietnam; are for (against) military victory in Vietnam, are for preservation of the Saigon regime, are willing to sacrifice Thieu-Ky regime, will withdraw from Vietnam, will change policy in Vietnam; will (will not) get prisoners of war back, will (will not) abandon prisoners of war.

2. Relations with the U.S.S.R.
   1128–1132
Democrats and/or McGovern (Republicans and/or Nixon) can handle Russia better (worse) because of more (less) experience; are for (against) understanding, détente, broadening of relationships with the Soviet Union.

3. Relations with Red China
   1123–1127
Democrats and/or McGovern (Republicans and/or Nixon) will handle Red China better (worse) because of more (less) experience; are for (against) understanding, thaw, détente, new relationship with Red China; are for admitting Red China to the UN; will defend Formosa, Chiang, Nationalists.

4. Military preparedness
   1106, 1107, 1110–1112, 1170–1172. Also included in YOUTH-RELATED ISSUES: 1170–1172
Democrats and/or McGovern (Republicans and/or Nixon) favor a strong (weaker) military position, preparedness, weapons systems, Pentagon spending, cutbacks on Pentagon spending, overkill, no overkill, reduced armed forces; are for (against) military aid to allies; are for (against) volunteer army, abolition of peacetime draft.

5. Internationalism
   1104, 1105, 1164–1166
Democrats and/or McGovern (Republicans and/or Nixon) are internationalists (isolationists), are interested in other countries' problems, would meddle (meddle less) in other

people's problems, are interested in nation's world role, are
pro-UN and allies, put America first, are for "Fortress
America," are for (against) free trade, high (reduced) tariffs,
would protect U.S. labor from foreign competition.

6. Foreign policy
   RELATIONS WITH THE U.S.S.R. + MILITARY PREPAREDNESS
   + RELATIONS WITH RED CHINA + INTERNATIONALISM +
   1101–1103, 1108, 1109, 1113–1122, 1167–1169, 1133–1154,
   1197, 0513, 0514, 0519, 0520. Also included in PARTISAN-
   SHIP: 0513, 0514, 0519, 0520
As for subjects noted above, and: Democrats and/or McGovern (Republicans and/or Nixon) have good (bad) foreign policies, foreign policy ideas, stands; have more (less) clear-cut
and decisive foreign policies; are more (less) bungling; are
more (less) cold-war-oriented; oppose (want) thaw, détente,
understanding with international communism; will fight international communism; are for (against) economic aid, foreign aid, nonmilitary aid; will handle Middle East better
(worse); are pro-Israel, anti-Arab; would raise (lower, not
maintain) American prestige; would deemphasize face-saving;
are for (against) trade with communists; would better handle
Eastern Europe, Latin America, Africa, Asia, India; are for
(against) defense of Iron Curtain countries; have pro (anti)
third-world posture; are for (against) colonialism; would continue (change) Democratic (Republican) foreign policies. References to other foreign policy reasons.

7. Government spending
   0605, 0606
Democrats and/or McGovern (Republicans and/or Nixon)
would spend less (more) than other party, would spend too
little (too much).

8. Monetary and fiscal policy
   0926–0933
Democrats and/or McGovern (Republicans and/or Nixon)
have good (bad) monetary policy; are for (against) loose
(tight) money; favor (are against) more (less) availability of

loans; are for higher (lower) interest rates; have good (bad) tax
policy; are for lower (higher) taxes; are for (against) tax reform, a fairer tax system, the end of loopholes, write-offs,
dodges.

9. Election's economic impact
   0934–0941

Wages, salaries, and income will be better (worse) under
Democrats and/or McGovern (Republicans and/or Nixon);
employment will be worse under him, them; prices for pro-
ducers will be better (worse) under him, them; "the times,"
general conditions, prosperity will be better (worse) under
him, them; inflation, the cost of living will be better (worse)
under him, them.

10. Economic issues
    GOVERNMENT SPENDING + MONETARY AND FISCAL POL-
    ICY + ELECTION'S ECONOMIC IMPACT + 0901

As for subjects noted above, and: Democrats and/or McGovern (Republicans and/or Nixon) have good (bad) economic
policies.

11. Farm policy
    0942–0945, 1215, 1216

Democrats and/or McGovern (Republicans and/or Nixon)
are for (against) higher levels, a fairer (change in) system of
price supports for farmers; are for (against) farmers, country
people.

12. Liberalism, conservatism
    0531–0536, 0815–0817, 0162–0165

McGovern is a northern (southern) Democrat, more liberal
(conservative) than most Democrats; Nixon is an eastern
(midwestern, western, southern) Republican, more liberal
(conservative) than most Republicans; McGovern (Nixon)
will bring in, listen to the party liberals (conservatives); Democrats and/or McGovern (Republicans and/or Nixon) are liberal (too liberal), radical (too radical), conservative (too conservative), reactionary, moderate, middle of the road, not
extremist or fanatic; are for slow change. Northerners, liberals
(southerners, conservatives) control the Democratic Party;

easterners, liberals, moderates (midwesterners, westerners, southerners) control the Republican Party.

13. Ideological stance
  LIBERALISM, CONSERVATISM + 0805–0814, 0818–0828, 0902–0904. Also included in YOUTH-RELATED ISSUES: 0821, 0822
As for subject noted above, and: Democrats and/or McGovern (Republicans and/or Nixon) are for (against) government activity, would spend more (wouldn't spend enough) on domestic needs, believe government should take care of things, are for big government; are (are not) humanistic; favor human rights over property rights; favor property rights over human rights; favor (are against) social change, reform, progress, improvement of social conditions; are for (against) socialism; are communistic (anticommunistic), soft on (hardliners on) communism, are apologists and dupes for communists; are extremist, fanatic, too far out, not too moderate, not fence-sitters; are pro far left, radicals, yippies, SDS; are encouraging anarchy, a guerrilla state; are pro (anti) far right, Birchers, reactionaries; encourage (discourage) fascist, police state; are for (against) extremists, nuts, bomb-throwers; are for (against) states' rights; are for (against) government economic controls, a planned economy, control of (interference in) private enterprise.

14. Welfare
  0905–0907, 1219, 1220
Democrats and/or McGovern (Republicans and/or Nixon) are for (against) government aid and activity in welfare programs; are for (against) government aid and activity to solve the problem of poverty; are for (against) people on welfare, ADC mothers, "chiselers."

15. Social security, the aged, workers' welfare programs
  0908–0913, 1221, 1222
Democrats and/or McGovern (Republicans and/or Nixon) are for (against) expansion of Social Security coverage and/or an increase in benefits; favor contraction or decrease in social security and pensions; are for (against) expansion of,

increase in benefits of unemployment compensation; are for (against) contraction of, reducing benefits of unemployment compensation; are for (against) old people, senior citizens.

16. Relationship to labor, unions
     0952–0958, 1207, 1208

Democrats and/or McGovern (Republicans and/or Nixon) have a good (bad) labor policy; are for (against) right-to-work laws; will have fewer (more) strikes, will handle strikes better (worse); are for (against) labor, unions, labor bosses, racketeers.

17. Relationship to Big Business, common man
     1201, 1202, 1205, 1206, 1209, 1210, 1233, 1234

Democrats and/or McGovern (Republicans and/or Nixon) favor (are against) special interests, privileged people, common man, little people, working people, Big Business, Wall Street, industry, the upper classes, the corporate rich, poor people.

18. New Deal issues
     ECONOMIC ISSUES + SOCIAL SECURITY, THE AGED, WORK-ERS' WELFARE PROGRAMS + WELFARE + RELATIONSHIP TO BIG BUSINESS, COMMON MAN + RELATIONSHIP TO LABOR, UNIONS + IDEOLOGICAL STANCE + FARM POLICY + 0920–0922, 0959–0961

As for subjects noted above, and: Democrats and/or McGovern (Republicans and/or Nixon) are for (against) more public housing, public power, utilities, TVA.

19. Law and order
     0968–0978. Also included in YOUTH-RELATED ISSUES: 0971, 0976; in RACE-RELATED ISSUES: 0970, 0975

Democrats and/or McGovern (Republicans and/or Nixon) take hard (soft) line on blacks, campus demonstrations, criminals, organized crime, hoodlums, street crime, power of police, court interference.

20. "Amnesty, acid, abortion"
     0982–0987, 1173, 1174, 1178. Also included in YOUTH-RELATED ISSUES: 0982–0984, 1173, 1174, 1178

Democrats and/or McGovern (Republicans and/or Nixon)
are for (against) legalization, decriminalization of drugs; are
hard (soft) liners on drugs; are for (against) legalization and
reform in abortion, birth control; have new (traditional) outlook on abortion, birth control; are for (against) amnesty,
draft dodgers.

21. Youth-related issues
    0821, 0822, 1223, 1224, 0971, 0976, 0982–0984, 1173,
    1174, 1178, 0979–0981, 1170–1172. Also included in MILI-
    TARY PREPAREDNESS: 1170–1172; in IDEOLOGICAL
    STANCE: 0821, 0822; in LAW AND ORDER: 0971, 0976; in
    "AMNESTY, ACID, ABORTION": 0982–0984, 1173, 1174,
    1178
Democrats and/or McGovern (Republicans and/or Nixon)
are for (against) far left, radicals, yippies, SDS; are encouraging (discouraging) anarchy, a guerrilla state; are for (against)
young people, kids, freaks, hippies; take a hard (soft) line on
campus demonstrations; are for (against) legalization, decriminalization of drugs; are hard (soft) liners on drugs; are for
(against) amnesty, draft dodgers; have permissive, newer,
modernistic outlook on morality; have strict, older, traditionalistic outlook on morality; are for (against) volunteer army,
abolition of peacetime draft.

22. Race-related issues
    0405, 0406, 0946–0948, 0970, 0975, 0991–0993, 1217,
    1218. Also included in LAW AND ORDER: 0970, 0975
Democrats and/or McGovern (Republicans and/or Nixon)
are (are not) racist, bigoted, prejudiced; are for (against) civil
rights, racial justice, integration, desegregation, voting rights;
take a soft (hard) line on law and order for blacks; are for
(against) busing, neighborhood schools; are for (against)
blacks, black people, Negroes.

23. The Social Issue
    LAW AND ORDER + "AMNESTY, ACID, ABORTION" + 0309,
    0310, 0405, 0406, 0423, 0424, 0821–0824, 0946–0948,
    0979–0981, 1170–1172, 1217, 1218, 1223, 1224,
    0991–0993. Also included in COMPETENCE OF CANDI-

DATES: 0309, 0310; in CANDIDATES' OTHER TRAITS: 0423, 0424; in IDEOLOGICAL STANCE: 0821–0824; in MILITARY PREPAREDNESS: 1170–1172. (Note that THE SOCIAL ISSUE includes all codes in YOUTH-RELATED ISSUES and RACE-RELATED ISSUES not included also in LAW AND ORDER and "AMNESTY, ACID, ABORTION")

As for subjects noted above, and: Democrats and/or McGovern (Republicans and/or Nixon) are good (bad) at communicating with blacks, young people, other "problem" groups; are (are not) racist, bigoted; are religious, moral (in religious sense), god-fearing, immoral (in religious sense); are pro (anti) far left, radicals, yippies, SDS; are encouraging (discouraging) anarchy, a guerrilla state; are for (against) extremists, nuts, bomb-throwers; are for (against) civil rights, racial justice, integration, desegregation, voting rights; are for strict (permissive), older (newer), traditionalistic (modernistic) outlook on morality; are for (against) blacks, black people, Negroes; are for (against) young people, kids, freaks, hippies; are for (against) busing, neighborhood schools; are for (against) volunteer army, abolition of peacetime draft.

24. Record, experience
    0211, 0212, 0215–0221, 0297, 0429
McGovern (Nixon) is experienced (inexperienced); is (is not) a military man; has a good (bad) military and war record; has no military or war record; has a good (poor) record in public service; has good (poor) record in previous offices; has (lacks) governmental and political experience; is (is not) a statesman; has (lacks) diplomatic experience. We shouldn't change horses in the middle of the stream, and other comments (unspecified) on the candidates' ability and experience.

25. Strength of leadership
    0303–0308, 0311, 0312
McGovern (Nixon) is strong (weak), decisive (indecisive), self-confident (not self-confident), aggressive, vacillating; will end all this indecision; is inspiring (uninspiring), (not) a man you can follow, (not) a leader; people have (don't have) confidence in him; knows (doesn't know) how to handle people.

26. Realism
    0413–0418
McGovern (Nixon) understands (doesn't understand) the nation's problems; is well (poorly) informed; is realistic, prag-
matic, down to earth, too (not too) idealistic, uses common
sense, makes a lot of sense, not sensible, impractical.

27. Competence of candidates
    RECORD, EXPERIENCE + STRENGTH OF LEADERSHIP + RE-
    ALISM + 0053, 0054, 0309, 0310, 0317–0320, 0407, 0408,
    0419–0422, 0601, 0602, 0431, 0432, 0707, 0708, 0213,
    0214, 0437, 0438, 0448, 0450–0454, 0425, 0609. Also in-
    cluded in THE SOCIAL ISSUE: 0309, 0310
As for subjects noted above, and: Democrats (Republicans)
have good (bad), young (old), experienced (inexperienced)
leaders; have a good (bad) ticket. McGovern (Nixon) is good
(bad) at communicating with blacks, young people, other
"problem" groups; is humble (not humble enough); knows his
limitations; doesn't pretend to know all the answers; is too
cocky and self-confident; is too careful (careless), too cautious
(impulsive); is a public servant, a man of duty, conscientious,
hard working; would be a full-time (part-time) president; does
not take public service seriously; is well (too well) educated,
scholarly; is poorly educated, unschooled, intelligent (unintel-
ligent), smart, stupid, dumb. Democrats and/or McGovern
(Republicans and/or Nixon) would bring a good (bad), efficient (inefficient), businesslike (unbusinesslike), wasteful, bureaucratic administration; McGovern (Nixon) is safe (unsafe),
stable (unstable), dictatorial, craves power. Democrats and
McGovern (Republicans and Nixon) are good (bad) protec-
tors; will (won't) know what to do. McGovern (Nixon) is dependable (undependable); is trustworthy (untrustworthy) in
his capabilities, reliable (unreliable); is likable (unlikable),
gets (doesn't get) along with people; is healthy (unhealthy);
is (too) old, (too) young, mature (immature); is self-made,
not well off, started out a poor boy; would do good (bad)
job, be good (bad) president, provide good (bad) administration.

28. Integrity, sincerity
    0313, 0401–0404

McGovern (Nixon) is a politician, too much in politics, a good
politician; is honest (dishonest), sincere (insincere); keeps
(breaks) promises; is (is not) a man of integrity; means
(doesn't mean) what he says; is (is not) tricky; is a man of high
principles, ideals, high moral purposes; lacks principles and
ideals; is not idealistic.

29. Appearance, family
    0445, 0446, 0449

McGovern (Nixon) has good (bad) family, wife; has a good
(poor) appearance, looks, face; makes (doesn't make) a good
appearance on TV.

30. Independence
    0315, 0316, 0502, 0503. Also included in PARTISANSHIP:
    0502

McGovern (Nixon) is (is not) independent; is (is not) run by
others; is (is not) his own boss; is (is not) controlled by party
regulars and bosses.

31. Candidate's other traits
    INTEGRITY, SINCERITY + APPEARANCE, FAMILY + INDE-
    PENDENCE + 0301, 0302, 0314, 0411, 0412, 0423, 0424,
    0426–0428, 0433–0436, 0439–0444, 0705, 0706, 0709,
    0710. Also included in THE SOCIAL ISSUE: 0423, 0424

As for subjects noted above, and: McGovern (Nixon) is digni-
fied (undignified); has (lacks) dignity; is not a politician, not in
politics, above politics, a bad politician; is patriotic (unpatrio-
tic); religious (irreligious), moral in religious sense (immoral
in religious sense), God-fearing; was born with a silver spoon
in his mouth; is old hat, a die-hard, a "loser" (in the past),
someone new, a fresh face; is democratic (undemocratic) in
nonpartisan sense; has a (has no) sense of humor; is humor-
less, serious (too serious); jokes a lot (too much); is kind, warm
(cold), gentle, aloof; is (is not) highfalutin; talks straight; talks
in circles; can (can't) talk to the common man; can communi-
cate ideas well; is highbrow (lowbrow); is (is not) well known;

is unknown. Democrats and/or McGovern (Republicans and/or Nixon) are good (bad) for the country, have (don't have) the country's interests at heart; will unite (divide) Americans.

32. Watergate affair
    0720
References to Watergate affair.

33. Governmental corruption
    WATERGATE AFFAIR + 0603, 0604
As for Watergate affair, and: Democrats and McGovern (Republicans and Nixon) will bring honest (dishonest) government; are (are not) corrupt; will bring a "mess" (no mess) in Washington.

34. Quality of stewardship
    INTEGRITY, SINCERITY + GOVERNMENTAL CORRUPTION + 0121, 0122, 0709, 0710. Also included in CANDIDATES' OTHER TRAITS: 0709, 0710
As for subjects noted above, and: You can (can't) trust the Democrats (Republicans); they keep (break) their promises; you know (don't know) where they stand; they will be good (bad) for the country; have (don't have) the country's interests at heart.

35. Partisanship
    0101, 0102, 0111, 0112, 0151, 0161, 0500, 0501, 0502, 0506, 0507, 0509–0520. Also included in FOREIGN POLICY: 0513, 0514, 0519, 0520; in INDEPENDENCE: 0502
R is (good, typical) Democrat (Republican), couldn't vote Democratic (Republican). References to Democrats (Republicans) in positive (negative) personal, affective terms, e.g., are good (bad) people, nice people, lazy people. References to local branch of party, how it has done in state, county, town. Reference to faction R sees as in control of party. McGovern (Nixon) is a Democrat (Republican), a good Democrat (Republican), a typical Democrat (Republican); is controlled (not controlled) by party regulars, bosses; can (can't) win, is (is not) good choice for party victory. McGovern (Nixon) would con-

tinue (change) Democratic (Republican) policies, Democratic (Republican) domestic policies, Democratic (Republican) foreign policies.

36. Party unity
     0131, 0132
Democrats (Republicans) are well (poorly) organized, united; stick together; are really two parties; are divided, factionalized.

37. Conduct of campaign
     0447, 0505, 0804
McGovern (Nixon) speaks well (poorly). R likes (dislikes) McGovern (Nixon) speeches, campaign tactics. Democrats and/or McGovern (Republicans and/or Nixon) are negative (too negative); are always tearing down the other side; have no solutions of their own.

38. Eagleton affair
     0541
References to Eagleton's resignation as a vice-presidential candidate.

39. Conventions, Eagleton affair
     EAGLETON AFFAIR + 0141
As for Eagleton affair, and: reference to 1972 national conventions, process of selecting candidates.

40. Vice-presidential candidates
     0009, 0010, 0033, 0542
References to Shriver, Agnew, and Eagleton.

INDEX

NOTE: Dates in parentheses indicate the year of the presidential election to which the indexed item refers.

Library of Congress Cataloging in Publication Data

Kelley, Stanley.
    Interpreting elections.

    Includes index.
        1. Presidents—United States—Election.   2. Elections—United
States.   3. United States—Politics and government—1945-   .
4. Voting research—United States.   I. Title.
JK524.K34   1983   324.973'092   82-25184
ISBN 0-691-07654-5
ISBN 0-691-02216-X (pbk.)